Junior
Dictionary
& Thesaurus

Author and consultant
Susan Purcell

Miles
Kelly

First published in 2011 by Miles Kelly Publishing Ltd
Harding's Barn, Bardfield End Green, Thaxted, Essex, CM6 3PX, UK

2 4 6 8 10 9 7 5 3 1

Publishing Director Belinda Gallagher

Creative Director Jo Cowan

Editors Carly Blake, Rosie McGuire, Sarah Parkin

Editorial Assistant Lauren White

Cover Designer Simon Lee

Designers Jo Cowan, Kayleigh Allen

Production Manager Elizabeth Collins

Reprographics Stephan Davis, Jennifer Hunt, Lorraine King

ISBN 978-1-84810-479-2

Printed in China

British Library Cataloguing-in-Publication Data
A catalogue record for this book is available from the British Library

Made with paper from a sustainable forest

www.mileskelly.net
info@mileskelly.net

www.factsforprojects.com

Junior
Dictionary
& Thesaurus

Introduction

The dictionary section of this book shows you how to spell words and explains what they mean. It also shows you how to use them. Many words will be familiar — the kind you use every day. Some will be new ones you are just beginning to learn. As you use your dictionary you will find fun things to do and look at. Each letter of the alphabet has its own cartoon, and throughout the book there are puzzles and word games.

The thesaurus section will help you to use new or different words. Each double page has a new keyword with a choice of related words called synonyms — these are words that have the same meaning as another word. Each synonym is explained and placed in an example sentence. You will also find opposites, cartoons and fact panels.

How to use your dictionary

Cartoons
Look out for the fun cartoons that appear in each letter. How many different things can you see starting with the same letter?

Entries
The words in **bold** are the entries, the words that you look up. There are more than 1700 entries in your dictionary.

Definitions
These come after each entry. They explain what the word means.

Example sentences
A sentence follows each definition. This gives you an example of the word within a sentence.

table ▶ take

How many things can you spot beginning with 't'?

a b c d e f g h i j k l m n o p q r s **t** u v w x y z

Tt

table (tables)
1 a piece of furniture with legs and a flat top
Please clear the table.
2 a list of numbers or words written in rows and columns
We measured the height of everyone in the class and wrote the results in a table.

tadpole (tadpoles)
a very young frog or toad
Tadpoles have big heads and l[ong] tails and live in water.

tail (tails)
the part of an animal at the [end] of its back
The dog has a long, white tail.

tail

take (taking, took, [taken])
1 to carry something
Take an umbrella with y[ou.]
2 to move something [or] someone to anothe[r place]
Can you take us to t[he] station?
3 to steal
The thieves took all the mon[ey.]

Different forms of a word

Some entries are followed by the same word in plural form. This is when there is more than one of something. The plural is shown after the entry within brackets.

talent ▶ teacher

talent (talents)
the ability to do something very well without having to learn it
Maya has a talent for drawing.

talk (talking, talked)
to speak
We talked on the phone for ages.

tall
1 higher than normal
My grandad is tall, and I am short.
2 having a certain height
How tall are you?

tambourine (tambourines)
a small round musical instrument that you shake or hit
I played the tambourine in the school concert.

tank (tanks)
1 a container for liquids
There's a leak in the petrol tank.
2 a strong truck used by soldiers
Tanks have metal tracks or belts instead of wheels.

tap (taps)
something that controls the flow of a liquid or gas
Turn the tap off; don't waste water.

tape
a flat, narrow strip of plastic that is sticky on one side
Put some sticky tape on the envelope.

taste (tasting, tasted)
1 to have a flavour
What does the soup taste like?
2 to try a little food or drink to see what it is like
Have you tasted the pizza?

taxi (taxis)
a car that takes people to different places, for money
We'll take a taxi.

tea
1 a hot drink made from leaves
Do you take milk in your tea?
2 a meal you eat in the early evening
What's for tea?

teacher (teachers)
a person who gives lessons in a subject
Our teacher's name is Mrs Griffiths.

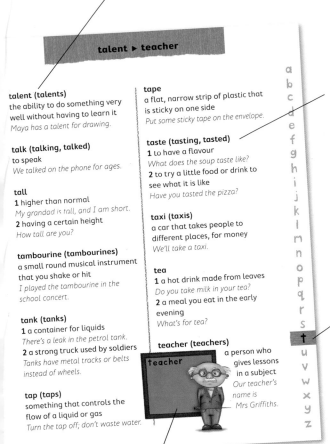

teacher

a
b
c
d
e
f
g
h
i
j
k
l
m
n
o
p
q
r
s
t
u
v
w
x
y
z

Verbs

If an entry is a verb (doing word) then other forms of the word will appear in brackets. For example, the verb 'taste' is followed by different endings.

Alphabetical order

All of the entries are in alphabetical order. The alphabet is listed down the side of each page. Use the highlighted letters to help you find your way around.

Illustrations and photographs

These help you to understand the meaning of a word. Each illustration or photograph has its own label to tell you exactly what it is.

Puzzle time
These are fun things to do and give you a chance to play with words. This helps you to learn and remember them.

a
b
c
d
e
f
g
h
i
j
k
l
m
n
o
p
q
r
s
t
u
v
w
x
y
z

How many things can you spot beginning with 'a'?

A a

above
1 in a higher place than something else
Annie lives in the flat above us.
2 more than
This ride is for children aged six and above.

absent
away from a place, not there
Sameer is absent today.

accident (accidents)
1 an unexpected event, often causing damage or injury
There was an accident on the road.
2 something that happens by chance
I dropped it by accident.

actor (actress; actors, actresses)
a person who plays a part in a film or play
My Dad is an actor.

add

add (adding, added)
1 to put something together with something else
Add the milk and sugar to the butter.

b
c
d
e
f
g
h
i
j
k
l
m
n
o
p
q
r
s
t
u
v
w
x
y
z

2 to put numbers together to find the total
If you add six to four it makes ten.

address (addresses)
the house number and street where you live
My address is 65 Chestnut Avenue.

65 Chestnut Avenue
Old Town
Southshire

address

adult (adults)
a grown-up, not a child
Only adults are allowed in the pool after six p.m.

adult

adventure (adventures)
an exciting experience
Flying is such an adventure.

advert (advertisement; adverts, advertisements)
words or pictures in newspapers or on television about things for sale
There are too many adverts on TV.

aerial (aerials)
a piece of metal or wire for receiving or sending radio or television signals
There is an aerial on our roof.

aeroplane (aeroplanes)
a large machine, with wings and an engine, that flies
When aeroplanes fly over our house it is very noisy.

afraid
scared, frightened
Are you afraid of snakes?

afternoon (afternoons)
the part of the day between midday and the evening
We'll go out this afternoon.

again
another time, once more
Shall we sing the song again?

age
the number of years someone has lived
At what age can I learn to drive?

air
the mixture of gases around us that we breathe
The air is clean and fresh.

a
b
c
d
e
f
g
h
i
j
k
l
m
n
o
p
q
r
s
t

aircraft (plural is the same)
machines that fly
Helicopters are a type of aircraft.

airport (airports)
a place where planes land and take off
The airport is very busy today.

alarm (alarms)
1 a machine that flashes or makes a noise as a warning
The burglar alarm is flashing!

alien (aliens)
something strange that comes from another planet
E.T. is a friendly alien.

alligator (alligators)
a type of large reptile that looks similar to a crocodile
Alligators spend much of their day in water, keeping cool and hidden from view.

alligator

alphabet (alphabets)
letters in a special order that form a language
'E' is a letter of the alphabet.

ambulance (ambulances)
a vehicle for taking people to and from hospital
Stop! There's an ambulance coming.

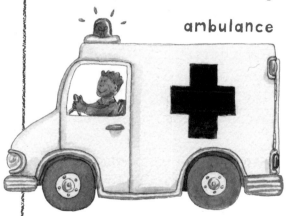
ambulance

anchor (anchors)
a heavy metal object on a rope or chain, which stops a boat moving.
Lower the anchor.

angel (angels)
a messenger from God, in some religions
In pictures, angels often have wings.

angry (angrier, angriest)
feeling or showing annoyance
My sister sometimes gets angry.

animal (animals)
a living thing that can move
Cows and horses are animals.

ankle (ankles)
the part of the body between the
leg and the foot
I twisted my ankle when I fell over.

answer (answers)
1 something you say or write
after a question
My answer is no.
2 the correct solution
Well done! That's the right answer.

answer (answering, answered)
1 to say or write something when
asked a question
*Where have you been? Please
answer my question.*
2 to pick up the telephone or go
to the door
Please answer the telephone.

ant (ants)
a tiny insect that lives in groups
Some types of ants cut up leaves.

appear (appearing, appeared)
1 to look or to seem
She appears to be better today.

2 to come into sight
My sister appeared from behind me.

applause (applauded)
clapping by a group of people to
show they enjoyed something
Everyone applauded at the end.

apple (apples)
a fruit that grows
on trees
*I always have an
apple after lunch.*

apple

apricot (apricots)
a small, fuzzy-skinned
yellow fruit
I like dried apricots on cereal.

apron (aprons)
a piece of cloth that you put over
your clothes to keep them clean
I wore an apron while I was painting.

arch

**arch
(arches)**
a curved
structure
*We sat on
the grass
under the
arch.*

a b c d e f g h i j k l m n o p q r s t u v w x y z

arena (arenas)
a large building where you can
see sports events or concerts
I saw a football match in an arena.

argue (arguing, argued)
to strongly disagree
Let's not argue about the meal.

arm (arms)
the part of your body between
your shoulder and hand
Dad has broken his right arm.

**armchair
(armchairs)**
a chair that has
places for you to
rest your arms
*I like to read when
I'm sitting in an armchair.*

armchair

army (armies)
the people that fight for a
country on land
The Roman army was very powerful.

arrest (arresting, arrested)
to take someone to a police
station because they have
committed a crime
The police arrested the thief.

arrow (arrows)
a pointed stick that you shoot
from a bow
We fired arrows at the enemy.

art
the making of paintings,
drawings and sculpture
My favourite subject at school is art.

artist (artists)
a person who makes art
He is a well-known artist.

ask (asking, asked)
1 to say something to someone
because you want them to tell
you something
"What is the time?" she asked.
2 to say you want something
I asked for a glass of water.

asleep
sleeping
*The baby is
fast asleep.*

asleep

assembly (assemblies)
a meeting of the whole school
*We have an assembly every
morning in the hall.*

astronaut (astronauts)
a person who travels into
space in a spacecraft
Astronauts walked on the Moon.

athlete (athletes)
a person who plays a sport
Athletes must train every day.

atlas (atlases)
a book with maps in
I use an atlas at school.

attack (attacking, attacked)
to be violent and fight someone
or something
Pirates attacked the ship.

aunt (auntie; aunts, aunties)
the sister of your mother or
father, the wife of your uncle
My aunt looks like my mother.

author (authors)
a person who writes books
*Philippa Pearce is the author of
Tom's Midnight Garden.*

autograph (autographs)
the name of a famous person,
written by them
Can I have your autograph?

automatic
if a machine is automatic
it works by itself
*The washing machine is
automatic.*

astronaut

autumn
the time of year between the
summer and the winter
The leaves turn red in autumn.

awake
not sleeping, not asleep
I tried to stay awake all night.

awful
very bad
This medicine tastes awful.

axe (axes)
a tool with a handle and a sharp
cutting edge that is used for
chopping wood
*Dad chopped
the tree down   axe
with an axe.*

a
b
c
d
e
f
g
h
i
j
k
l
m
n
o
p
q
r
s
t
u
v
w
x
y
z

a
b
c
d
e
f
g
h
i
j
k
l
m
n
o
p
q
r
s
t
u
v
w
x
y
z

How many things can you spot beginning with 'b'?

B b

baboon (baboons)
a large monkey
Baboons are very noisy.

baby (babies)
a young child that has not yet learnt to talk or walk
There is a new baby in the family.

baboon

babysitter (babysitters)
a person who looks after children while their parents are out
Our babysitter plays games with us.

back (backs)
1 the part of your body behind you, between your shoulders and bottom
I can swim on my back.
2 the part of something that is furthest from the front or from the way it is facing
The wires are at the back of the computer.

backwards
the direction opposite to the way something is facing
Take four steps backwards.

bacon
meat from a pig
We have bacon and eggs for breakfast.

bad (worse, worst)
not good or pleasant
It's bad news.

badge (badges)
something that you put on your clothes to show who you are or what you have done
I have four swimming badges.

badger (badgers)
an animal with black-and-white fur that lives underground
There is a family of badgers living in the wood.

badly
not done well
I play the piano badly.

badminton
a game that is played with rackets and a small object called a shuttlecock
We play badminton every day.

bag (bags)
a container made of plastic, paper, cloth or leather
Let's put the vegetables into this bag.

baggy (baggier, baggiest)
loose, not tight
My jumper is too big and baggy.

bake (baking, baked)
to cook food in an oven
Bake the cake for 40 minutes.

balance
the ability to stay still without falling over
If I close my eyes I lose my balance.

balance (balancing, balanced)
1 to hold yourself still without falling over
Can you balance on this narrow bar?
2 to keep something steady without dropping it
The seal balanced a ball on its nose.

badminton

a
b
c
d
e
f
g
h
i
j
k
l
m
n
o
p
q
r
s
t
u
v
w
x
y
z

balcony (balconies)
an area outside a window where
you can sit or stand
*You can see the beach from
the balcony.*

bald
without hair
My dad is going bald.

bald

ball (balls)
a round object
that you throw, hit
or kick in games
The ball went into the net.

ballet
a type of dancing that tells a
story with no words
A very famous ballet is Swan Lake.

balloon (balloons)
a thin, rubber bag
filled with air that is
used as a decoration
*We had balloons at
the party.*

banana (bananas)
a long, curved
yellow fruit
I like bananas for breakfast.

balloons

band (bands)
1 a thin strip of material
Megan has got a band in her hair.
2 a group of people who play
music together
*My brother plays the drums
in a band.*

bandage (bandages)
a piece of material that
you wrap around an injury
*The nurse put a bandage on
Matthew's leg when he fell over.*

bang (bangs)
a sudden loud noise
The door shut with a bang.

bank (banks)
1 a place to keep
money
*There is a bank in
the town.*
2 the land alongside a river
*People sit on the bank and
catch fish.*

barbecue (barbecues)
a meal cooked over a flame
outside
*The weather's good. Let's have a
barbecue.*

bark
the hard material on a tree trunk
The bark is peeling off the tree in some places.

bark (barking, barked)
to make a short, loud noise, like a dog
My dog barks when someone knocks at the door.

barn (barns)
a farm building for keeping animals or crops
The cows are in the barn.

basket (baskets)
a container made of thin strips, to hold or carry things
Put the bread in the basket.

basketball
a game played by two teams that score points by throwing a ball through a round net
Basketball is a fast game.

bat (bats)
1 a small animal that usually flies at night
Bats have big ears and good hearing.

2 the wooden stick used to hit a ball in games such as rounders
I got a cricket bat for my birthday.

bath (baths)
a long container that you fill with water and sit in to wash your body
In our bathroom there's a bath, washbasin and toilet.

battery (batteries)
an object that makes electricity
My torch needs two batteries.

beach (beaches)
the area of land that is next to the sea
We built a sandcastle on the beach.

bean (beans)
the seed of a climbing plant that is eaten as food
I like baked beans on toast.

beans

a
b
c
d
e
f
g
h
i
j
k
l
m
n
o
p
q
r
s
t
u
v
w
x
y
z

bear (bears)
a large, strong wild animal that is covered in fur
Bears sleep all winter.

beard (beards)
hair that grows on a man's chin and cheeks
My Dad has a beard.

beard

beautiful
lovely to look at
Roses are beautiful flowers.

bed (beds)
a piece of furniture for sleeping on
There are two beds in my room.

bedroom (bedrooms)
the room where you sleep
My bedroom is next to the bathroom.

bee (bees)
an insect with yellow-and-black stripes
Bees make honey.

beef
meat from a cow
We had roast beef for dinner.

begin (beginning, began, begun)
to start
The story begins in the forest.

behind
at the back of someone or something
She's hiding behind the garden fence.

bell (bells)
a metal object that makes a ringing sound
The church bells ring every Sunday.

below
in a lower place than something else
The gym is on the floor below.

belt (belts)
a piece of clothing that you wear around your waist
My belt holds my trousers up.

Puzzle time
Untangle the bees to see which one gets home

a b c d e f g h i j k l m n o p q r s t u v w x y z

bench (benches)
a long seat for two or more
people to sit on
*I'll sit on the bench and
wait for you.*

berry (berries)
a small, soft fruit that
grows on bushes or trees
*Blackberries and raspberries
are types of berries.*

better (best)
of a higher standard or quality
*The new game is better
than the last one.*

between
in a place or time that
separates two things
or people
You can sit between us.

**bicycle (bike; bicycles,
bikes)**
a machine with two
wheels that you sit on
and move by pushing
on pedals
*I'd like a new bicycle
for my birthday.*

bicycle

big (bigger, biggest)
1 large in size, not small
*I need a big
bag to carry
all these books.*
2 important
There's a big match today.

bird

bird (birds)
a creature that has wings,
feathers, and lays eggs
There's a bird in the tree.

birthday (birthdays)
the day of the year on which a
person is born
My birthday is 25 September.

biscuit (biscuits)
a dry, thin cake that is
usually sweet
*My Mum likes a biscuit
with a cup of tea.*

**bite (biting, bit,
bitten)**
to cut into
something with your
teeth
Be careful of the dog. He bites!

a b c d e f g h i j k l m n o p q r s t u v w x y z

a
b
c
d
e
f
g
h
i
j
k
l
m
n
o
p
q
r
s
t
u
v
w
x
y
z

bitter
having a strong, sharp taste such as coffee
Dark chocolate sometimes tastes very bitter.

blanket (blankets)
a piece of material on a bed that you use to keep warm
I'd like an extra blanket on my bed.

blind
not able to see
Some blind people carry white sticks.

blister (blisters)
a raised piece of skin, filled with liquid, caused by burning or rubbing
I have a blister on my foot.

blizzard (blizzards)
a very heavy snow storm
People shouldn't drive in a blizzard.

blood
red liquid that the heart pumps through your body
I cut my finger and now there's blood on my shirt.

blouse (blouses)
a shirt that girls and women wear
Our school blouse is blue and white.

blow (blowing, blew, blown)
to push air out of your mouth
It's fun to blow bubbles!

boat (boats)
a small ship
You get to the island by boat.

body (bodies)
1 the whole of a person
Skin covers your body.
2 a dead person
They covered the body with a sheet.

boat

bone (bones)
a hard, white part under the skin of a person or animal
Your skeleton has more than 200 bones.

bonfire (bonfires)
a fire outside
Dad made a bonfire in the garden.

book (books)
1 sheets of paper with writing on, joined together for reading
This is a book about spiders.
2 sheets of paper joined together for writing on
Write your name on the cover of your exercise book.

books

boot (boots)
1 a strong shoe that covers your foot and ankle
Wear your boots in the rain.
2 the part of a car for carrying things
The bags are in the boot.

bored
not interested
I'm bored, let's play a game.

boring
not interesting
This programme's boring. Let's turn the television off.

born
starting life
My Dad was born in 1970.

borrow (borrowing, borrowed)
to take something that belongs to another person and give it back to them later
You can borrow the books for two weeks.

bottle (bottles)
a tall container for storing liquid
I have a water bottle on my bike.

bottom (bottoms)
1 the part of your body that you sit on
I fell on my bottom.
2 the lowest part of something
The number is at the bottom of the page.

bounce (bouncing, bounced)
to move back quickly after hitting or falling on something
The children bounced up and down on the trampoline.

bow (rhymes with low; bows)
1 a knot with loops
I tied my shoelaces in a bow.
2 a long, thin stick with string for shooting arrows or playing an instrument
You play the violin with a bow.

a
b
c
d
e
f
g
h
i
j
k
l
m
n
o
p
q
r
s
t
u
v
w
x
y
z

bow (rhymes with cow; bowing, bowed)
to bend your body or your head to show respect
The servants all bowed to the king.

bowl (bowls)
a deep, curved dish
You eat cereal out of a bowl.

box (boxes)
a container with four sides
I keep my crayons in a box.

boxing
the sport of fighting with closed hands
My Dad likes watching boxing on TV.

boy (boys)
a male child or a young man
There are two boys in their family.

bracelet (bracelets)
a piece of jewellery worn around the wrist
My bracelet has my name on it.

boy

brain (brains)
the part of your body inside your head that you use for thinking, feeling and moving
When you touch something hot, nerves send a message to your brain and you pull your hand away.

branch

branch (branches)
the part of a tree that grows out from the trunk
Leaves, flowers and fruit grow on branches.

brave
not afraid to do dangerous things
Soldiers are very brave.

bread
a type of food made with flour, water and yeast
I like jam on bread.

break (breaking, broke, broken)
to make something separate into two or more pieces
I dropped the glass and broke it.

breakfast (breakfasts)
the first meal of the day
We always have cereal for breakfast.

breath (breaths)
the air that goes in and out of your body
Take a deep breath and smell the fresh air.

breathe (breathing, breathed)
to take air into your body and let it out
Breathe in, and slowly breathe out.

breeze (breezes)
a light wind
There's a lovely warm breeze blowing.

brick (bricks)
a block of baked clay used for building
The wall is made with bricks.

bridge (bridges)
a structure built to join two things
There is a bridge over the river.

bright
1 full of light
It's a bright, sunny day.
2 strong and easy to see
Yellow and orange are bright colours.
3 clever, intelligent
That's a bright idea.

brilliant
1 very bright and strong
There was a brilliant light in the sky.
2 very good at doing something
She's a brilliant scientist.
3 very good or enjoyable
This is a brilliant book, you should read it.

bring (bringing, brought)
to take something with you
Don't forget to bring a packed lunch for the trip.

broccoli
a green vegetable that looks like a little tree
Let's have broccoli with our dinner.

bridge

a b c d e f g h i j k l m n o p q r s t u v w x y z

a
b
c
d
e
f
g
h
i
j
k
l
m
n
o
p
q
r
s
t
u
v
w
x
y
z

broom (brooms)
a brush with a handle
Sweep the floor with a broom.

brother (brothers)
a boy or a man who has the same
parents as another person
Nadia has two brothers.

bruise (bruises)
a blue or purple mark on the skin
that appears after something has
hit you
I've got a big bruise on my arm.

brush (brushes)
a tool that has stiff hairs fastened
to a handle that is used for
sweeping, painting or cleaning
*When you've
finished
painting, put
the brush in the
jar of water.*

**bubble
(bubbles)**
a small ball of
air in a liquid
*Lemonade has
got lots of little
bubbles in it.*

bucket (buckets)
a round, open container with a
handle
The bucket was full of water.

**budgie
(budgerigar;
budgies,
budgerigars)**
a small, brightly
coloured bird
that some people
keep as a pet
Our budgie lives in a cage.

budgie

build (building, built)
to make something, such as a
house, by putting pieces together
*There are plans to build a new
school next year.*

building (buildings)
a place with a roof and
walls
*Houses, shops and
schools are all buildings.*

bull (bulls)
a male cow, elephant
or whale
*We saw a bull with a
ring in his nose.*

Puzzle time
Which of these brushes
is the odd one out?

answer:
broom, it
doesn't end
in 'brush'

bunch (bunches)
a group of things that are attached together
There's a bunch of grapes in my lunchbox.

bunch

burger (burgers)
a flat cake of meat or vegetables
We had burgers and chips for dinner.

burglar (burglars)
a person who goes into buildings to steal things
A burglar stole the money.

burn (burning, burnt, burned)
1 to be on fire
The candles are burning.
2 to destroy something with fire
We burnt all the rubbish on a bonfire.

bus (buses)
a vehicle that carries passengers
I get the bus to school.

bush (bushes)
a small tree with lots of branches
Berries grow on bushes.

busy (busier, busiest)
1 doing things, working hard
Mum's busy on the computer.
2 lively, full of people
The town centre is always very busy on a Saturday.

butcher (butchers)
a person who cuts up and sells meat
Our butcher always wears a striped apron.

butter
yellow food that is made from milk
Use a knife to spread butter on the bread.

butterfly (butterflies)
an insect with large wings
Butterflies drink from flowers.

button (buttons)
a round object that fastens clothes
My shirt has six buttons.

buy (buying, bought)
to get something by paying money for it
Shall we buy some sweets?

a b c d e f g h i j k l m n o p q r s t u v w x y z

a b **c** d e f g h i j k l m n o p q r s t u v w x y z

How many things can you spot beginning with 'c'?

C c

cabbage (cabbages)
a large vegetable with thick, round leaves
Rabbits love eating cabbages.

cabin (cabins)
1 a small house made of wood, usually in the country
The cabin is halfway up the mountain.

2 the place where the passengers sit inside an aeroplane
The pilot walked back through the cabin.
3 a small room to sleep in on a ship
The cabin has two beds.

cactus (cacti or cactuses)
a plant that grows in hot, dry places, and that has needles instead of leaves
Cacti don't need much water.

café (cafés)
a place that serves drinks and simple meals
Why don't we stop and have lunch at a café?

cabbage

cage (cages)
a room or box with bars in which
to keep animals or birds
Pet hamsters and mice live in cages.

cake (cakes)
a sweet food made of flour, sugar
and eggs that is baked in an oven
*Mum baked me a chocolate cake for
my birthday.*

calculator (calculators)
a machine that adds up numbers
and does other sums
*I use a calculator in
maths lessons.*

calculator

**calendar
(calendars)**
a chart that shows the days,
weeks and months of the year
*We wrote everyone's birthday on
the calendar.*

calf (calves)
1 a baby cow, elephant or whale
The calf is two days old.
2 the back part of your leg
between your ankle and knee
I've pulled a muscle in my calf.

call (calling, called)
1 to shout or say something in a
loud voice
Dad called out to us.
2 to telephone
I'll call you when I get home.
3 to visit
*The doctor calls when
someone is very ill.*
4 to give
someone or
something
a name
*They called the
baby Luke.*

camel

camel (camels)
a large animal
with one or two humps that can
carry heavy loads
*A camel can go without water for a
long time.*

camera (cameras)
a piece of equipment used for
taking photographs or filming
*The teacher brought her camera on
the school trip.*

camp (camps)
a place where people stay in tents
The camp is over the hill.

a b c d e f g h i j k l m n o p q r s t u v w x y z

a
b
c
d
e
f
g
h
i
j
k
l
m
n
o
p
q
r
s
t
u
v
w
x
y
z

camp (camping, camped)
to stay in a tent
Every summer the Scouts camp in this field.

can (cans)
a metal container
We collect drink cans for charity.

can (could)
1 to be able to do something
Aziz can play the violin.
2 to be allowed to do something
We can come to your party.

candle (candles)
a stick of wax with a string through it that you burn for light
Let's light the candles on the cake.

candles

canoe (canoes)
a small boat which is pointed at both ends
You use a paddle to make a canoe move through the water.

capital (capitals)
the main town in a country
Paris is the capital of France.

capital letter (capital letters)
a large letter of the alphabet
THIS SENTENCE IS WRITTEN IN CAPITAL LETTERS.

captain (captains)
1 someone who leads a team
Who is captain of the football team this year?
2 a person who is in charge of a ship or a plane
The captain has told us the flight will take two hours.

car (cars)
a machine on wheels that has an engine and that people can ride in
There is a car in the driveway.

car

caravan (caravans)
a small house on wheels that can be pulled behind a car
Jack and Katie have taken their caravan on holiday.

card (cards)
1 thick, stiff paper (no plural)
We stuck the pictures onto card.
2 a piece of card with words and a picture that you give or send someone
My brother gave me a birthday card.
3 a piece of stiff paper or plastic that you use to buy things or to identify yourself
I have a library card.
4 a piece of stiff paper with pictures and numbers that you use to play games
Each player has seven cards.

cards

cardigan (cardigans)
a piece of clothing like a jumper with buttons down the front
Wear a cardigan if it's cold.

careful
paying attention to what you are doing so that you don't make a mistake or have an accident
Be careful! That knife is sharp.

caretaker (caretakers)
a person who looks after a building
The caretaker locks up the school at night.

carnival (carnivals)
a big party in the street with music and dancing
People often wear fancy dress at a carnival.

carnival

carol (carols)
a religious Christmas song
My favourite carol is Silent Night.

carpet (carpets)
a thick cover for the floor
The carpet in my bedroom is blue.

carrot (carrots)
a long, orange vegetable that grows under the ground
Carrots are a healthy food to eat.

carry (carrying, carried)
to move something from one place to another
Can you help me carry these bags?

a
b
c
d
e
f
g
h
i
j
k
l
m
n
o
p
q
r
s
t
u
v
w
x
y
z

a b **c** d e f g h i j k l m n o p q r s t u v w x y z

cartoon (cartoons)

1 a funny drawing in a newspaper or comic

There is a cartoon every day in most newspapers.

2 a film with drawings instead of real actors

I like watching cartoons on television.

castle (castles)

a large, strong building with thick walls

Sleeping Beauty lived in a castle.

cat (cats)

a small, furry animal with a long tail and sharp claws

My cat likes to climb trees.

cat

catch (catching, caught)

1 to get hold of something when someone throws it

I'll throw the ball and you can try to catch it.

2 to get an illness

People often catch cold in winter.

3 to get on a bus, train or plane and go somewhere

We usually catch the bus to school.

caterpillar (caterpillars)

an animal, like a worm with legs, that turns into a butterfly or a moth

Caterpillars eat leaves.

castle

cave (caves)

a hole in a mountainside or under the ground

Caves are usually dark and damp.

CD (compact disc; CDs, compact discs)

a circular piece of plastic for storing sound

Have you bought their latest CD? It's really good!

CD-ROM (compact disc read-only memory; CD-ROMs)

a circular piece of plastic for storing information to be used by a computer

CD-ROMs hold lots of information.

celery

a long, green, crunchy vegetable

Mum chopped up some celery.

cellar (cellars)
a room underneath a house or other building
We keep our bikes in the cellar.

cello (cellos)
a large musical instrument that you sit down to play
Cellos look like big violins.

cereal
a breakfast food that is made from wheat, oats or rice
I always put sugar on my cereal.

chair (chairs)
a piece of furniture for sitting on
Pull your chair close to the desk.

chalk
a soft, white rock
I drew a picture using chalk.

chameleon (chameleons)
a lizard that changes colour so its skin matches the things around it
A chameleon catches its prey using its long, sticky tongue.

chameleon

change (changing, changed)
1 to become different or to make something different
You haven't changed at all!
2 to put on different clothes
I'm cold – I'll change my top.

cheap
not expensive
My watch was cheap. I bought it in the sale.

cheese
a food that is made from milk
Can I have cheese on toast for tea?

cheese

cheetah (cheetahs)
a wild animal of the cat family with black spots
Cheetahs can run very fast.

cherry (cherries)
a small, round, reddish fruit with a stone in the centre
We had cherries and ice cream for dessert.

chess
a board game for two people
Chess is my favourite game.

a b c d e f g h i j k l m n o p q r s t u v w x y z

chimpanzees

chest (chests)
1 the part of your body between your neck and your stomach
Men have hair on their chests.
2 a strong box with a top that locks
The pirates hid the gold in a chest.

chestnut (chestnuts)
a big, brown, shiny nut which grows on trees
We had roasted chestnuts at the party.

chicken (chickens)
a farm bird kept for its eggs and meat, or the meat from this bird
A female chicken is called a hen.

child (children)
1 a young person
Every child has to go to school
2 someone's son or daughter
My eldest sister has just one child.

chimney (chimneys)
an opening over a fire that takes smoke out through the roof of a building
Smoke was coming from the chimney.

chimpanzee (chimp; chimpanzees, chimps)
a small ape with fur and no tail
Chimpanzees are closely related to humans.

chin (chins)
the part of your face under your mouth
His beard hides his chin.

chips
pieces of potato fried in oil
Do you like fish and chips?

chocolate
a sweet food made from cocoa beans
Would you like a piece of chocolate?

chocolate

choir (choirs)
a group of singers
I sing in the school choir.

Christmas
a Christian holiday in December
I got lots of presents for Christmas.

church (churches)
the place where Christians meet
to worship
My uncle got married in a church.

cinema (cinemas)
a place you go to see films
Shall we go to the cinema?

circus (circuses)
a show with people
and animals, held
in a big tent
The circus is in town!

city (cities)
a large town
London is the biggest city in Britain.

claws

clap (clapping, clapped)
to make a loud sound by hitting
the palms of your hands together
We clapped at the end of the show.

class (classes)
1 a group of people who learn
together
We're in the same class.

2 a group of things or animals
that are similar
*People belong to the class of
animals called mammals.*

classroom (classrooms)
a room in a school where you
have lessons
Our classroom is next to the hall.

claw (claws)
a sharp, hard nail on an animal's
foot
My cat scratched me with her claws.

clean
not dirty
The car is clean and shiny.

clean (cleaning, cleaned)
to make something tidy, to
take dirt away
*Mum told me to clean my room
because it was very messy.*

clear
1 easy to understand, hear or
read
The instructions are clear.
2 easy to see through
*You can see the fish swimming in the
clear water.*

a
b
c
d
e
f
g
h
i
j
k
l
m
n
o
p
q
r
s
t
u
v
w
x
y
z

a b **c** d e f g h i j k l m n o p q r s t u v w x y z

clever
able to learn or understand things quickly or well
Well done. You're very clever.

cliff (cliffs)
a rock or mountain next to the sea
The road runs along a cliff.

climb (climbing, climbed)
to move upwards
She climbed to the top of the ladder.

cloakroom (cloakrooms)
a room where you hang your coat
We each have our own peg in the cloakroom.

clock (clocks)
a machine that tells the time
The clock said 5:55 a.m.

clock

close (rhymes with dose)
near
The hotel is close to the beach.

close (closing, closed) (rhymes with rose)
to shut
The shops close at six o'clock.

cloth (cloths)
1 a soft material
The chair is covered in cloth.
2 a piece of cloth for a special purpose
Clean the window with a cloth.

clothes
things that people wear
I've grown and now my clothes don't fit me.

cloud (clouds)
a white or grey object in the sky that is made of tiny drops of water
There are a few clouds in the sky.

clown (clowns)
someone who makes people laugh
There was a clown at Tom's party.

coach (coaches)
1 a large bus
We went to the zoo by coach.
2 a person who trains people in sport
The football team is looking for a new coach.

coast
the land next to the sea
The village is on the coast.

coat (coats)
a piece of clothing you wear over
your clothes to stay warm
*I hang my coat on my peg when I
get to school.*

cobweb

cobweb (cobwebs)
a thin net that a spider
spins to catch insects
*There are cobwebs in
the cellar.*

coconut (coconuts)
the nut of the palm tree
*Coconuts have a white juice inside
them.*

cocoon (cocoons)
the bag around an insect that
protects it while it is growing into
an adult
*The cocoon broke open and a
butterfly flew out.*

coffee
a hot drink made from the brown
beans of a plant
Do you take sugar in your coffee?

coin (coins)
a piece of money that is made of
metal
They keep coins from their holidays.

cold
not warm or hot
Brrr – this water is very cold.

collect (collecting, collected)
to put things together in one
place
Some people collect stamps.

colour (colours)
blue, green, red or yellow
What colour is your jacket?

colour (colouring, coloured)
to make something a colour, for
example with paint or crayons
We coloured the picture in.

comb

comb (combs)
an object for making
your hair tidy
Don't let anyone use your comb.

comic (comics)
a magazine with pictures that tell
a story
The story in this comic is very funny.

a
b
c
d
e
f
g
h
i
j
k
l
m
n
o
p
q
r
s
t
u
v
w
x
y
z

a
b
c
d
e
f
g
h
i
j
k
l
m
n
o
p
q
r
s
t
u
v
w
x
y
z

compass (compasses)
an object that shows you what direction you are travelling in
Read the compass to find the treasure!

competition (competitions)
a test to see who is best at something
There was a singing competition on the radio.

complain (complaining, complained)
to say that something is wrong and that you are unhappy with it
He complained to the waiter.

computer (computers)
a machine for storing information and doing jobs such as writing letters
You can play games on computers.

concentrate (concentrating, concentrated)
to pay attention to what you are doing
I can't concentrate on my work because it's so noisy.

concert (concerts)
a show where people play music
I'm playing the violin in the concert tonight.

confused
a feeling of not being sure
I was confused by the question.

container (containers)
something that holds something else in it
Jars, tins and boxes are containers.

continent (continents)
one of the seven large areas of land in the world
Asia, Africa and Europe are all continents.

cook (cooks)
a person who prepares food
The cook has to make meals for 200 children every day.

cook (cooking, cooked)
to make food hot so it can be eaten
Ahmed is cooking dinner for us.

cook

cool
a little bit cold
There is a cool breeze.

copy (copying, copied)
to do something the same as
something else
*The teacher writes a sentence and
we copy it.*

corn
the seeds of plants such as wheat
and oats
*Popcorn and cornflakes are made
from corn.*

cottage

cottage (cottages)
a small house, usually in the
country
My granny lives in a little cottage.

cough (coughing, coughed)
to force air from your throat
*She's still coughing. Give her a drink
of water.*

count (counting, counted)
to find out how many
The teacher counted the books.

country (countries)
1 a place with its own
government
*France and Italy are European
countries.*
2 land away from cities and
towns
We live in a village in the country.

cousin (cousins)
the child of your aunt or uncle
Charlie is my cousin.

cow (cows, cattle)
a large, female farm
animal that gives milk
Cows eat grass.

cowboy (cowboys)
a man who rides a horse
and takes care of cattle
*The cowboy is wearing
a big hat and boots.*

crab (crabs)
a sea creature that moves
sideways and has big claws
I saw a crab in a pool on the beach.

crab

a b c d e f g h i j k l m n o p q r s t u v w x y z

crack (cracks)
a line where something
is broken
There's a crack in this mug.

**crack (cracking,
cracked)**
to break something so
that a line appears on it
I've cracked this mug. Sorry!

crane (cranes)
a large machine that lifts very
heavy things
*The crane lifted the huge box and
put it on the ship.*

crash (crashes)
1 an accident when two or more
things bump into each other
My uncle had a crash in his car.
2 a loud noise
The loud crash hurt my ears.

crash (crashing, crashed)
1 to have an accident by
bumping into something
The car crashed into a tree.
2 to suddenly stop
working
*The computer has crashed and
now I've lost all my work.*

cracks

**crawl (crawling,
crawled)**
to move around
on your hands
and knees
*The baby is
starting to crawl.*

crayon (crayons)
a small pencil made from
coloured wax
Use crayons to finish the picture.

cream
1 the thick yellowish-white liquid
at the top of milk
*I love strawberries and cream in
summer.*
2 a thick substance that you rub
in your skin
Don't forget to put sun cream on.

creature (creatures)
any animal
The blue whale is a huge creature.

crash

creep (creeping, crept)
to move so that no one sees or
hears you
We crept quietly through the bushes.

cricket
1 a game played by two teams.
The aim is to hit the ball and
score runs
*At my school we play football in
winter and cricket in summer.*
2 (crickets) an insect which
makes a noise by rubbing its
wings together
Crickets live under rocks and logs.

crisps
fried, thin slices of potato
I love eating crisps.

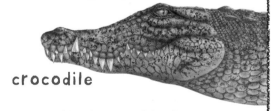
crocodile

crocodile (crocodiles)
a large animal with a long body,
short legs and big teeth
Crocodiles like floating in the water.

crooked
not straight
The fence is very crooked.

crop (crops)
plants that are grown for people
and animals to eat, or that are
used to make things
*The weather is very important to
farmers who grow crops.*

cross (crosses)
two lines that go over each other
like the letter x
*There is a cross on the map where
the treasure is hidden.*

cross (crossing, crossed)
to go from one side of something
to the other
*We looked both ways then crossed
the road.*

crowd (crowds)
a lot of people in one place
*There was a big crowd of
people outside the shop.*

crown

crown (crowns)
a metal circle that kings
and queens wear on their heads
The king is wearing a gold crown.

cruel (crueller, cruellest)
not kind
We must not be cruel to animals.

a b c d e f g h i j k l m n o p q r s t u v w x y z

a b **c** d e f g h i j k l m n o p q r s t u v w x y z

crumb (crumbs)
a small piece of something such as bread or cake
Who's eaten the cake? There are only a few crumbs left.

cry (crying, cried)
1 to have tears coming from your eyes, usually because you feel sad or are hurt
The little boy cried when he fell over.
2 to shout
"Help! Help!" they cried.

crying

cucumber (cucumbers)
a long, thin green vegetable that you put in salads
Cucumbers contain a lot of water.

cuddle (cuddling, cuddled)
to hold someone in your arms to show you care
Chloe cuddled her friend to cheer her up.

cup (cups)
a container with a handle for drinking from
I'd like a cup of hot milk please.

cupboard (cupboards)
a piece of furniture for storing things
Please dry the dishes and put them in the cupboard.

curious
wanting to know or find out about something
Cats are very curious.

curls

curl (curls)
a piece of hair that is curved at the end
She has beautiful curls.

curtain (curtains)
cloth that hangs across or over a window
We close the curtains at night.

cushion (cushions)
a bag with soft material inside for sitting or lying on
This chair is hard. I'm going to put a cushion on it.

cut (cutting, cut)
to use a knife or scissors to break something or make it smaller
We all sang 'Happy Birthday', then she cut the cake.

How many things can you spot beginning with 'd'?

D d

damage (damaging, damaged)
to spoil or break something
A big dog damaged the garden fence.

dance (dancing, danced)
to move your body to music
Let's dance to this music.

daffodil (daffodils)
a yellow flower
that comes out
in spring
*I bought my mum a
bunch of daffodils.*

daffodils

**dandelion
(dandelions)**
a wild flower with
thin, yellow petals
and fluffy seeds
*There are dandelions
growing on the lawn.*

daisy (daisies)
a flower with white
petals and a yellow centre
*Sophie picked some daisies to make
a daisy chain.*

dangerous
not safe
Playing with matches is dangerous.

a b c **d** e f g h i j k l m n o p q r s t u v w x y z

dark
not light
It's too dark to play outside.

date (dates)
1 the number of a day in a month
What's the date today?
2 a sweet fruit from a palm tree
Dates are sticky and chewy.

daughter (daughters)
a female child
Mr and Mrs Patel have two daughters.

day (days)
1 a 24-hour period
We're staying here for three days.
2 the time between the early morning when the sun rises and the time it sets
Bats do not fly during the day.

dead
not alive
This plant looks dead. Did you water it?

deaf
not able to hear
Many deaf people can read lips.

dear
1 a word to start a letter
Dear Aran, How are you?
2 much loved
She's a very dear friend.
3 expensive
This dress is too dear, let's find a cheaper one.

deep
a long way from the top to the bottom
I'm not afraid to swim in the deep end of the pool.

deer

deer
an animal that lives in forests
Deer are gentle animals.

delicious
tasting very good
This ice cream is delicious.

delighted
very happy
I'm delighted with my new bike.

den (dens)
1 a wild animal's home
The fox went back to its den.
2 a structure that children play or hide in
We made a den out of cardboard boxes.

dentist (dentists)
a person who looks after people's teeth
I go to the dentist every six months.

desert (deserts)
a place where there is very little or no rain
Camels live in the desert.

desk (desks)
a piece of furniture that you sit at to read, write or use a computer
There's a lamp on my desk.

dessert (desserts)
sweet food that you eat at the end of a meal
What's for dessert? Is it ice cream?

dessert

detective (detectives)
a person who follows clues to find out about a crime and who did it
The detective asked everyone questions.

diamond (diamonds)
a very hard, clear stone which is used to make jewellery
Diamonds are very expensive.

diary (diaries)
a book with the days of the year in it where you write what you plan to do, or what you have done
I write in my diary before I go to bed each night.

dice

die (dice)
a cube with spots on each side that is used for playing games
It's your turn – throw the dice.

die (dying, died)
to stop living
Water the plant before it dies.

a
b
c
d
e
f
g
h
i
j
k
l
m
n
o
p
q
r
s
t
u
v
w
x
y
z

a
b
c
d
e
f
g
h
i
j
k
l
m
n
o
p
q
r
s
t
u
v
w
x
y
z

different
not the same
The two sisters are very different.

difficult
not easy
*I hope the spelling test isn't
too difficult.*

dig (digging, dug)
to make a hole in the ground
Let's dig a hole in the sand.

digital
1 showing information using
numbers that can change
This is a digital watch.
2 storing information using a
special computer code
My mum uses a digital camera.

dining room (dining rooms)
the room in which you eat your
meals
*The dining room is next to the
kitchen in our house.*

dinner (dinners)
the main
evening meal
*We're having lasagne
and salad for dinner.*

dinner

dinosaur (dinosaurs)
an animal that became extinct
millions of years ago
*We learnt all about dinosaurs at
the history museum.*

dinosaur

dirty (dirtier, dirtiest)
not clean
*Please take your dirty shoes off
before you come in.*

disabled
a disabled person cannot use
part of their body
*This parking space is for disabled
drivers only.*

**disappear (disappearing,
disappeared)**
to go out of sight or become
impossible to find
*The sun disappeared behind
a cloud.*

disco (discos)
a place or a party where
people dance
There's a disco on Saturday.

discover (discovering, discovered)
to find something for the first time
The farmer discovered some old coins in his field.

disease (diseases)
an illness
Injections stop you from getting some diseases.

disguise (disguises)
something that you wear to hide who you really are
He came to the party in disguise.

dive

dish (dishes)
a bowl or plate, used for serving food
Please dry the dishes.

disk (disks)
a thin, round piece of plastic for storing computer information
Save the file on a disk.

district (districts)
an area of a town or country
Emily and I live in the same district.

disturb (disturbing, disturbed)
to speak to someone when they are doing something
Please don't disturb James while he's doing his homework.

ditch (ditches)
a long, narrow hole in the ground along the side of a road or field
Don't fall into the ditch!

dive (diving, dived)
to go into water headfirst
I can dive to the bottom of the pool.

divide (dividing, divided)
to separate or share something
Let's divide the pizza between us.

dizzy (dizzier, dizziest)
feeling that things are turning around you or that you are going to fall
That ride makes me dizzy.

doctor (doctors)
a person who looks after sick people
My uncle is a doctor. He works at the hospital.

a b c d e f g h i j k l m n o p q r s t u v w x y z

a
b
c
d
e
f
g
h
i
j
k
l
m
n
o
p
q
r
s
t
u
v
w
x
y
z

document (documents)
1 a set of papers that contain official information
We keep important documents in this cupboard.
2 a piece of work that is saved in a file on a computer
You can attach a document to an email.

dog (dogs)
an animal that people keep as a pet
Our dog is called Prince.

dog

doll (dolls)
a toy in the shape of a person
Let's play with our dolls.

dolphin (dolphins)
a large, warm-blooded creature that lives in the ocean
A dolphin looks like a fish but it is an air-breathing mammal.

domino (dominoes)
a piece of black wood or plastic with white spots that is used to play games
Each person has five dominoes.

donkey (donkeys)
an animal that looks like a small horse with long ears
Every day we feed carrots to the donkey in the field near our house.

door (doors)
something that you open and close to go into or out of a room, house or car
It's cold, shall we shut the door?

doughnut (doughnuts)
a small, round, sugary cake that has been fried in hot oil
Some doughnuts have a hole in the middle.

dolphins

down
towards a lower place
Get down off the ladder.

download (downloading, downloaded)
to put information from the Internet onto your computer or other electronic device
I downloaded the song to my iPod.

dragon

dragon (dragons)
an imaginary animal like a big lizard that breathes fire
The story is about a princess trapped in a dragon's cave.

dramatic
very exciting with lots of action
The programme had a very dramatic ending.

draughts
a board game for two people
In draughts, each player has twelve pieces.

draw (drawing, drew, drawn)
to make a picture
I can't draw people very well.

drawer (drawers)
part of a piece of furniture that slides in and out that is used for storing things
Put the socks in the drawer.

dream (dreams)
a story that happens in your mind when you are asleep
I had a bad dream last night.

dream (dreaming, dreamt, dreamed)
1 to see things in your sleep
I dreamt that I could fly.
2 to hope for something
We dream of winning the World Cup.

dress (dresses)
a piece of clothing for girls or women that has a top and skirt
I'm wearing a dress for the party.

dress

dress (dressing, dressed)
to put clothes on yourself or someone else
My mum dresses us alike because we're twins.

a b c **d** e f g h i j k l m n o p q r s t u v w x y z

a b c **d** e f g h i j k l m n o p q r s t u v w x y z

dressing gown (dressing gowns)
a long, loose garment like a coat that you wear over pyjamas
She opened the door in her dressing gown.

drink (drinks)
liquid that you take in your mouth and swallow
I'm thirsty. Can I have a drink please?

drink (drinking, drank, drunk)
to take liquid into your mouth and swallow it
I drank a glass of water.

drive (driving, drove, driven)
to control a vehicle, such as a car
Our mum drives us to and from school every day.

drop (dropping, dropped)
to fall or to let something fall
Don't drop that vase.

drum (drums)
a musical instrument that you hit with a stick or your hand
My brother got a drum for his birthday.

dry (drier, driest or dryer, dryest)
not wet
The washing is nearly dry.

duck (ducks)
a bird with webbed feet that lives near water
We feed bread to the ducks.

ducks

dustbin (dustbins)
a big container for storing rubbish
The dustbin needs emptying.

duvet (duvets)
a large bag of feathers or other soft material that you put on a bed
I curled up under the duvet.

DVD (digital versatile disk; DVDs)
a circular piece of plastic used for storing and playing music and films
We watched a DVD last night.

How many things can you spot beginning with 'e'?

a b c d **e** f g h i j k l m n o p q r s t u v w x y z

E e

eagle (eagles)
a bird that hunts for its food
An eagle has sharp claws called talons.

ear (ears)
one of two parts of your body that you hear with
Amy's hair covers her ears.

early (earlier, earliest)
before the normal time
I wake up early in the summer.

earn (earning, earned)
to get money for work
I earn extra pocket money for washing the car.

earring (earrings)
a piece of jewellery that is worn on the ear
My mum got a pair of earrings for her birthday.

eagles

Earth (earth)
1 the planet we live on
Earth travels around the Sun.
2 soil
A worm is moving through the earth.

Earth

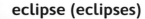

earthquake (earthquakes)
a strong shaking of the earth
The earthquake did lots of damage.

Easter
a Christian holiday in March or April
We're spending Easter at home.

easy (easier, easiest)
not difficult
This book is easy to read.

eat (eating, ate, eaten)
to take food into your mouth and swallow it
We eat our lunch in the canteen.

echo (echoes)
a sound that bounces off something and can be heard again
Can you hear an echo?

eclipse (eclipses)
a situation where the Moon passes in front of the Sun and hides it for a short time
Next week there will be an eclipse of the Sun.

eel (eels)
a long fish that looks like a snake
Eels swim thousands of miles across the Atlantic Ocean.

egg (eggs)
1 an oval object with a shell that some animals lay, and from which their babies hatch
The hen has just laid an egg.
2 an egg used as food
Fried eggs are definitely my favourite breakfast.

egg

elbow (elbows)
the place where your arm bends
Ouch; I bumped my elbow.

electricity
power that is used to make lights and machines work
Lightning is a big spark of electricity.

elephant (elephants)
a large, wild animal with a long nose called a trunk
There's a new baby elephant in the zoo.

elephants

email (emails)
a message sent by computer
I received emails from all my friends.

email (emailing, emailed)
to send a message by computer
Could you email me the information?

emergency (emergencies)
something very serious that happens suddenly and which needs people to take action immediately
The guide told us what to do in an emergency.

empty
with nothing inside
The box is empty.

end (ends)
the place or time when something stops
Keep walking to the end of the road.

end (ending, ended)
to finish or stop
The film ends at 6:30 p.m.

enemy (enemies)
someone who does not like you, or wants to hurt you
We are enemies, not friends.

energy
strength or power
We're trying to save energy, so we've switched the lights off.

engine (engines)
1 a machine that makes something work
Most cars have their engines at the front.

2 the part of a train that pulls the other carriages
Thomas is the name of a fictional tank engine in a series of stories.

empty

a b c d **e** f g h i j k l m n o p q r s t u v w x y z

a
b
c
d
e
f
g
h
i
j
k
l
m
n
o
p
q
r
s
t
u
v
w
x
y
z

enjoy (enjoying, enjoyed)
to like to do something
I enjoy playing tennis.

enormous
very, very big
Whales are enormous creatures.

enough
as much as you need
There is enough for everyone.

enter (entering, entered)
1 to go into a place
The children entered the hall and sat down.
2 to put information into a computer
You need to enter your name and address on this form.

entrance (entrances)
the door or way in to a place
The entrance to the cave was dark.

envelope (envelopes)
a paper cover for letters and cards
Put a stamp on the envelope.

equal

environment
everything around us, such as land, air or water
They live in a hot environment.

equal
the same as something else in number or amount
One kilogram is equal to 1000 grams.

equal (equalling, equalled)
to be the same as something else in number or amount
One hundred centimetres equal one metre.

Equator
an imaginary line round the centre of the Earth
Countries near the Equator are very hot.

equipment
things that are used to do a job or activity
Our school has lots of new computer equipment.

envelopes

error (errors)
a mistake
There are lots of errors in your work.

escalator (escalators)
a staircase that moves
We went up the escalator.

escape (escaping, escaped)
to get away from a place and
be free
A tiger escaped from the zoo.

**estimate (estimating,
estimated)**
to guess the size or cost of
something
We estimated the height of the tree.

evening (evenings)
the time of day between
afternoon and night time
*We don't go to school in
the evening.*

exercise

**exaggerate
(exaggerating,
exaggerated)**
to say that something is bigger or
better than it really is
*Don't exaggerate! It didn't cost
that much.*

excellent
very good
*This is an excellent book. I really
like it.*

excited
happy and interested in
something
I am excited about tomorrow.

excursion (excursions)
a trip or an outing
*We're going on an excursion to a
theme park tomorrow.*

excuse (excuses)
a reason you give for something
that you have said or done
*Her excuse for being late is that she
couldn't find her bag.*

exercise
activity that keeps you
fit and healthy
*Don't watch television.
Go and do some exercise.*

exhibition (exhibitions)
a show where people can look at
things like paintings
*There is an exhibition of things we
made at school.*

a b c d e f g h i j k l m n o p q r s t u v w x y z

a
b
c
d
e
f
g
h
i
j
k
l
m
n
o
p
q
r
s
t
u
v
w
x
y
z

exit (exits)
the way to leave a place
Don't use this door. The exit is over there.

expensive
costing a lot of money
Diamonds are expensive.

experiment (experiments)
a test that you do to learn something or find out if something is true
We did an experiment to see what happens when you put a magnet near a compass.

explain (explaining, explained)
to say what something means or why it has happened
Our teacher explained how the equipment worked.

explanation (explanations)
something that explains what something means or why it happened
There is a good explanation for the accident.

explode (exploding, exploded)
to suddenly burst or blow up into small pieces
The fireworks exploded in the night sky.

explore (exploring, explored)
to look around a new place
We explored the cave.

explosion (explosions)
a loud bang that you hear when something blows up
There was an explosion and then we saw a lot of smoke.

extinct
no longer existing
The dodo is an extinct bird.

extra
more than is necessary
If a lot of people come to the show we'll need some extra chairs.

eye (eyes)
the part of the body that we use to see
I have got blue eyes.

eye

How many things can you spot beginning with 'f'?

a b c d e **f** g h i j k l m n o p q r s t u v w x y z

Ff

face (faces)
the front part of your head
I wash my face every morning.

fact (facts)
something that is true or that
really happened
We need to know all the facts.

factory (factories)
a place where things are made in
large numbers by machines and
people
Dad works at the car factory.

faint
1 not strong or easy to hear, see
or smell
*I can't see it well because the
writing is very faint.*
2 feeling weak and dizzy
I feel faint because I'm very hungry.

faint (fainting, fainted)
to suddenly become weak or
dizzy and fall down
It was so hot that Sophie fainted.

fair
1 good and reasonable
*It's not fair that you've got
more sweets than me.*
2 light-coloured
He has fair hair.
3 fine, pleasant
*The forecast says
that the weather will be fair today.*

fair

a b c d e **f** g h i j k l m n o p q r s t u v w x y z

fairground (fairgrounds)
a place in the open air with rides and stalls
There are dodgems and a rollercoaster at the fairground.

fairy (fairies)
a person with magic powers in stories
There are good fairies and a bad fairy in Sleeping Beauty.

fairy

fairy tale (fairy tales)
a story for children about magical things
Cinderella is my favourite fairy tale.

fake
not real
Her coat is made of fake fur.

fall (falling, fell, fallen)
to drop downwards
The leaves fall from the trees in autumn.

false
not true, correct or real
He gave a false name.

family (families)
a group of people who are related to each other
There are nine people in their family.

famous
very well-known
He's a famous singer.

fan (fans)
1 an object that you hold in your hand and wave, or a machine that moves the air to make it cooler
Sit in front of the fan if you're hot.
2 someone who likes a particular thing or person very much
My dad is a fan of Manchester United.

fancy dress
clothes that you wear to a party to make you look like another person or like an animal
Are you wearing fancy dress to the party?

fang

fang (fangs)
an animal's long, sharp tooth
Wolves and snakes have fangs.

far (farther, farthest; further, furthest)
not near, at a distance away
The station is in the High Street; it's not far.

farm (farms)
a place where people grow crops and keep animals
My uncle's farm has a lot of cows.

fast
quick, not slow
Racing cars are very fast.

fat (fatter, fattest)
1 weighing more than is good or normal
It isn't healthy to be too fat.
2 thick, big or wide
Our teacher reads to us from a big, fat book.

father (fathers)
a male parent, your dad
My father was born in India.

favourite
liked the best
Blue is my favourite colour.

father

fax (faxes)
1 a machine that sends documents down a telephone line
The secretary sent the document by fax.
2 a document sent by fax
There's a fax for you.

fear (fearing, feared)
to be afraid that something bad is going to happen
Don't worry; there is nothing to fear!

feast (feasts)
a large, special meal to celebrate something
Christmas dinner is a feast at our house.

feather

feather (feathers)
one of the soft, light things that cover a bird's body
The feather floated slowly to the ground.

feed (feeding, fed)
to give food to a person or an animal
It's fun to feed the ducks.

a b c d e **f** g h i j k l m n o p q r s t u v w x y z

a b c d e **f** g h i j k l m n o p q r s t u v w x y z

feel (feeling, felt)
1 to have an emotion
I feel happy!
2 to touch something
The doctor felt my arm.

female (females)
a woman, girl or animal that can
have babies when adult
*The farmer separated the females
from the males.*

fence (fences)
a wall made of
wood or wire
*There is a fence
between our garden
and the road.*

fence

ferry (ferries)
a type of ship that carries
passengers over a short distance
We went to France by ferry.

few
not many, a small number
There are only a few tickets left.

fiction
a story which is made up and not
about real people
J K Rowling writes fiction for children.

fidget (fidgeting, fidgeted)
to keep moving and wriggling
about
Don't fidget, please. Sit still!

field (fields)
a piece of land for growing crops,
raising animals or playing sports
There is a bull in that field.

fierce
angry and strong, or violent
Guard dogs can be very fierce.

fight (fights)
a situation where people try to
hurt each other
There was a fight in the car park.

fight (fighting, fought)
when people fight they hit and
try to hurt each other
*Some people were fighting in the
car park.*

figure (figures)
1 a written number
*Two hundred and fifty one in figures
is 251.*
2 a person's shape
*She saw the figure of a woman in
the shadows.*

file (files)
1 a cardboard folder or a box to keep papers in
I keep my postcards in this green file.
2 information on a computer
Move your files to a new folder.

fill (filling, filled)
to put things into something until it is full
Fill the vase with water before putting the flowers in.

film (films)
1 a movie that you watch at the cinema or on the television
There's a Harry Potter film on the television tonight.
2 thin plastic that you put into a camera to take photographs
Digital cameras don't use film.

final (finals)
the last match in a competition
Our team is playing in the final.

final
last, happening at the end
You'll find out what happens in the final chapter.

find (finding, found)
to see or get something that you are looking for
I've lost my bag. Can you help me find it?

fine
1 very thin or in small pieces
The beach is covered with fine, white sand.
2 very good
They are fine singers.

finger (fingers)
one of the five long parts on your hand
Some people wear rings on their fingers.

fingers

finish (finishing, finished)
to end
Put your pencil down when you have finished.

fire (fires)
something that burns, giving out heat and flames
We sat around the fire.

fire

fire engine (fire engines)
a truck used to put out fires
The fire engine went along the road flashing its lights.

firework (fireworks)
a small object that explodes into bright colours in the sky
We're going to see the fireworks in the park tonight.

fish (plural is the same)
a creature that lives in water
Fish have fins to help them swim, and they breathe through gills.

fist (fists)
a closed hand
Make a fist with your hand.

fish

fit (fitter, fittest)
healthy and strong
I am very fit because I walk a lot.

fit (fitting, fitted)
to be the right size
My shoes don't fit; they're too small.

fix (fixing, fixed)
1 to mend, to repair
Dad fixed the broken tile in the kitchen.

2 to stick or attach
Fix the picture to the wall.

fizzy (fizzier, fizziest)
having a lot of tiny bubbles
Fizzy drinks aren't very healthy.

flag (flags)
a piece of cloth that is used as a signal, or the sign of a country
The British flag is red, white and blue.

flame (flames)
burning gas from a fire, or bright light from a candle
The candle flames lit up the room.

flash (flashes)
a burst of light
There was a flash of light in the sky.

flash (flashing, flashed)
to shine very brightly, but only for a short time
A light flashed on and off in the distance.

flat (flats)
a room or rooms in a bigger building
My uncle lives in a third-floor flat.

fix

flat (flatter, flattest)
not bumpy or hilly, smooth
The ground is very flat round here.

flavours

flavour (flavours)
the taste of something
*Chocolate and vanilla
are flavours of ice cream.*

flour
powder made from wheat which
is used to make bread and cakes
*Mix the flour and
butter together.*

Puzzle time
Can you guess these
flavours?
1. v_nilla   2. choc_l_te
3. str_wberr_   4. ban_n_

Answers: 1. vanilla
2. chocolate 3. strawberry
4. banana

flower (flowers)
the brightly
coloured part of a
plant that makes
the seeds or fruit
*Roses and daffodils
are flowers.*

flight (flights)
a journey in a plane
Our flight leaves at 9 o'clock.

float (floating, floated)
to lie on the water without
sinking
We floated in the pool.

flood (floods)
a lot of water in a place that is
usually dry
*There were heavy rains and then a
flood.*

floor (floors)
part of a room that you stand on
There was a carpet on the floor.

flu (influenza)
an illness like a very bad cold
*I was off school last week because I
had flu.*

fly (flies)
a small insect with wings
A fly buzzed past me.

fly (flying, flew, flown)
to move through the air
*Some birds fly south in
the winter.*

flying

fog
mist or cloud
*We can't see anything
because of the fog.*

a b c d e **f** g h i j k l m n o p q r s t u v w x y z

fold (folding, folded)
to turn or bend something over on itself
Fold your clothes before you put them in the drawer.

follow (following, followed)
to move after or behind someone or something
The ducklings followed their mother.

follow

food
something that people or animals eat
This food tastes delicious.

foolish
silly
It is a foolish idea.

foot (feet)
the part of your body at the end of your leg that you stand and walk on
My father has very big feet.

football
a game that is played by two teams who try to kick a ball into a net to score goals
We play football every day.

forest (forests)
a large area of land with lots of trees growing close together
Hansel and Gretel got lost in the forest.

forget (forgetting, forgotten)
to fail to remember something
Don't forget to do your homework.

fork (forks)
1 something with a handle and points that is used for eating or digging
Use your knife and fork.
2 the place where a road or river divides in two
Which way do we go? There's a fork in the road.

forwards
towards the front
Take a step forwards.

fossil (fossils)
the print of an animal or plant that lived long ago
Fossils show us about living things millions of years ago.

fossil

fountain (fountains)
a jet of water that is pushed up
into the air
There is a fountain in the city centre.

fox (foxes)
a wild animal that looks
like a dog with a bushy tail
I saw a fox in the bushes.

fox

fraction (fractions)
a part of something
*One half, one third and
one quarter are fractions.*

frame (frames)
a wood or metal thing that fits
around a door, window or picture
Granny put my photo in a frame.

freckle (freckles)
a small, reddish-brown spot on a
person's skin
I have freckles on my face.

free
1 not controlled, being able to do
what you want
*I have free time on Wednesday
afternoon.*
2 not costing anything
It's free to get in the museum.

freeze (freezing, froze, frozen)
to turn to ice because the
temperature is very cold
Water freezes at 0˚C.

fresh
1 just picked, grown or made
*Fresh fruits and vegetables are
healthy foods.*
2 clean and pure
*I'm going outside to get some
fresh air.*

**fridge (fridges; refrigerator,
refrigerators)**
a machine to keep food cool
Put the milk back in the fridge.

friend (friends)
a person you know and like
My friends are coming to my party.

friendly (friendlier, friendliest)
kind and easy to get on with
We have very friendly neighbours.

**frighten (frightening,
frightened)**
to scare, to
make afraid
*Storms may
frighten animals.*

frighten

a b c d e f g h i j k l m n o p q r s t u v w x y z

full

frog (frogs)
a creature, often green, that has long legs and lives on land and in water
There are frogs in the pond.

front
the part of something that is the most forward
I sit at the front of the class.

frost
white, icy powder that forms when it is very cold outside
The trees are covered in frost.

frown (frowning, frowned)
to have a sad, angry or worried look on your face
What's the matter? Why are you frowning?

fruit (fruits or fruit)
part of a plant that has seeds
Apples, oranges and grapes are all types of fruit.

fry (frying, fried)
to cook something using oil
Fry the fish until it is cooked.

full
containing as much as possible
Is the tank full yet?

fun
an enjoyable activity
We had great fun at the party.

funny (funnier, funniest)
making you laugh
The cartoon is very funny.

fur
soft, thick hair on the skin of an animal
The kitten has soft, fluffy fur.

furniture
things such as chairs, tables, beds and desks
We have some new furniture.

future
the time after now
I wonder what life will be like in the future.

fuzzy (fuzzier, fuzziest)
1 not clear
These pictures are fuzzy.
2 curly and soft
My hair is fuzzy.

fruit

How many things can you spot beginning with 'g'?

G g

game (games)
an activity with rules that you play for fun
What game shall we play?

garage (garages)
1 a building to keep a car
The garage is next to the house.
2 a place where cars are repaired
The car is at the garage.

gallop (galloping, galloped)
to run very fast, like a horse does
The horse galloped across the field.

garden (gardens)
land where flowers and plants can be grown
The garden is full of flowers.

galloping

a b c d e f **g** h i j k l m n o p q r s t u v w x y z

a
b
c
d
e
f
g
h
i
j
k
l
m
n
o
p
q
r
s
t
u
v
w
x
y
z

gate (gates)
a door in a fence or wall
*There is a gate between our garden
and our neighbour's garden.*

gentle
1 kind and careful not to hurt or
disturb people or things
She is gentle with the animals.
2 not loud or strong
There is a gentle breeze blowing.

geography
the study of the Earth,
countries and people
*I like geography because we read
about different people and places.*

ghost (ghosts)
a dead person's spirit
Do you believe in ghosts?

giant (giants)
an imaginary person who is
very big
The story is about a giant.

gift (gifts)
something given to
someone, a present
*That's a lovely gift,
thank you.*

giraffe (giraffes)
a very tall wild animal with a
long neck
Giraffes live in Africa.

girl (girls)
a female child
*There are 15 girls
in our class.*

girls

give (giving, gave, given)
to let someone have something
We gave our teacher a present.

glad (gladder, gladdest)
happy about something
He was glad to see us.

gift

glass (glasses)
1 hard, clear material that is used to make windows, bottles and mirrors
The bowl is made out of glass.
2 a container that you drink from
Can I please have a glass of water?

glasses
two pieces of glass or plastic that you wear to protect your eyes or to see better
I wear glasses for reading.

glitter
tiny pieces of sparkly material
We could make a birthday card and put glitter on it.

glitter (glittering, glittered)
to sparkle and shine brightly
Her necklace glittered in the sunlight.

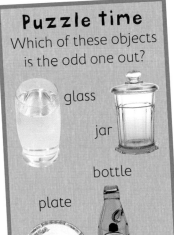

globe

Puzzle time
Which of these objects is the odd one out?

glass

jar

bottle

plate

Answer:
plate

globe (globes)
1 the world
He sailed around the globe.
2 a map of the world in the shape of a round ball
Turn the globe round to find Australia.

gloomy (gloomier, gloomiest)
1 dark
It's a gloomy day.
2 sad
Don't look so gloomy. Smile!

glove (gloves)
a piece of clothing to wear on your hands
You need your gloves today; it's cold.

glue
a thick liquid that sticks things together
Put a dot of glue in each corner of the picture.

glue (gluing, glued)
to stick things together
I'm going to glue these pictures in my scrapbook.

a b c d e f **g** h i j k l m n o p q r s t u v w x y z

a b c d e f **g** h i j k l m n o p q r s t u v w x y z

goal (goals)

1 the net and posts in a game such as football or hockey, where the player tries to place the ball
The goalkeeper stands in front of the goal.
2 the point given to a team when it puts the ball inside the goal
The striker scored another goal.
3 something you hope to do
My goal in life is to be a teacher.

goal

goat (goats)

a farm animal that usually has horns
Goats will eat almost anything.

gold

a valuable, yellow metal
The ring is made of gold.

goldfish (goldfish or goldfishes)

a small orange fish that people like to keep as a pet
I feed my goldfish once a day.

good (better, best)

1 of high quality
It's a very good school.
2 pleasant
I'm having a good time.
3 well-behaved
They have been really good children.

goodbye (bye)

something you say when you are leaving someone
Goodbye and good luck!

goose (geese)

a bird that looks like a big duck
There are geese on the farm.

goose pimples (goosebumps)

little bumps on your skin that appear when you are cold or frightened
I've got goose pimples on my arms.

gorilla (gorillas)

the biggest type of ape
We saw a huge gorilla at the zoo.

gorilla

GP (general practitioner; GPs)
a doctor who looks after the health of people in a local area
Mum took me to see the GP when I had earache.

grandfather

grandchild (grandson, granddaughter)
the child of your children
Grandparents love seeing their grandchildren.

grandchildren

grandparent (grandfather, grandmother)
the parent of your mother or father
Our grandparents live with us.

grape (grapes)
a small, round, juicy fruit that grows in bunches
Grapes can be green or purple.

grass
a green plant with thin leaves that grows over the ground
My brother is cutting the grass.

gravity
the force that pulls things towards the earth
Gravity is what makes things fall to the ground.

gravy
a brown, meaty sauce
I like gravy poured over mashed potato.

great
1 very good
This is a great song.
2 very big
There was a great storm.

greedy (greedier, greediest)
wanting or taking more food or money than is necessary
He was a greedy king.

grapes

ground
1 the earth that is under your feet
Lie on the ground and look up at the stars.
2 a piece of land used for a purpose
The football ground is on the edge of town.

a b c d e f **g** h i j k l m n o p q r s t u v w x y z

a b c d e f **g** h i j k l m n o p q r s t u v w x y z

group (groups)
people or things
that are together
or connected
*The children are sitting
in groups of four.*

group

grow (growing, grew, grown)
to become bigger or longer
The flowers are growing very well.

grown-up (grown-ups)
a child's word for a man or a
woman who is no longer a child
*Some grown-ups aren't very good
at using computers.*

grumpy (grumpier, grumpiest)
in a bad mood
He's always grumpy in the morning.

guard (guards)
a person who protects something
or someone
*Four guards stood outside
the palace.*

**guard (guarding,
guarded)**
to protect something
or someone
Soldiers guard the palace.

**guess (guessing,
guessed)**
to try to give the right
answer when you are
not sure if it is correct
Guess which hand it is in.

guest (guests)
a person you invite to your house
*We've got some guests coming this
weekend.*

guinea pig (guinea pigs)
a furry animal with no tail that
people keep as a pet
*We have a guinea pig in our
classroom.*

guitar (guitars)
a stringed musical
instrument with a long neck
He plays the guitar in a band.

gun (guns)
a weapon that fires bullets
In the film the cowboy had a gun.

gym (gyms)
a place where people go to
exercise
*There are lots of different
machines at the gym.*

guitar

How many things can you spot beginning with 'h'?

a b c d e f g **h** i j k l m n o p q r s t u v w x y z

H h

habit (habits)
something that you do often and
do without thinking about it
Biting your nails is a bad habit.

habitat (habitats)
the place where an
animal or plant
lives in the wild
*A frog's natural
habitat is in or near
a pond.*

hailstones
little balls of ice that fall like rain
from the sky
*Hailstones the size of tennis balls
sometimes fall in India.*

hair

**hair
(hairs)**
thin threads that grow on your
skin and head
She has long, curly hair.

half (halves)
one of two equal parts
*Would you like half an
orange?*

half

a
b
c
d
e
f
g
h
i
j
k
l
m
n
o
p
q
r
s
t
u
v
w
x
y
z

hall (halls)
1 the room next to the main door of a house
I always take my shoes off in the hall.
2 a big room used for meetings or parties
We do PE in the hall.

ham
meat from a pig's leg
Would you prefer ham or cheese in your sandwich?

hamburger (hamburgers)
minced beef cooked and served in a round bun
We cooked hamburgers when we were at camp.

hammer (hammers)
a tool used for hitting nails into wood
Don't drop the hammer on your toe. It's heavy!

hammock (hammocks)
a piece of material that hangs between two poles or trees which is used as a bed
It's fun to swing in a hammock.

hamster

hammock

hamster (hamsters)
a small, furry animal like a mouse
Hamsters keep food in their cheeks.

hand (hands)
the part of your body at the end of your arm
Your fingers and thumb are attached to your hand.

handbag (handbags)
a bag used for keeping things in
Mum keeps a hairbrush and keys in her handbag.

handle (handles)
the part of a bag, door or jug that you hold on to
Hold the kettle by its handle.

handsome
nice-looking
He's a very handsome man.

hang (hanging, hung)
to attach the top part of something, leaving the lower part free or loose
The teacher hung my picture on the wall.

hangar (hangars)
a big building where aeroplanes are kept
There are lots of hangars at the airport.

hanger (hangers)
a curved piece of wood or plastic to hang clothes on
Pick your shirt up and put it on a hanger.

happen (happening, happened)
to be, to take place
What a lot of noise. What's happening?

happy (happier, happiest)
feeling pleased
I'm happy because we're going on holiday tomorrow.

harbour (harbours)
a safe place for ships and boats near land
The fishing boats leave the harbour early in the morning.

hard
1 not soft
This bed is very hard.

2 difficult, not easy
The questions are very hard.

harvest (harvests)
the time of the year when farmers cut and collect crops that have been growing, or the crops themselves
The farmer had a good harvest of potatoes last year.

hat (hats)
a piece of clothing that you wear on your head
You must wear a hat in the sun.

hate (hating, hated)
to strongly dislike something or someone
Our cat hates going to the vet for her injections.

haunted
if a building is haunted people think ghosts live in it
Some people say that the house on the corner is haunted.

hay
dry grass which is cut and used to feed animals
Horses and cows eat hay.

hat

a b c d e f g **h** i j k l m n o p q r s t u v w x y z

a
b
c
d
e
f
g
h
i
j
k
l
m
n
o
p
q
r
s
t
u
v
w
x
y
z

head (heads)
1 the part of your body above your neck
Put your hands on your head.
2 a person who is the leader
The head of the school has her own office.

headphones
things that cover or go into the ears and through which you can listen to music without other people hearing it too
I can never hear people talking to me when I'm wearing my headphones.

healthy (healthier, healthiest)
1 well and strong
My grandad walks 3 miles every day to keep healthy.
2 good for you
Fruit and vegetables are very healthy foods.

hear (hearing, heard)
to be aware of sounds by using your ears
Can you hear a noise?

heart (hearts)
1 the part of your body that pumps your blood
Your heart beats faster when you run.
2 the main part of something
The theatre is in the heart of the city.
3 a shape that means love
Valentine cards often have hearts on them.

heart

heat (heating, heated)
to make something warm
Heat the soup but don't boil it.

heavy (heavier, heaviest)
weighing a lot
These books are heavy.

hedge (hedges)
a line of bushes along the side of a field or garden
The ball went over the hedge.

heavy

hedgehog (hedgehogs)
a small, wild animal with sharp hairs on its back
Hedgehogs curl up in a ball.

heel (heels)
1 the back part of your foot
Your heel is under your ankle.
2 the part of a shoe that is under your heel
Mum's shoes have high heels.

height
how tall something is
What is your height in centimetres?

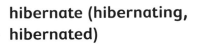

height

helicopter (helicopters)
an aircraft with blades on top that spin and make it fly
The helicopter landed in the field.

hello
what you say when you see or meet someone, or when you answer the telephone
Hello! How are you?

helmet (helmets)
a hat that protects your head
Always wear a helmet when you ride your bike.

helmet

help (helping, helped)
to make it easier for someone to do something
Let me help you carry those books.

hen (hens)
a female chicken
Hens lay eggs.

hen

here
in this place
I like it here.

hibernate (hibernating, hibernated)
to sleep during cold weather
Some animals hibernate in winter.

hide (hiding, hid, hidden)
to put yourself or something out of sight
Hide the presents, she's coming.

high
1 how long something is from the bottom to the top
How high is the mountain?
2 a long way above
The plane is high above us.

a b c d e f g **h** i j k l m n o p q r s t u v w x y z

a b c d e f g **h** i j k l m n o p q r s t u v w x y z

hill (hills)
a high piece of ground
Run down the hill.

**hippopotamus (hippo;
hippopotamuses or
hippopotami)**
a large animal that lives near
rivers and lakes in Africa
*Hippos like to
splash in
mud.*

hippo

history
things that have happened in the
past
*The history of our town is very
interesting.*

hit (hitting, hit)
to swing your hand or something
you are holding against
something else
Hit the ball as hard as you can.

hive (hives)
a box where bees live and
where they keep their honey
Thousands of bees live in each hive.

hive

hobby (hobbies)
something that you enjoy doing
in your spare time
*My hobbies are skateboarding and
listening to music.*

hockey
a game played on a field by two
teams that hit a ball using curved
wooden sticks
*We play hockey in winter and cricket
in summer.*

hold (holding, held)
to have something in your hands
or arms
Hold my coat, please.

hole (holes)
an opening or an empty space
There's a hole in the bag.

holiday (holidays)
1 a special day
Easter is a religious holiday.
2 a time when you do not have to
work or go to school
We're going on holiday next week.

hollow
empty inside
The log is hollow.

holly
holly
a plant with shiny,
prickly leaves and
red berries
*People use
holly to make
Christmas
decorations.*

hologram (holograms)
a picture made with a laser
There is a hologram on the sticker.

home
the place where you live
What time will you get home?

homework
school work you do at home
*I do my homework when I get
home from school.*

honey

honey
a sweet, sticky
food made by bees
I like honey on my porridge.

hood (hoods)
a piece of clothing that covers
your head, usually part of a coat
or jacket
Put your hood up, it's raining.

hoof (hooves)
the foot of an animal, such as a
deer, horse or goat
Horses have very thick hooves.

hook (hooks)
a piece of metal
or plastic for
hanging up or
catching things
*Hang your jacket
on the hook.*

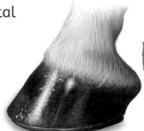
hoof

hoop (hoops)
a large ring of metal, wood or
plastic
It's fun to play with hoops.

hop (hopping, hopped)
to jump on one foot
*I can hop
across the
room.*

**hope
(hoping,
hoped)**
to wish for
something
*I hope you
have a good
time.*

hop

a
b
c
d
e
f
g
h
i
j
k
l
m
n
o
p
q
r
s
t
u
v
w
x
y
z

horizon
a line in the distance where the sky appears to touch the sea
You can see a boat on the horizon.

horn (horns)
1 one of the hard, pointed things on an animal's head
Bulls have horns.
2 part of a car that makes a loud noise
The driver beeped his horn.

horrible
bad or unpleasant
What a horrible colour.

horse (horses)
a large animal with four legs, a mane and a tail
My brother can ride a horse.

hospital (hospitals)
a place where sick or injured people go to get better
Have you ever stayed in hospital?

hot (hotter, hottest)
at a very high temperature
Egypt is a hot country.

hot dog (hot dogs)
a sausage in a long bun
Would you like a hot dog?

horns

hotel (hotels)
a place people pay to stay in
We stayed in a hotel near the beach.

hour (hours)
sixty minutes
The television programme lasts an hour.

house (houses)
a building that people live in
My house is at the top of the hill.

house

housework
cleaning and other jobs that need to be done every day in the house
Most people hate housework.

hurricane

huge
very big
There is a huge crowd waiting outside.

human (human being)
a person, not an animal
My cat is cleverer than some humans.

hump (humps)
a large bump
Some camels have two humps and others have just one.

hungry (hungrier, hungriest)
feeling that you need food
I'm hungry. What's for dinner?

hunt (hunting, hunted)
1 to look for something or someone
We hunted everywhere for the other shoe.

2 to try to catch wild animals
Owls hunt mice at night.

hurricane (hurricanes)
a very strong wind storm
Hurricanes can cause lots of damage.

hurry (hurrying, hurried)
to do something quickly
Hurry and get your coat.

hurt (hurting, hurt)
1 to cause pain to someone
The injection won't hurt you.
2 to feel pain
My knee hurts.

husband (husbands)
the man who a woman is married to
Dad is Mum's husband.

hutch

hutch (hutches)
a box where pet rabbits live
I clean my rabbit's hutch once a day.

a b c d e f g **h** i j k l m n o p q r s t u v w x y z

a b c d e f g h **i** j k l m n o p q r s t u v w x y z

How many things can you spot beginning with 'i'?

Ii

ice
water that is so cold that
it has frozen and
become hard
*Let's go skating
on the ice.*

iceberg (icebergs)
a huge piece of ice
that floats in the sea
*We saw the tip of an
iceberg.*

iceberg

ice cream
a sweet, frozen food
that is usually made
from milk or cream
*Ice cream tastes
good on hot days.*

ice
cream

ice hockey
a game that two teams
play on ice. Players use
sticks to try to hit a disc into
the goal
*The rubber disc used in ice
hockey is called a puck.*

ice skate (ice skates)
a boot with a metal blade
on the bottom for moving
across ice
You can hire ice skates at the rink.

ice-skate (ice-skating, ice-skated)
to move across ice wearing ice skates
We're learning how to ice-skate.

icicle (icicles)
a thin, pointed stick of ice
There were icicles hanging from the roof.

icing
a sweet covering for cakes
Mum put chocolate icing on the cake.

icicles

idea (ideas)
a plan or a thought about how to do something
Have you any ideas about how we can raise money for the school outing?

identical
exactly the same
Tommy and Charlie are identical twins.

identical

igloo (igloos)
a house made of blocks of snow and ice
The Inuit people live in igloos in winter.

ill
not well, sick
He's feeling ill so is going to see the doctor.

imaginary
not real
The story is about an imaginary cat with magical powers.

imagine (imagining, imagined)
to make a picture of something in your mind
Try to imagine what life was like a hundred years ago.

imitate (imitating, imitated)
to copy
The children imitated the monkeys' behaviour.

immediately
now, at once, right away
Please put your clothes away immediately.

a b c d e f g h i j k l m n o p q r s t u v w x y z

a b c d e f g h i j k l m n o p q r s t u v w x y z

important
1 serious, useful or valuable
It is a very important discovery.
2 powerful
The mayor is an important person in our town.

impossible
not able to be or to happen
That's impossible – you can't be in two places at once!

improve (improving, improved)
to get better
Your spelling is improving.

increase (increasing, increased)
to get bigger
The population of our town has increased a lot in the last ten years.

increase

infectious
if an illness is infectious other people can catch it easily
Measles is an infectious illness caused by a virus.

information
facts or knowledge about someone or something
There is a lot of information on our website.

impossible

initial (initials)
the first letter of a person's name
My initials are J M.

injection (injections)
a way of putting medicine into your body using a special needle
My baby sister had an injection yesterday.

injure (injuring, injured)
to hurt yourself or someone else
The footballer fell and injured his leg.

ink
coloured liquid that is used for writing or printing
Sign your name in ink.

innocent
an innocent person hasn't done anything wrong
He's not guilty; he's innocent.

insect (insects)
a small creature with six legs
Beetles, butterflies and bees are all
types of insects.

insects

Puzzle time
Can you find three insects
hidden in this wordsearch?

t	r	b	e	e	o
s	d	l	e	f	w
e	u	a	y	a	a
c	a	n	d	d	s
a	e	t	r	o	p
z	x	c	t	n	o

Answers: ant bee wasp

inside
in or into a place
or container
Come inside the house; it's very cold
out there.

instrument (instruments)
1 something people
use to do a job
A stethoscope is an
instrument that a
doctor uses to listen to
sounds in your body.
2 something that
makes music
Guitars and violins
are instruments.

instruments

interactive
an interactive computer program
allows users to change things
In this interactive game
you click on the ball to
try to score a goal.

interested
wanting to pay
attention to something
or someone so that
you can learn more
Sam is interested in
sport.

interesting
exciting in a way that keeps your
attention
This book is really interesting.

Internet
a huge system of linked
computers all over the
world that lets
people
communicate with
each other
We use the Internet
at home and at
school.

a b c d e f g h **i** j k l m n o p q r s t u v w x y z

interrupt (interrupting, interrupted)
to stop someone who is speaking
The phone call interrupted our conversation.

invade (invading, invaded)
to attack or go into a place in large numbers
The Vikings invaded Britain in the 8th century.

invent (inventing, invented)
to make something that has not been made before
The Chinese invented paper nearly 2000 years ago.

invention (inventions)
something new that someone makes, or produces, for the first time
The scientist is working on her new invention.

iron

investigate (investigating, investigated)
to examine something carefully to find out the truth about it
The police are still investigating the burglary.

invisible
not possible to see
You can't read it, it is written in invisible ink!

invitation (invitations)
a note or a card that asks you to go to a party
Have you replied to the party invitation?

invite (inviting, invited)
to ask someone to come somewhere with you
Ellie always invites lots of people to her parties.

iron
1 a strong, hard metal
The spade is made of iron.
2 (irons) a machine for making clothes smooth
Be careful! The iron gets very hot.

island (islands)
a piece of land that has water all around it
There's a small island in the middle of the lake.

island

How many things can you spot beginning with 'j'?

a b c d e f g h i **j** k l m n o p q r s t u v w x y z

J j

jail (jails)
a prison, a place where people
are kept by the police
*The thief was put in jail for seven
months.*

jam
a sweet food made from fruit
We have toast and jam for breakfast.

jacket (jackets)
a short coat
*Take a jacket with you;
it might be cold.*

jar (jars)
a glass container for storing
food
Jam and honey are sold in jars.

jackpot (jackpots)
the biggest prize in
a lottery or
competition
*If I win the jackpot
I'll buy you a
present.*

jars

jealous
feeling angry or bad because you want something that someone else has
He is jealous because I got a prize.

jeans

jeans
trousers made of denim, a strong material
My favourite clothes are jeans and a T-shirt.

jeep (jeeps)
an open vehicle that is used for driving over rough ground
It was a bumpy ride in the jeep.

jelly (jellies)
a clear, sweet solid food made from fruit juice
We had jelly and ice cream at the party.

jellyfish (jellyfish or jellyfishes)
a sea creature with a soft, clear body that may sting
It's difficult to see jellyfish in the water.

jet (jets)
a fast aeroplane
The pop star flew to America in a private jet.

jewel (jewels)
a stone that is very valuable, such as a diamond or ruby
The crown was covered in beautiful jewels.

jewels

jewellery
necklaces, bracelets and earrings that you wear for decoration
My mum likes to wear jewellery.

jigsaw (jigsaws)
a puzzle made from pieces that fit together to make a picture
The jigsaw has 100 pieces.

jellyfish

job (jobs)
1 work that you get paid for doing
She has a new job at the hospital.
2 something that you have to do
It's my job to take out the rubbish.

jockey (jockeys)
someone who rides a horse in a race
The winning jockey collected her prize.

jockey

jog (jogging, jogged)
to run slowly for exercise
My dad jogs three miles every morning.

join (joining, joined)
1 to become a member of a club or other group
I've joined the chess club.
2 to stick or fasten together
Join the two pieces of card with sticky tape.

joke (jokes)
a funny story that makes people laugh
Do you know any good jokes?

jolly (jollier, jolliest)
happy, always smiling
He's a jolly person.

journey (journeys)
a trip from one place to another
We were very tired after the long journey.

judge (judges)
1 the person in a court who says how to punish a guilty person
Judges often wear wigs in court.
2 a person who chooses the winner in a competition
The judges gave him nine points.

judge (judging, judged)
to say how good something is
The headmistress is going to judge the art competition.

Puzzle time

Look at this joke. Use the code to find out what the answer is.

A	B	C	D	E	F	G	H	I	J
1	2	3	4	5	6	7	8	9	10

K	L	M	N	O	P	Q	R
11	12	13	14	15	16	17	18

S	T	U	V	W	X	Y	Z
19	20	21	22	23	24	25	26

What did one road say to the other?
13/5/5/20   25/15/21   1/20   20/8/5
3/15/18/14/5/18!

Answer: Meet you at the corner!

a b c d e f g h i **j** k l m n o p q r s t u v w x y z

judo
a Japanese fighting sport
In judo people try to throw each other to the floor.

jug (jugs)
a container with a handle for liquids
Fill the jug with water.

juice   jug

juggle (juggling, juggled)
to throw several things up in the air and catch each one quickly without dropping them
The acrobat juggled with four balls.

juice
liquid from fruit or vegetables
You can have orange juice or apple juice.

jump

jump (jumping, jumped)
to push yourself off the ground with both feet
Jump as high as you can.

jumper (jumpers)
a piece of warm clothing that covers your upper body that you pull over your head
My granny knitted me a jumper.

jungle (jungles)
a thick forest in a hot country
The trees and plants in a jungle grow very close together.

junior
for younger people
I play in the junior orchestra.

junk
things you don't want any more because they are old or no good
The garage is full of junk.

just
1 happened a very short time ago
I've only just arrived.
2 exactly the right amount or thing
There was just enough flour to make a cake.
3 only
No, it's not a fly. It's just a bit of fluff.

How many things can you spot beginning with 'k'?

Kk

kaleidoscope (kaleidoscopes)
a tube with pictures or pieces of coloured glass or plastic at one end that you look through and turn to see changing patterns
The kaleidoscope was invented in 1816.

kaleidoscope

kangaroo (kangaroos)
an Australian animal that keeps its young in a pouch on the front of its body
Kangaroos have big, strong back legs.

kangaroo

karaoke
the playing of the music of songs without the words, so people can sing the words into a microphone
Karaoke started off in Japan.

karate
a Japanese fighting sport
In karate you fight using your hands and feet.

a b c d e f g h i j **k** l m n o p q r s t u v w x y z

a b c d e f g h i j **k** l m n o p q r s t u v w x y z

kebab (kebabs)
pieces of meat or vegetables on
a stick
Let's have a takeaway kebab.

keep (keeping, kept)
1 to continue to have something
*You can keep the books for two
weeks.*
2 to continue to do something
Don't keep staring at that man.
3 to store something in a certain
place
We keep the paints in the cupboard.

kennel (kennels)
a small structure, usually made
out of wood, for a dog to sleep in
*The man next door is making a
kennel for his dog.*

ketchup
a thick, cold, sauce
made out of tomatoes
*I'd like some ketchup on my
burger, please.*

kettle (kettles)
a container with a lid for boiling
water
*Come in. I'll put the kettle on and
make some tea.*

key

key (keys)
1 a piece of
metal used to open
a lock
Have you seen my door key?
2 one of the parts of a computer
or piano that you press with your
fingers
*Type the file name and then press
the 'enter' key.*
3 a set of answers or an
explanation of symbols
There is a key at the back of the book.

keyboard (keyboards)
the set of keys on a computer or
a piano that you press to type or
make a sound
*This is a special keyboard with
letters and pictures.*

kick

**kick (kicking,
kicked)**
to swing your foot
at something
*Kick the ball into
the goal!*

kill (killing, killed)
to cause someone or
something to die
Some weeds kill other plants.

kind
helpful, pleasant and thoughtful
It's very kind of you to think of me.

king (kings)
a royal man who rules a country
Do you think the prince will become king?

king

kiss (kissing, kissed)
to touch someone with your lips
Mum kissed us all goodnight.

kitchen (kitchens)
the room in a house for preparing food
There are nice smells coming from the kitchen.

kite (kites)
a toy for flying in the air, made of light wood and cloth, paper or plastic and that has a long string
Shall we fly the kite today?

kite

kitten (kittens)
a baby cat
Our cat has just had a litter of kittens.

kiwi fruit (kiwi fruits)
a green fruit with a brown, hairy skin
Mum sliced a kiwi fruit to put in the fruit salad.

kitten

knee (knees)
the part of your leg that bends
When you walk, you bend your knees.

kneel (kneeling, knelt)
to get down on your knees
Dad knelt down to stroke the cat.

knife (knives)
a tool with a blade for cutting things into pieces
Use a knife to cut the meat.

Puzzle time

How many kitchen things can you find in this word puzzle?

sinkbathovencupboardtable
chairsofashelfcupbedsaucer

Answer: 8

a b c d e f g h i j **k** l m n o p q r s t u v w x y z

a
b
c
d
e
f
g
h
i
j
k
l
m
n
o
p
q
r
s
t
u
v
w
x
y
z

knight (knights)
a type of soldier
who lived hundreds
of years ago
*Knights wore armour
when they rode into
battle.*

knight

knit (knitting, knitted)
to make clothes or
other things using wool and two
long needles
Jodie knitted a scarf.

knob (knobs)
1 a round handle on a door,
cupboard or drawer
*I opened the drawer and the knob
came off in my hand.*
2 a round switch on a radio or on
a machine
Turn the knob to make it louder.

knock (knocking, knocked)
to hit something to make a noise
Someone is knocking on the door.

knot (knots)
the place where two pieces of
string or rope are tied together
There's a knot in my shoelaces.

know (knowing, knew, known)
1 to have information and facts in
your mind
*I know that Rome is the capital of
Italy.*
2 to have met someone before
or be familiar with them
*Do you know our neighbour
Mrs Smith?*

knuckle (knuckles)
one of the bony places in your
hand where the fingers bend
*When you make a fist you can see
your knuckles.*

koala (koalas)
an Australian animal that looks
like a small grey bear
Koalas live in trees.

koala

How many things can you spot beginning with 'l'?

a b c d e f g h i j k l m n o p q r s t u v w x y z

Ll

ladder (ladders)
a piece of equipment made from two long bars joined together by short bars, which you climb to reach high places
Dad uses a ladder when he paints the house.

label (labels)
a piece of paper or cloth that gives information about the thing it is attached to
Always put a label on your folders.

ladybird (ladybirds)
an insect that is red with black spots
Ladybirds are good for the garden.

ladybird

lace
fine cloth made with patterns of tiny holes
The doll's dress is made of lace.

lake

lake (lakes)
a big area of water that has land all around it
There are lots of rowing boats on the lake.

lamb
1 (lambs) a young sheep
Lambs are born in the spring.
2 meat from lambs
We had roast lamb for dinner.

lamb

lamp (lamps)
a light that you can carry around
I have a lamp on my desk.

land
1 ground
They built a house on a plot of land.
2 the dry part of the Earth
The sailors were happy to see land.
3 (lands) a place or a country
The castle is in a magical land.

land (landing, landed)
to reach the ground after being in the air
The plane lands at 2:45 p.m.

language (languages)
words people use when they speak and write
French and English are languages.

lap (laps)
1 the top of your legs when you are sitting down
My cat sits on my lap.

2 once around a track
They ran 12 laps of the track.

laptop (laptops)
a small computer that you can carry around with you
Some people use laptops on trains.

large
big
We ate a large piece of cake.

laptop

larva (larvae)
a very young form of an insect
The larva of a butterfly is called a caterpillar.

laser (lasers)
a powerful light or the machine that makes it
Doctors sometimes use lasers in operations.

lasso (lassos)
a long rope with a loop at one end
The cowboy used a lasso to round up all the cattle.

lasso

last
1 after the others
We came last in the egg and spoon race.
2 the most recent, the one that happened the shortest time ago
We went to Italy for our last holiday.

last (lasting, lasted)
to continue to work or to happen
How long do you think this good weather will last?

late
1 after the normal or correct time
Sorry I'm late!
2 towards the end of a period of time
It was late on Sunday afternoon when we left for town.

laugh (laughing, laughed)
to make a sound that shows you are happy, or when you think something is funny
We laughed at Dad's silly joke.

law (laws)
a rule made by the government
There are laws about children working before the age of 14.

lawn (lawns)
an area of grass that is kept short in a garden or a park
We play football on the lawn.

lay (laying, laid)
1 to put in a place
Lay out your pencils in a row.
2 to make an egg
The hens lay eggs most days.

lazy (lazier, laziest)
1 not wanting to work
Don't be lazy. Get up out of the armchair.
2 not busy, relaxed
We had a nice, lazy weekend.

lead (leads)
a strap that you put on a dog when taking it for a walk
Please keep your dog on a lead!

lead

lead (leading, led)
1 to show someone the way
The guide led us through the cave's passageways.
2 to be in the front
The black horse is leading the race.

a b c d e f g h i j k l m n o p q r s t u v w x y z

leaf

leaf (leaves)
one of the many flat, green
things on a plant or tree
Dad swept up all the leaves.

lean (leaning, leant, leaned)
1 to bend your body
Lean over to reach the ball.
2 to rest against something
Chris was leaning against the wall.

leap (leaping, leapt)
to jump into the air
or over something
*The fish leapt out
of the water.*

leap

**learn (learning,
learnt, learned)**
to get knowledge or information
about a subject
We are learning French at school.

leather
the skin of an animal that is used
to make bags, shoes and other
things
My belt is made of leather.

leave (leaving, left)
1 to go away from a place
What time are you leaving?

2 to put a thing in a place or
to let a thing stay in a place
You can leave your bike here.

leg (legs)
1 the part of your body between
your hip and your foot that you
stand on
You've got longer legs than me.
2 the part of a table or chair that
holds it up
One of the chair legs is broken.

legend (legends)
a very old story about things that
happened a long time ago
*There are many legends about
Robin Hood.*

lemon (lemons)
a yellow fruit with a sour taste
I put a slice of lemon in my drink.

lemonade
a cold, sweet, fizzy drink
We drank lemonade at the party.

lend (lending, lent)
to let someone have or use
something that they will return
after using
Could you lend me a pen, please?

a b c d e f g h i j k **l** m n o p q r s t u v w x y z

length
how long something is
This table is one metre in length.

leopard (leopards)
a wild cat with yellow
fur and black spots
*Leopards are fast runners
and can climb trees.*

leopard

leotard (leotards)
a stretchy piece of clothing like a
swimming costume with sleeves
We wear leotards to do ballet.

lesson (lessons)
a time when you are learning
something from a teacher
We had two lessons in the morning.

let (letting, let)
1 to allow someone to do
something
Will your mum let you come over?
2 to allow something to happen
Just let the ball drop.

letter (letters)
1 one of the signs of the alphabet
used in writing
*There are five letters in the word
'catch'.*

2 a written message that you put
in an envelope and send or give
someone
*You can either send a
letter or an email.*

lettuce (lettuces)
a green, leafy vegetable
eaten in salads
We're growing lettuce this year.

library (libraries)
a place where you can borrow
books
*A mobile library comes to our
village twice a week.*

lick (licking, licked)
to put your tongue
on something
Lick your ice cream, it's going to drip.

lick

lie (lies)
something you say that you know
is not true
I told a lie and said I liked her dress.

lie (lying, lay, lain)
to have your body flat on the
floor, ground or bed
*We put our towels on the sand and
lay down.*

a b c d e f g h i j k l m n o p q r s t u v w x y z

lie (lying, lied)
to say something that you know is not true
They lied about their age.

life
1 (lives) the time between when you are born and when you die
He had a long and happy life.
2 the state of being alive
Is there is life on other planets?

lifeboat (lifeboats)
a boat that helps people who are in danger at sea
The lifeboat rescued the fishermen just in time.

lifeboat

lift (lifts)
1 a machine that takes you up and down in a building
Take the lift to the fourth floor.
2 a ride in a car
Do you need a lift?

lift (lifting, lifted)
to move something to a higher place
It took four people to lift our piano.

lift

light
1 energy or brightness from the Sun or a lamp that lets you see things
Is it light enough to take a photo?
2 (lights) a device with a bulb that gives out light
Turn off the light, it's time for bed.

light (lighter, lightest)
not heavy
My bag is light because there's nothing in it.

lighthouse (lighthouses)
a tower on the coast that has a bright light that flashes to warn ships
There's a lighthouse at the end of the beach.

lightning
electrical light in the sky during a storm
We could see lightning in the distance.

like (liking, liked)
1 to enjoy something or be fond of someone or something
I really like skateboarding.

2 to want
What would you like for your birthday?

limb (limbs)
an arm or a leg
I felt dizzy and all my limbs were shaking.

line (lines)
1 a long, thin mark
Draw a line through the mistakes.
2 a piece of string, rope or wire
Hang the clothes on the line.
3 a row
There is a line of trees by the park.

lion (lions)
a large wild cat that lives in Africa
Male lions have long hair on their head called a mane.

lion

lip (lips)
one of the two edges of your mouth
The cat came in, licking his lips.

liquid (liquids)
something, such as water that and can be poured
Milk, juice and water are liquids.

listen (listening, listened)
to pay attention to sound
Are you listening to me?

litter

litter
1 rubbish lying on the ground
We picked up all the litter.
2 (litters) the group of babies that an animal has at one time
Our dog had a litter of puppies.

little
1 small, not large
My little brother is so funny.
2 not much
We gave the cat a little milk.

live (living, lived)
1 to be alive
My uncle lived to be 90 years old.
2 to have your home in a certain place
They live in France now.

living room (living rooms)
a room in a house for sitting and relaxing in
The TV is in the living room.

a b c d e f g h i j k l m n o p q r s t u v w x y z

a b c d e f g h i j k **l** m n o p q r s t u v w x y z

lizard (lizards)
a small reptile with a long tail
Lizards have dry, scaly skin.

lizard

llama (llamas)
an animal from
South America
that has a soft, woolly coat
Llamas can carry heavy loads.

loaf (loaves)
bread that is baked in one piece
Get a loaf of bread from the shop.

lobster (lobsters)
a sea creature with
eight legs and two claws
*We saw a lobster through
the glass-bottomed boat.*

loaf

lock (locks)
an object that closes something
that you can only open with a key
There's a lock on the diary.

lock

lock (locking, locked)
to close or fasten
something with a key
*Have you locked the
door?*

locker (lockers)
a narrow metal cupboard
We left our suitcase in a locker.

loft (lofts)
the inside of the roof of a house
There's some old books in the loft.

log (logs)
a thick piece of a tree
It's cold. Put another log on the fire.

lollipop (lollipops)
a hard, round sweet on a stick
I bought an orange lollipop.

lonely (lonelier, loneliest)
feeling sad that you are alone
Old people sometimes get lonely.

long
1 measuring a big distance from
one end to the other
We sit at a long table for lunch.
2 continuing for a large amount
of time
It's a very long film.

look (looking, looked)
to pay attention to
something that you see
Look at that hot-air balloon.

loose
1 not tight
These trousers are loose.
2 escaped, free
The bull is loose in the field.

loose

lorry (lorries)
a large vehicle for carrying things
My uncle drives a big lorry.

lose (losing, lost)
1 not to be able to find something
I've lost my key.
2 not to win a competition or a game
Our team lost the match.

lottery (lotteries)
a game where you can win a big prize if the numbers on your card match the winning numbers
If I win the lottery I'll buy a car.

loud
not quiet, making a lot of noise
There was loud music coming from upstairs.

loud

love (loving, loved)
to like someone or something very much
We love our new baby.

lovely (lovelier, loveliest)
beautiful or pleasant
It's a lovely day.

low
close to the ground, not high
The Sun was low in the sky.

lucky (luckier, luckiest)
1 fortunate, having good things happen to you
They're lucky they won the lottery.
2 giving good luck
These are my lucky football boots.

luggage
the bags and suitcases you take with you when you are travelling
I can't carry all this luggage.

lunch (lunches)
a meal that you eat in the middle of the day
What's for lunch today?

lung (lungs)
one of two parts of your body inside your chest that help you to breathe
Your two lungs are protected by bones called ribs.

a b c d e f g h i j k l m n o p q r s t u v w x y z

a b c d e f g h i j k l **m** n o p q r s t u v w x y z

How many things can you spot beginning with 'm'?

Mm

macaroni
pasta shaped like small tubes
I like macaroni with cheese sauce.

machine (machines)
a piece of equipment
that is used to
do a job
*Washing
machines
wash, rinse and
spin your clothes.*

magazine (magazines)
a thin book with a paper cover
containing pictures and stories
*My mum buys her favourite
magazine every week.*

magic
a power to make strange things
happen
The coin disappeared by magic.

magician (magicians)
a person who does magic tricks
We had a magician at my party.

magnet (magnets)
a piece of metal that makes
some other metal objects move
towards it
A magnet will pick up all these pins.

magnet

magpie (magpies)
a big, black-and-white bird with
a long tail
*Magpies sometimes
steal shiny
objects.*

magpie

mail
all the letters, cards and parcels
you send or receive in the post
He sat at his desk reading his mail.

main
the most important or the
biggest
*We'll meet you in front of the main
entrance.*

make (making, made)
1 to create or build something
I made a model of an aeroplane.
2 to cause something to happen
or be a certain way
That joke always makes me laugh.

male (males)
a man, boy or an animal that
cannot produce eggs
or have babies
*The male peacock is
the one with the big,
colourful tail.*

mammal (mammals)
a type of animal that gives birth
to live babies and makes milk
for them to drink
*The elephant is the
largest land mammal.*

mammal

man (men)
an adult male
A man knocked at the door.

many (more, most)
large in number
I've been to France many times.

map (maps)
a drawing that shows where
things and places are in a
building, town, country or other
place
We studied a map of the world.

marble
1 a type of hard stone
The statue is made of marble.
2 (marbles) a small glass or
metal ball used to play a game
*I won two marbles in that
last game.*

marbles

a b c d e f g h i j k l **m** n o p q r s t u v w x y z

march

march (marching, marched)
to walk with regular steps
The soldiers marched in the parade.

mark (marks)
1 a sign or shape
Put a mark to show where your house is.
2 a letter or number that a teacher puts on a piece of work to show how good it is
She's getting good marks this term.
3 a spot or a dark patch on something that makes it look bad
There is a mark on the carpet where we spilled the juice.

market (markets)
a place where you can buy food, clothes, plants and other things
Most markets are outdoors.

marmalade
jam that is made from oranges
My mum likes toast and marmalade.

marry (marrying, married)
to become husband and wife
They married three years ago.

mask (masks)
something that you put over your face to hide or protect it
She wore a mask to go to the fancy-dress party.

mast (masts)
a tall pole on a boat that holds up the sail
The pirate climbed up the mast.

mat (mats)
a piece of material, like a small carpet, that you put on the floor
Wipe your feet on the mat.

match (matches)
1 a small stick that makes a flame when you rub it against something rough
We have special long matches for lighting the fire.
2 a contest or game
That's the best tennis match I've ever seen.

match

match (matching, matched)
to go well together or be the same
Does my shirt match my trousers?

mathematics (maths)
the study of numbers or shapes
Mathematics is my favourite subject at school.

mattress (mattresses)
the soft, thick part of a bed that you sleep on
My mattress is too hard and I can't get to sleep.

mayonnaise
a cold, thick, creamy sauce that you put on salads
Could I have mayonnaise in my sandwich, please?

mayor (mayors)
the leader of the town or city council
The mayor came to our autumn fair.

maze (mazes)
a lot of confusing paths that it is difficult to find your way through
We couldn't find our way out of the maze, but it was fun.

meadow

meadow (meadows)
a field with grass and flowers
There are lots of pretty flowers growing in the meadow.

meal (meals)
the food you eat at certain times of the day
Our main meal was roast chicken.

meal

mean
1 cruel or unkind
Don't be mean to each other.
2 not wanting to spend money
The king is very mean and counts his money every day.

mean (meaning, meant)
1 to explain something or say what something is
What does this word mean?
2 to want or plan to do something
I didn't mean to hurt him.

a b c d e f g h i j k l **m** n o p q r s t u v w x y z

meaning (meanings)
the information that you get
from words and signs
*Can you explain the meaning
of this sentence?*

measles

measles

a serious illness
that that can give
you a high temperature and lots
of red spots
*When we had measles, we had to
stay in bed.*

measure

measure
**(measuring,
measured)**
to find out the
size or amount of something
We measured the line with a ruler.

meat
food that comes from the bodies
of animals
*Chicken, beef and pork are all types
of meat.*

mechanic (mechanics)
a person who fixes cars and
machines
*My dad works as a mechanic at the
garage.*

medal (medals)
a piece of metal that is given as a
prize for winning a competition
or for doing something special
He won a medal for bravery.

medicine
1 something that you take
when you are not well so that
you will get better
*You have to take this medicine three
times a day.*
2 the study of illness and injury
*She is studying
medicine because
she wants to be a
doctor.*

medium
middle sized, between large and
small
I'd like a medium popcorn, please.

meet (meeting, met)
1 to get to know someone for the
first time
*I met my best friend Theo on the
first day of school.*
2 to go to the same place as
another person
*Let's meet at 10 o'clock in front of
the swimming pool.*

melody (melodies)
a song or the tune of a song
The song has a strange but
beautiful melody.

melon (melons)
a large fruit with a hard skin and
flat seeds
Melons can
be green,
yellow or
orange.

melt

melt (melting, melted)
to change from a solid to a liquid
when the temperature rises
The ice in my drink has melted.

memory (memories)
1 something that you remember
from the past
Photographs bring back memories.
2 the ability to remember things
Do you have a good memory?
3 the part of a computer where
information is stored
This computer has more
memory than our old one.

mend (mending, mended)
to repair
Could you help me mend the tyre?

menu (menus)
1 the list of food in a
café or restaurant
The waiter brought
us each a menu.
2 a list of things seen
on a computer screen
Click here to go back to the main
menu.

menu

mermaid (mermaids)
in stories, a sea creature with a
woman's body but a fish's tail
instead of legs
The mermaid was sitting on a rock
combing her hair.

message (messages)
information for a person from
someone else
I sent you a message by email.

messy (messier, messiest)
untidy
This room is very messy.

metal
hard material such
as gold, silver,
copper or iron
Coins are made
out of metal.

metal

microphone (microphones)
something that is used for recording sounds or making them louder
Sing into the microphone.

— microphone

microscope (microscopes)
something that makes small things look much bigger
We looked at a hair under the microscope.

microwave (microwaves)
an oven that cooks food very quickly
Heat the soup in the microwave.

midday
12:00 in the middle of the day
We'll have our lunch early – at about midday.

middle (middles)
the centre or the part of something that is halfway between the beginning and the end
We sat down in the middle of the row.

midnight
12:00 in the middle of the night
We stay up until midnight on New Year's Eve.

mild
1 not too strong or serious
She had a mild case of flu.
2 not tasting too strong or too spicy
It's a mild curry.
3 not too cold, quite warm
The weather is mild today.

milk
white liquid that female mammals produce to feed their babies
The milkman leaves two pints of milk on the doorstep every day.

milk

mime (miming, mimed)
to act or tell a story without using any words
The children mimed scenes from the story.

mind (minds)
the part of you that helps you think and remember
I said the first thing that came into my mind.

mind (minding, minded)
1 not to like something, or to be worried by it
I don't mind what we play.
2 to be careful
Mind your head when you go through the door.
3 to look after something or someone
I'll mind your cat while you're on holiday.

mind

minus
1 the sign used in maths when taking one number away from another
Twenty-five minus five equals twenty.
2 in temperature, below zero
It's cold today, it's minus one outside!

minute (minutes)
sixty seconds
We waited for twenty minutes but they didn't come.

miracle (miracles)
a wonderful thing that happens that you can't explain
It's a miracle that no one was killed in the plane crash.

mirror

mirror (mirrors)
special glass in which you can see your reflection
Go and look in the mirror; you look really pretty.

miserable
very unhappy
Don't look so miserable.

miss (missing, missed)
1 not to hit a target
He threw the ball but missed the basket.
2 to feel sad because you are not with someone
My dad is away in the army and I miss him.

mist
light fog caused by tiny drops of water forming a cloud near the ground
The mist soon cleared and the sun came out.

a b c d e f g h i j k l **m** n o p q r s t u v w x y z

mistake (mistakes)
something that is wrong
If you make a mistake, cross it out.

mitten (mittens)
a glove that does not have separate places for each finger
Wrap up well and wear your mittens.

mix (mixing, mixed)
to put different things together and stir them
Mix the eggs and sugar together.

moat (moats)
a ditch or deep hole around a castle
The people in the castle built the moat to keep out their enemies.

mobile phone (mobile phones)
a small telephone that people carry around
Call me on my mobile phone.

model (models)
1 a small copy of something such as a plane or a building
We made a model of a jet plane at the weekend.

2 a person whose job is to show clothes
She wants to be a model.
3 one type of something
This computer is the most up-to-date model.

money
coins and paper that you use to buy things
Have you spent all your money already?

moat

monitor (monitors)
1 the part of a computer that shows the screen
It's easier to see on a big monitor.
2 a pupil who has a special job to do
I'm the book monitor this term.

monkey (monkeys)
an animal with a long tail that is good at climbing trees
We watched the monkeys at the zoo.

monkey

monster (monsters)
a frightening creature
in stories and films
*The monster chased
them into the forest.*

monster

month (months)
one of the twelve parts of
the year
*June and July are
summer months.*

Moon

moon (Moon; moons)
the round shining
object that you see in the sky at
night
*The Moon goes round the Earth and
takes four weeks to go round once.*

mop (mops)
a sponge or lots of strips of cloth
on the end of a handle that you
use for cleaning floors
*Put the mop back in the bucket
when you've finished.*

more (most)
1 stronger or greater than
*This book is more interesting than
the one I was reading last week.*

2 a bigger amount or number
Is there any more cake?

morning (mornings)
the part of the day between the
time the sun comes up and noon
*We get up at the same time every
morning.*

mosque (mosques)
a building where Muslims pray
*Ali goes to the mosque every
Friday.*

moth (moths)
an insect that looks like a
butterfly
Moths fly around at night.

mother

mother (mothers)
a woman who has a
child or a female
animal that has
young
*My mother
looks after me.*

motor (motors)
the part of a machine that uses
power to make it work
*The washing-machine motor is
broken.*

a
b
c
d
e
f
g
h
i
j
k
l
m
n
o
p
q
r
s
t
u
v
w
x
y
z

motorbike (motorcycle; motorbikes, motorcycles)
a vehicle with two wheels and an engine
Dad has a new motorbike.

motorway (motorways)
a road where cars can drive fast and travel a long way
There aren't any traffic lights or roundabouts on a motorway.

mountain (mountains)
a very high piece of land, bigger than a hill
Some mountains have snow on top all year round.

Puzzle time
Spot five differences between these two pictures

mouse

mouse (mice)
1 a small animal with a long tail and a pointed nose
There are mice in the field.
2 part of a computer that you click on to move things around on the screen
You need a mouse to play this game.

moustache (moustaches)
the hair that grows above a man's lip
My dad has a little moustache.

mouth (mouths)
the part of your face with lips, teeth and your tongue
You talk and eat using your mouth.

move (moving, moved)
to change your position or the position of something else
Can you move your head, please? I can't see.

movie (movies)
a film, a story that is told using pictures that move
Let's watch a movie tonight.

much (more, most)
a lot
Thank you so much for coming.

mud
wet soil or earth
I'm covered in mud!

mug (mugs)
a big cup with tall sides
Do you want a mug of hot chocolate?

mugs

multiply (multiplies, multiplying, multiplied)
to add a number to itself, often more than once
What number do you get if you multiply two by four?

music

munch (munches, munching, munched)
to eat something noisily
The rabbit munched on carrots.

muscle (muscles)
one of the parts of the body that tightens and relaxes to cause movement
My brother has got big muscles because he goes to the gym.

museum (museums)
a place where old, important, valuable or interesting things are kept so that people can go and look at them
There is a toy museum in our town.

mushroom (mushrooms)
a small fungus with a stem with a round top that you can eat
Do you want mushrooms on your pizza?

music
a pattern of sounds that is sung or played on special instruments
The orchestra played such beautiful music.

must
to have to do something
You must put your books away.

mustard
a yellow or yellowish-brown sauce that tastes hot and spicy
I'd like mustard on my hot dog.

mysterious
strange, secret or difficult to understand
He is a mysterious person; we don't know much about him.

myth (myths)
a very old story about gods, goddesses and heroes
The story Pandora's Box *is an ancient Greek myth.*

a
b
c
d
e
f
g
h
i
j
k
l
m
n
o
p
q
r
s
t
u
v
w
x
y
z

a b c d e f g h i j k l m **n** o p q r s t u v w x y z

How many things can you spot beginning with 'n'?

Nn

nail (nails)
1 a thin, sharp piece of metal with one flat end that you hit with a hammer
Hammer a nail into the wall so we can hang up the picture.
2 the hard covering on the ends of your fingers and toes
He bites his nails.

nail

name (names)
what a person or object is called
What's your name?

narrow
having only a short distance from one side to the other
The road is very narrow.

name

nasty (nastier, nastiest)
very unpleasant or bad
That's a very nasty cut.

nation (nations)
a country and the people who live there
Teams from all nations take part in the Olympic Games.

national
to do with a country
or the whole country
*We waved the national
flag of our country.*

national

nature
all the animals, plants, rivers,
mountains and other things in
the world that are not made by
people
I like reading books about nature.

**naughty (naughtier,
naughtiest)**
badly behaved
Don't be naughty.

naughty

navy (navies)
the ships and people that fight
for a country at sea during a war
My cousin is in the navy.

near
close by, not far
There's a bus stop near the zoo.

neat
clean or organized
His room is always neat and tidy.

necessary
if something is necessary you
really need it or it must be done
*It's useful to have your own
computer, but it isn't necessary.*

Puzzle time
Someone has been very
naughty and written this
message backwards. Can
you work out what it says?

ouy dlouhs od ruoy
krowemoh yreve yad

Answer: you should do your
homework every day

neck (necks)
the part of your
body that attaches
your head to your
shoulders
*Put a scarf around
your neck.*

**necklace
(necklaces)**
a piece of jewellery
that you wear
around
your
neck
*That's a
beautiful
necklace.*

necklace

nectarine (nectarines)
a fruit like a peach but with a
smooth skin
This nectarine is lovely and juicy.

need (needing, needed)
if you need something, you must
have it
*I need another exercise book; this
one is full.*

needle

needle (needles)
1 a thin, sharp
piece of metal
with a hole
through it
used for sewing
*Could you thread
this needle for me, please?*
2 a thin, sharp piece of metal
through which injections are
given
The needle will not hurt you.

**neighbour
(neighbours)**
a person who
lives near you
*We invited all our
friends and
neighbours to the
party.*

nephew (nephews)
the son of your sister or brother
*My nephew is staying with us for a
few days.*

nerve (nerves)
part of your body like a long
string, which carries messages
between the brain and other
parts of the body
*There are millions of nerves in the
human body.*

nervous
worried or frightened, not able to
relax
*She's a little nervous about being in
the school play.*

nest (nests)
a place birds make to lay their
eggs
There's a robin's nest in that tree.

nest

net (nets)
material that is made
by joining pieces of
string or thread
together, leaving
spaces between them
*We use a small net
when we go fishing.*

netball
a game played by two teams of seven players, usually women or girls. The aim is to throw a ball through a net hanging on a pole
My hobbies are netball and swimming.

nettle (nettles)
a wild plant whose leaves sting if you touch them
You can make tea and soup from nettles.

nettle

network (networks)
a system of things or people that are connected
This computer is part of a network.

never
not at any time, not ever
I've never been to China.

new
recently made or bought, not old
I love your jacket. Is it new?

new

news
information about something that is happening now or that happened a short time ago
Write soon and send us all your news.

newspaper (newspapers)
large sheets of paper which tell you what is happening in the world

newspapers

Have you read today's newspaper?

next
1 the one that is nearest to you
There's an empty seat next to Susie.
2 the one that is immediately after someone or something else
Who's next on the list?

nice
enjoyable, good, pleasant
Did you have a nice time?

nickname (nicknames)
a name which your friends and family call you
My brother Rory's nickname is Rozza.

a
b
c
d
e
f
g
h
i
j
k
l
m
n
o
p
q
r
s
t
u
v
w
x
y
z

niece (nieces)
the daughter of your sister or brother
Her niece works in a bank.

night (nights)
the time between sunset and sunrise, when it is dark
You can see the stars on a clear night.

nightdress (nightie; nightdresses, nighties)
a dress to sleep in
Put your nightdress on and get into bed.

nightdress

nightmare (nightmares)
a bad dream
Nightmares can be very scary.

nil
a score of nothing in sport
Our team won four-nil.

nobody
no one, no person
There's nobody home.

nod (nodding, nodded)
to move your head up and down
You can nod your head instead of saying 'yes'.

noise (noises)
a loud sound
Did you hear that noise?

noisy

noisy (noisier, noisiest)
very loud or making a lot of noise
There were lots of noisy people on the beach.

none
not any, not one
I wanted some bread but there was none left.

nonsense

nonsense
something that does not make any sense, or mean anything
The idea that animals can drive is complete nonsense.

no one
nobody, not one person
I have no one to talk to.

noodles
long, thin strips of pasta
*Do you want rice or
noodles with
your beef?*

noon
midday, 12:00
*The bell goes at
noon.*

noodles

normal
something that is ordinary or
usual
*It's normal to feel tired first thing in
the morning.*

nose (noses)
the part of your face that you use
for breathing and smelling things
*Breathe in deeply through
your nose.*

nose

nostril (nostrils)
one of the two openings at
the bottom of your nose
*The horse wrinkled its
nostrils and tossed its head back.*

note (notes)
1 a short written message
Mum wrote a note to the school.
2 a piece of paper money
This machine doesn't take notes.
3 a musical sound or the mark to
show a musical sound
She played three notes on the piano.

nothing
not anything, zero
*There's nothing in the box; it's
empty.*

notice (notices)
a sign that tells people
something
*The notice says that the play starts
tomorrow.*

notice (noticing, noticed)
to see something, or be aware
that it is there
*Did you notice if anyone was in the
shop?*

novel (novels)
a book that tells a
long story
*Her latest novel is
about a family in
India.*

a b c d e f g h i j k l m **n** o p q r s t u v w x y z

now
this time, the present
My dad used to work in a factory, but he works at home now.

nowhere
not anywhere
There's nowhere else to go.

number (numbers)
1 a word or symbol that you use when you count things
Some people think seven is a lucky number.
2 the group of numbers you press when you phone someone
What's your mobile number?

nurse (nurses)
a person whose job is to look after people who are sick or hurt
The nurse put a bandage on my finger.

Puzzle time

What are the missing words in these nursery rhymes?

1. Jack and Jill went up the – – – –
2. Humpty – – – – – – sat on a wall
3. Mary, Mary, quite – – – – – – – –

Answers: 1. hill 2. Dumpty 3. contrary

numbers

nursery (nurseries)
1 a place where small children are looked after while their parents are at work
My little brother goes to nursery.
2 a place where people grow and sell plants
My dad bought some strawberry plants at the nursery.

nursery rhyme (nursery rhymes)
a poem or song for young children
My favourite nursery rhyme is Humpty Dumpty.

nut (nuts)
a seed that you can eat
Peanuts, cashews and almonds are all different types of nuts.

nuts

How many things can you spot beginning with 'o'?

a b c d e f g h i j k l m n **o** p q r s t u v w x y z

oasis (oases)
an area in the desert where there is water and where trees and plants grow
There are lots of oases in the Sahara desert, but you might travel for days without seeing one.

oak (oaks)
a big tree with seeds called acorns
That oak is over two hundred years old.

oar (oars)
a pole which is wide and flat at one end that you use when you row a boat
I let go of the oar and it fell into the water.

oak

ocean
1 the salt water that covers most of the Earth
Strange fish live at the bottom of the ocean.
2 (oceans) a large sea
The Pacific is the largest ocean in the world.

octopus (octopuses)
a sea creature that has eight legs
*The legs of an octopus are called
tentacles.*

octopus

off
1 away from somewhere
Take the glass off the table.
2 not in use, not switched on
*Switch the computer off if you're
finished with it.*

office (offices)
a place where people
work at desks
*There are four people in
my mum's office.*

ogre

ogre (ogres)
a frightening
giant in stories
*The ogre roared until
the mountains shook.*

oil
1 a thick liquid made from plants
or animals and used for cooking
Pour a little oil into the pan.
2 a thick liquid that comes out of
the ground and is used to make
petrol
They discovered oil there last year.

3 a thick liquid that is used on
metal or wood so that parts
move better or more easily
*This door is squeaking.
Can you put some oil on
it, please?*

okay (OK)
1 fine, healthy, well
Are you okay?
2 all right
*Is it okay if I copy my work to your
computer?*

old
not young, not new
We live in an old house.

once
1 one time
We've met only once before.
2 one time in a fixed period
We go swimming once a week.

onion (onions)
a vegetable that has a strong
smell and taste
Peeling onions makes you cry.

online
using the Internet
I bought these trainers online.

open
not closed or covered over
They must be at home; all the windows are open.

open (opening, opened)
1 to move a door or window so it is no longer closed
We opened the window because it was too hot.
2 to let customers in to buy things
What time does the shop open?

operation (operations)
when a doctor cuts open a person's body to mend or remove something
I've got to have an operation on my eye.

open

opponent (opponents)
the person you are playing against in sport
In judo you try and throw your opponent to the ground.

opposite
1 completely different
The opposite of near is far.

2 across from, facing
They live in the house opposite the garage.

orange
1 (oranges) a round, juicy fruit with a thick skin
Oranges are much sweeter than lemons.
2 the colour between red and yellow
She's wearing an orange jacket.

orbit (orbiting, orbited)
to travel round and round something, like a planet in space
The Earth orbits the Sun.

orchestra (orchestras)
a group of people playing musical instruments together
He plays the violin in the school orchestra.

order (ordering, ordered)
1 to ask for something in a restaurant or shop
Can I order a coffee, please?
2 to tell someone what to do
The captain ordered the men to attack the ship.

a
b
c
d
e
f
g
h
i
j
k
l
m
n
o
p
q
r
s
t
u
v
w
x
y
z

ordinary
nothing special, normal
It's just an ordinary house.

ostrich (ostriches)
a large, African bird with a
long neck
Ostriches cannot fly.

ostrich

otter (otters)
a brown,
furry wild
animal that swims and eats fish
Otters feed mainly at night.

out
1 away from
The mouse got out of his cage.
2 not at home
She's out at the moment.

outdoors
not inside a building, in the open
air
It's much cooler outdoors.

oven (ovens)
something that you use to bake
or roast food
*Bake the cake in the oven for
45 minutes.*

over
1 above, on top of
We live over a cake shop.
2 finished, ended
Is the film over yet?
3 from one side to another
She crossed over the road.

**overtake (overtaking,
overtook, overtaken)**
to go past someone or something
It's dangerous to overtake on a bend.

owl (owls)
a bird that hunts at night
*Sometimes you can
hear an owl hooting.*

**own
(owning, owned)**
to have something
that you bought or
were given
We own our house.

owl

oxygen
a gas that animals and plants
need to live
Fire needs oxygen in order to burn.

How many things can you spot beginning with 'p'?

P p

paddle (paddling, paddled)
1 to move a boat through water using oars or your hands
I paddled the dinghy across the lake.
2 to walk in shallow water
My little brother can't swim yet, but he likes to paddle.

pack (packing, packed)
to put things into boxes, bags or suitcases
Don't forget to pack your suitcases.

paddling

padlock (padlocks)
a type of lock with a metal loop that fastens things together

package (packages)
a small parcel
This package has your name on it.

I chained my bike to the railings with a padlock.

a b c d e f g h i j k l m n o **p** q r s t u v w x y z

page (pages)
one side of a sheet of paper in a book, magazine or newspaper
This book has 384 pages.

pain (pains)
the feeling you have when you are hurt or ill
I have a bad pain in my side.

paint (paints)
paint
a sticky liquid that you brush onto things to colour them
Don't spill paint on the carpet.

pair (pairs)
1 two things that go together
I need a new pair of trainers.
2 something that is made of two similar things joined together
I've bought a new pair of sunglasses for my holiday.

palace (palaces)
a big house where a king, queen or other important person lives
The princess lived in an old palace.

palm (palms)
1 the inside part of your hand
Fortune tellers read palms.

2 a kind of tree with leaves only at the top
Our tent was under a row of palms on the beach.

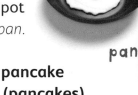

pan (pans)
a round cooking pot
Fry an egg in the pan.

pan

pancake (pancakes)
a thin, flat cake that is cooked in a frying pan
I like pancakes with sugar.

panda (pandas)
a large, black-and-white animal that is part of the bear family
Pandas come from China.

pantomime (pantomimes)
a funny musical show that is performed around Christmas
The pantomime this year is 'Aladdin'.

paper
1 thin sheets of material for writing or printing on
There is no paper in the printer.
2 (papers) a newspaper
My dad buys a paper every day.

a b c d e f g h i j k l m n o **p** q r s t u v w x y z

parachute (parachutes)
a piece of equipment made of cloth that people wear to let them fall slowly through the air
The parachute opens automatically.

parade (parade)
a lot of people walking or marching in a long line to celebrate a special occasion
There is a parade every year.

parade

parcel (parcels)
something which is wrapped up in paper and often sent in the post
My parcel arrived today.

parent (parents)
a mother or father
My parents are both dentists.

park (parks)
a piece of ground with trees and grass
Let's go to the park to play.

park (parking, parked)
to put a car or bike in a place for a time
You can park in front of the library.

parrot (parrots)
a bird with coloured feathers that usually lives in hot countries
My parrot can say my name.

parrot

part (parts)
1 one of the pieces or sections that something is divided into
Would you like part of my newspaper?
2 the role of an actor in a film or a play
Who is playing the part of the princess?

partner (partners)
a person you work or do something with
Will you be my partner for this dance?

party (parties)
a group of people who meet to enjoy themselves
I'm having a party on Saturday.

a b c d e f g h i j k l m n o **p** q r s t u v w x y z

a
b
c
d
e
f
g
h
i
j
k
l
m
n
o
p
q
r
s
t
u
v
w
x
y
z

pass (passing, passed)
1 to go beyond or past a person, place or thing
You'll pass the bakery on your way.
2 to succeed in doing something such as a test or an examination
I hope you pass your driving test.
3 to give someone something
Could you please pass the salt?

passengers

passenger (passengers)
someone who travels in a vehicle that is driven by someone else
This coach has seats for 48 passengers.

Passover
a Jewish holiday held in the spring
The family get together for Passover.

passport (passports)
a little book that shows who you are, that you need when you travel to another country
You have to show your passport at the airport.

past
1 after a certain hour
Let's meet at half past six.
2 on the far side of something
The bank is on this street, just past the supermarket.
3 the time before the present
In the past, email didn't exist.

pasta
food made from flour, eggs and water, cut into shapes
We had pasta with tomato-and-mushroom sauce for lunch.

pasta

paste
1 a type of glue *I made a paste of flour and water.*
2 a soft, spreadable mixture
He likes fish paste on his sandwiches.

patch (patches)
1 a small piece of material to cover a hole in something
I put a patch on my jeans.

2 a small area which is different from the area around it
There are damp patches on the wall.

patient (patients)
a person who is in hospital or visiting a doctor
This car park is for patients only.

patient
able to wait without complaining or getting bored
Please be patient! Dinner will be ready soon.

patio (patios)
an area outside a house with paving stones instead of grass
We sometimes have our meals on the patio.

pattern (patterns)
1 lines, shapes or colours arranged in a certain way
The dinner plate has a pattern painted on it.
2 a shape that you copy or use as a guide to make something
Mum used a pattern to make this jacket for me.

pattern

pavement (pavements)
the path you walk on next to a road
Be sure to walk on the pavement.

paw (paws)
the foot of an animal
Our dog has a sore paw.

paw

pay (paying, paid)
to give someone money for something that you are buying, or because someone has done work for you
I'll pay for the theatre tickets now.

peas

pea (peas)
a small, round green seed that is eaten as a vegetable
I had fish, chips and peas for dinner.

peace
1 no war or fighting
There has been peace between them for many years.
2 quiet, calmness
She needed a little peace and quiet.

a b c d e f g h i j k l m n o **p** q r s t u v w x y z

peach (peaches)
a soft fruit with a large seed inside it
This is a sweet, juicy peach.

peacock

peacock (peacocks)
a male bird with long, brightly coloured tail feathers that spread out like a fan
Peacocks usually have green and blue feathers.

peanut (peanuts)
a small nut with a soft, bumpy shell
You can buy salted peanuts in small packs.

pear (pears)
a fruit with green skin that grows on a tree and that is narrow at the top and wide at the bottom
We had pears with chocolate sauce for dessert.

pebble (pebbles)
a small, smooth, round stone
We threw pebbles into the sea.

pedal (pedals)
1 part of a bicycle that you push with your feet to make the wheels go round
Can you reach the pedals?
2 part of a car that you push with your feet to make it stop and go
The middle pedal stops the car.

peel
the skin on fruit and vegetables
You can eat the peel of an apple.

peel (peeling, peeled)
to take the skin off a fruit or a vegetable
I peeled the potatoes for lunch.

peel

peg (pegs)
1 a clip for fastening clothes to a washing line
Clothes pegs are made of wood or plastic.
2 a small hook where you can hang things
I hung my coat up on a peg.

pen (pens)
an object for drawing and writing
with ink
Sign this with a black pen.

pen

pencil (pencils)
an object with a sharp
point used for drawing
and writing
*I drew the outline using a
pencil.*

pencil

penguin (penguins)
a black-and-white sea bird that
cannot fly
Penguins are brilliant at swimming.

people
human beings; men, women and
children
*There were a lot of people in town
today.*

pepper
1 a hot powder used to flavour
food
Please pass the salt and pepper.
2 (peppers) a sweet or
hot-tasting vegetable
*Peppers can be green,
red, yellow or orange.*

peppers

perfume (perfumes)
a liquid with a pleasant smell
that you put on your skin
What perfume are you wearing?

person (people, persons)
a human being; a man, woman or
child
*Our geography teacher is a very
interesting person.*

pet (pets)
an animal that is kept at
someone's home
*Do you have
any p*

pets

petal (petals)
one of the coloured parts of a
flower
Daffodils have yellow petals.

petrol
liquid fuel that makes a car
engine run
We need to stop for petrol.

phone (phones)
a telephone
Be quiet! I'm on the phone.

a b c d e f g h i j k l m n o **p** q r s t u v w x y z

phone (phoning, phoned)
to call someone on the telephone
Joe phoned while you were out.

pickle

photo (photograph; photos, photographs)
a picture made with a camera
We had our photos taken for our passports.

phrase (phrases)
a group of words coming together
The phrase 'a piece of cake' means easy.

piano

piano (pianos)
a large musical instrument with black and white keys
I play the piano.

pick (picking, picked)
1 to choose
The teacher picked me for the team.
2 to break off a flower or a piece of fruit from a plant
We picked blackberries in the woods.

pickle (pickles)
vegetables in vinegar which keep fresh for a long time
I like cheese and pickle at lunchtime.

picnic (picnics)
food that you take outdoors to eat
We had a picnic in the park.

picture (pictures)
a drawing, painting or photograph
The best picture will be in the paper.

pie (pies)
food made with fruit, vegetables, fish or meat that is baked inside pastry
Would you like another piece of pie?

piece (pieces)
a part of something that has been separated or broken
Careful! There are some pieces of glass on the floor.

pig (pigs)
a farm animal with pink skin and a curly tail
A baby pig is called a piglet.

pig

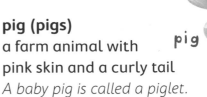

pigeon (pigeons)
a grey bird that lives in towns
Please don't feed the pigeons!

pile (piles)
a lot of things put on
top of each other
*There's a pile of
washing on the floor.*

pile

pillow (pillows)
a cushion to put your
head on in bed
I put my tooth underneath my pillow.

pilot (pilot)
the person who is in
control of a plane
*The pilot showed us the
plane's control panel.*

pilot

pin (pins)
a sharp, thin piece of metal that
is used to fasten things or hold
pieces of cloth together
*Take all the pins out before you try
the shirt on.*

pin

pinch (pinching, pinched)
to squeeze between your thumb
and fingers
Ow! He pinched my arm.

pineapple (pineapples)
a brown fruit that is yellow inside
and has pointed leaves that stick
out of the top
*This slice of pineapple is
very juicy.*

pirate (pirates)
a person who goes
onto boats and ships
to steal the things they
are carrying
*The ship was attacked by a group of
pirates.*

pitch (pitches)
a piece of
ground painted
with lines
where you can play
football, hockey or
another sport
Fans ran on to the pitch.

pizza (pizzas)
a thin, flat round bread that is
covered with tomatoes, cheese
and other toppings then baked in
an oven
*We're going to have pizza at the
party.*

a b c d e f g h i j k l m n o p q r s t u v w x y z

a b c d e f g h i j k l m n o **p** q r s t u v w x y z

place (places)
1 a town, area or building
What's the name of the place where we went on holiday last year?
2 a point or position
I broke my arm in two places.

plain
1 made of one colour, having no pattern or decoration
The curtains are plain green.
2 easy to understand
Can you tell me in plain English?
3 not fancy or complicated
It's a plain room, but very clean and neat.

plan (plans)
1 an idea about what will happen in the future
What are your plans for the weekend?
2 a drawing of a room, building or other space
We drew a plan of our playground.

plan (planning, planned)
to think about what you want to do and how to do it
Let's plan what we're going to do this weekend.

plane (planes)
an aeroplane
The plane took off from the airport on time.

planet (planets)
one of the very large, round objects that moves around the Sun
Venus and Mars are planets.

plant (plants)
a living thing that has roots, leaves and seeds and can make its own food
Water the plants every day.

plant

plant (planting, planted)
to put seeds or plants into the ground or containers so they will grow
Plant the seeds in early summer.

plaster
1 a thick paste that hardens when it dries
The builder spread plaster on the walls.
2 (plasters) a thin piece of plastic or cloth that you put over a cut or sore
The nurse put a plaster on my knee.

plaster

plastic
a light material that is made from chemicals
The bucket is made of plastic.

plastic

plate (plates)
a flat dish to eat food from
Take the plates into the kitchen.

play (plays)
a story performed by actors in a theatre or on the radio
I hope I get a part in the school play.

play (playing, played)
to do things that you like such as games or sports
Let's play outdoors.

playground (playgrounds)
a place for children to play
There are swings and a slide at the playground.

play

please
a word to use when you are asking for something politely
Please wait here.

plenty
enough or more than enough
There are plenty of sandwiches, so take two.

plough (ploughs)
a piece of equipment that farmers use to turn the soil before they plant
Modern ploughs can cut through the earth very quickly.

plug (plugs)
1 a piece of plastic or rubber that stops water going out of a sink or bath
Put the plug in the bath, then turn on the water.
2 a piece of plastic connected to an electrical wire that you put into a wall
Which one is the plug for the computer?

plum (plums)
a small, red, green or purple fruit with a stone
We had plums and custard for dessert.

plums

a b c d e f g h i j k l m n o **p** q r s t u v w x y z

a
b
c
d
e
f
g
h
i
j
k
l
m
n
o
p
q
r
s
t
u
v
w
x
y
z

plumber (plumbers)
a person whose job it is to fix
water taps and pipes
The plumber repaired the leak.

plus
and, added to, the symbol +
Eleven plus six equals seventeen;
11 + 6 = 17.

pocket (pockets)
a small, flat bag
sewn into a piece of
clothing or luggage
Put your key in your
pocket.

poem (poems)
writing that uses
words that sound
good together. The
words often rhyme
This poem is very funny.

point (points)
1 a sharp end on something
Use a pencil with a sharp
point.
2 a certain place
or time
There's a meeting
point at the airport.

polar bear

3 the reason for something
The whole point was to raise money
for the school.
4 a mark for counting a score in a
game
The answer is worth one point.

point (pointing, pointed)
to use your hand or finger to
show where something is
Point to where the gate is.

poison (poisons)
something that will kill
you or make you very
ill if you swallow it
In the film the cook put
poison in the soup.

Puzzle time
Can you unscramble the
lines of this poem?

a. Roses red are
b. are blue Violets
c. sweet is Sugar
d. And are you so

Answer:
a. Roses are red
b. Violets are blue
c. Sugar is sweet
d. And so are you

poisonous

poisonous
harmful, containing poison
Some wild mushrooms are poisonous.

polar bear (polar bears)
a large, white bear that
lives near the North Pole
Polar bears hunt fish and seals.

pole (poles)
a long narrow piece of wood, plastic or metal
We forgot to take the tent poles.

police
people whose job it is to make sure everyone obeys the law
Do you think we need to call the police?

polite
speaking or acting in a pleasant and not rude way
It is polite to say please, thank you and excuse me.

pollen
yellow or orange powder found inside flowers
Bees carry pollen from one flower to another.

pollen

pond (ponds)
a small area of water
There are fish in the pond.

pony (ponies)
a small horse
I had a ride on a pony.

pool (pools)
1 a place filled with water for swimming
I like playing in my pool when the weather is warm.
2 a puddle or another small area of water
We saw tiny fish in the pools on the beach.

poor
1 not having enough money
It's a very poor country.
2 not as good as it should be
The food was poor.

pop
1 (pops) a sudden noise
There was a loud pop when they opened the bottle.
2 a short form of popular
They are a famous pop band.
3 a fizzy drink
Do you want a bottle of pop?

poppy (poppies)
a wild, red flower with black seeds
The field is full of poppies.

poppy

a b c d e f g h i j k l m n o **p** q r s t u v w x y z

popular
liked by a lot of people
Fishing is a popular hobby.

porcupine (porcupines)
a wild animal with long sharp
hairs like needles on its back
Some porcupines can climb trees.

pork
meat from a pig
*We had roast
pork and apple
sauce for dinner.*

potato

porridge
a warm breakfast
food that is made from oats
I like honey on porridge.

postcard (postcards)
a small piece of card
with a picture on one
side. You write on the
other side.
*I sent my grandparents
a postcard.*

poster (posters)
a large picture or notice that you
put up on the wall
I've posters on my bedroom wall.

post office (post offices)
a place where people buy stamps
and send letters and parcels
*Can you get me some stamps at the
post office?*

potato (potatoes)
a roundish white vegetable that
grows under the ground
Let's have baked potatoes for lunch.

pour (pouring, poured)
to make a liquid move out of or
into something
Pour the milk into the jug.

powerful
1 very strong
*A powerful tornado swept through
town.*

2 able to control other people
and things that
happen
*It is one of the most
powerful countries in
the world.*

powerful

practice
something that you do again and
again to get better at something
What time is swimming practice?

practise (practising, practised)
doing something regularly to
improve a skill
Keep practising your serve.

pram (prams)
a little bed on wheels for moving
a baby around
I'm taking the baby out in the pram.

prefer (preferring, preferred)
to like something better than
another thing
I prefer apple juice to lemonade.

prepare (preparing, prepared)
to get ready or to make
something ready
I'm preparing for the test.

presents

present
1 (presents) a gift, a
thing that you are given without
asking for it
Thank you for all the presents.
2 now
The story is set in the present.

president (presidents)
the leader of an organization or a
country
She is president of the club.

press (pressing, pressed)
to push something
Press the button on the machine.

**pretend (pretending,
pretended)**
to act like something is true when
it is not
She pretended to be asleep.

pretty (prettier, prettiest)
nice to look at
What pretty flowers!

price (prices)
the amount of money that
   something costs
   The prices are high.

prince (princes)
   the son or grandson of a king
   or queen
*The prince rode
through the forest.*

princess (princesses)
the daughter or
granddaughter of a
king or queen
*The princess dreamt
of a faraway place.*

princess

a
b
c
d
e
f
g
h
i
j
k
l
m
n
o
p
q
r
s
t
u
v
w
x
y
z

a b c d e f g h i j k l m n o **p** q r s t u v w x y z

print (printing, printed)
1 to put letters, numbers or pictures on paper with a machine
Print five copies of the story.
2 to write words without joining the letters
Print your name in full.

printer (printers)
1 a machine connected to a computer that makes copies on paper
The printer is out of paper.
2 a person who prints books, newspapers, leaflets and other things
Take the poster to the printer.

prison (prisons)
a place where people are kept under guard as punishment
The thief was sent to prison.

prison

private
only for some people, not for everyone
The beach is private; it belongs to the hotel.

prize (prizes)
something that you win in a game or competition
First prize is a gold trophy.

prize

problem (problems)
something that is wrong and needs to be corrected
We have a problem.

programme (programmes)
1 a show on the radio or television
This is my favourite programme.
2 a thin book that tells you about a play or a show at the theatre
I'll look in the programme to see what the actor's name is.

promise (promises)
something you say you will definitely do
I always keep my promises.

promise (promising, promised)
to tell someone that you will definitely do something
Daniel promised his dad that he would behave at school.

protect (protecting, protected)
to take care of someone or something and not let it be hurt or damaged
Penguins protect their chicks.

proud
feeling happy that you or someone else has done something
My parents are proud of me.

public
for everyone
The public transport in this town is very good.

puddle (puddles)
a little pool of water on the ground or floor
There are puddles after the rain.

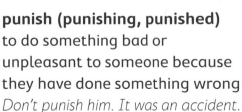
puddle

pull (pulling, pulled)
to move something towards you or drag something behind you
The puppy pulled its.blanket on the floor.

pull

pump (pumps)
a machine that pushes a liquid or gas from one place to another
Take your bicycle pump with you.

pumpkin (pumpkins)
a big, round, orange vegetable
The children made a lantern out of a pumpkin.

pumpkin

puncture (punctures)
a hole made by a sharp object, especially in a tyre
We had a puncture on the way home.

punish (punishing, punished)
to do something bad or unpleasant to someone because they have done something wrong
Don't punish him. It was an accident.

pupil (pupils)
1 a child that goes to school
The pupils wear a dark blue uniform.
2 the black circle in the middle of your eye
Your pupil gets smaller when you look at a bright light.

a b c d e f g h i j k l m n o **p** q r s t u v w x y z

puppet (puppets)
a toy that people move by
putting their hand inside it or by
pulling strings attached to it
*Pinocchio is a puppet at the
beginning of the story.*

puppy (puppies)
a young dog
Puppies love to play.

pure
not mixed with anything else
This is pure apple juice.

puppets

purr (purring, purred)
to make a soft, low sound like a
happy cat
Our cat purrs when you stroke her.

purse (purses)
a little bag to keep money in
*I'll have to pay you later; I left my
purse at home.*

push (pushing, pushed)
1 to move something away from
you or out of the way
He pushed past everyone.
2 to press down on something
such as a key or a button
Push the restart button.

put (putting, put)
to move a thing to a place
Put the bags in the corner.

pyjamas
loose clothes that
you wear to bed
*Have a bath and put
on your pyjamas.*

pylon (pylons)
a tall, steel tower that holds up
electricity wires
*You see more pylons in the country
than in towns.*

pyramid (pyramids)
1 a very old stone building with
triangular walls that form a
point
at the top
*The Egyptian pyramids were built
4000 years ago.*
2 something with this shape
The tent is shaped like a pyramid.

python (pythons)
a large snake that kills
animals for food by
squeezing them
*Some pythons are
eight metres long.*

python

How many things can you spot beginning with 'q'?

Qq

quack (quacking, quacked)
to make the loud sound a duck makes
The ducks quacked when they saw me coming.

quarrel (quarrels)
an angry argument
The quarrel started over whose turn it was.

quarter (quarters)
one of four equal, or nearly equal, parts of something
Divide the apple into quarters.

queen (queens)
the royal female ruler of a country or the wife of a king
The queen lives in a palace.

queen

question (questions)
something that you ask someone
We'll try to answer all your questions.

a b c d e f g h i j k l m n o p **q** r s t u v w x y z

**question mark
(question marks)**
a sign like this ? that
you write at the end of
a sentence
*You need a question
mark at the end of a
sentence that begins
with the word 'why'.*

quilt

queue (queues)
a line of people waiting
*There was a long queue at the
cinema.*

quiche (quiches)
a tart that is filled
with eggs, cheese
and vegetables,
meat or fish
*There's bacon in this
quiche and salmon
in that one.*

quick
fast, taking a short
time
Email is quick and easy.

quiet
1 not making a noise
Please be quiet.

2 calm and still, not
busy
*The lake is quiet and
peaceful at this time of day.*

quilt (quilts)
a warm cover for a bed
*Patchwork quilts are made by
sewing lots of small pieces of
cloth together.*

quit (quitting, quit)
to stop doing something or to
leave a computer program
To quit, press Ctrl + Q.

quiz (quizzes)
a game or
competition that
tests your
knowledge
*Shall we see if we
can answer the
questions in the
quiz?*

quote (quoting, quoted)
to repeat the words that
someone else has said or written
*The English teacher quoted a line
from one of Shakespeare's plays to
the class.*

Puzzle time
Can you answer all the
questions in this quiz?
1. What is a baby pig called?
2. Can penguins fly?
3. Is a tomato a fruit or
a vegetable?
4. What are the spines on
a porcupine called?

Answers: 1. piglet 2. no 3. fruit
4. quills

How many things can you spot beginning with 'r'?

a b c d e f g h i j k l m n o p q **r** s t u v w x y z

Rr

rabbit (rabbits)
a small furry animal with long ears
There are rabbits living in the wood.

race (races)
1 a competition to see who can do something the fastest
The race starts in 15 minutes.

rabbit

2 a group of people with similar physical features
People of all races and beliefs can live together happily.

race

race (racing, raced)
1 to take part in a race
There were ten drivers racing in the opening heats.
2 to do something very quickly
Jessica raced through the first part of the test.

racket

racket (rackets)
1 a flat, hard net on the end of a stick that you use to play some sports
Hit the ball hard with the racket.
2 a lot of loud noise
Who's making that racket?

radio (radios)
a piece of equipment that receives sounds
I listen to the radio in the car.

raft (rafts)
a simple flat boat made of pieces of wood tied together
They crossed the river on a raft.

rail (rails)
1 a metal or wooden bar that you can hang things on
I hang my clothes on the rail in my wardrobe.
2 one of two metal tracks that a train runs on
They put new rails along the track.

railway (railways)
1 a train track
The railway runs to the coast.
2 a system of trains
A railway is being built in the city.

rain
water that falls from clouds in the sky
Look at that heavy rain!

rain

rain (raining, rained)
when it rains, small drops of water fall from clouds in the sky
It's raining so we can't play outside.

rainbow (rainbows)
the curve of colours that you see in the sky after it rains and the sun comes out
The colours of the rainbow are red, orange, yellow, green, blue, indigo and violet.

raise (raising, raised)
to lift or put something in a higher place
Raise your hand if you know the answer.

Ramadan
the ninth month of the Muslim
year
*Muslims do not eat or drink during
the day in the month of Ramadan.*

**raspberry
(raspberries)**
a small, soft, red fruit
*I like raspberries with
ice cream.*

raspberries

rat (rats)
an animal that looks
like a big mouse with a long tail
There are rats in the barn

rattle (rattles)
a toy that makes a knocking
noise when you shake it
Babies like playing with rattles.

raw
not cooked
*Raw vegetables make a
healthy snack.*

rats

read (reading, read)
to understand words
printed on a page
The teacher is reading to the class.

recipe (recipes)
a set of instructions telling you
how to cook something, and what
you need to make it
Can I have the recipe for this cake?

**record
(recording,
recorded)**
to write down or
tape information
*We recorded a
song on the
computer.*

recorder (recorders)
a small musical instrument that
you blow to make music
I play the recorder in the orchestra.

**recycle (recycling,
recycled)**
to use something again
*We're recycling
newspapers and
magazines at school.*

referee (referees)
a person who makes sure
that players in a game
don't break the rules
The referee blew his whistle.

a b c d e f g h i j k l m n o p q **r** s t u v w x y z

reflection (reflections)
an image, like a copy of
something, that you
see in a mirror
or in water
*The dog
saw its reflection
in the pond.*

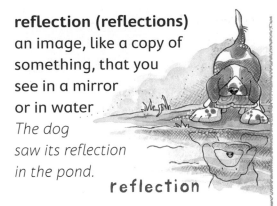

r e f l e c t i o n

rehearsal (rehearsals)
a time when actors or singers
practise before appearing in front
of an audience
There's a rehearsal at lunchtime.

reindeer (reindeer)
a deer with big antlers that lives
in cold countries
Reindeer live in groups called herds.

relative (relatives)
a person in your family
We have relatives staying overnight.

remember (remembering, remembered)
1 to keep information about the
past in your mind
I remember our holiday last year
2 to bring back information to
your mind
I've just remembered; my dad is out.

remind (reminding, reminded)
to cause someone to remember
something
Remind me to buy sugar.

repeat (repeating, repeated)
to say or do something again
Please repeat the question

reptile (reptiles)   r e p t i l e
a cold-blooded animal
with dry, scaly skin
Lizards are reptiles.

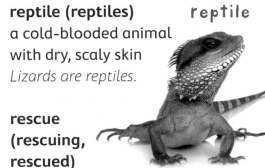

**rescue
(rescuing,
rescued)**
to save someone or something
from danger
The lifeguard rescued the children.

rest
1 a period of time when you relax
or do nothing
I'm tired. Let's have a rest.
2 the other things or people that
are left
You can have the rest of the sweets.

rest (resting, rested)
to relax, to sit or lie still
I wasn't asleep; I was just resting.

restaurant (restaurants)
a place where people eat and pay for meals
A new Thai restaurant has opened.

result (results)
1 something that happens because of something else
This beautiful garden is the result of a lot of hard work.
2 a final score
Have you heard the football results?

return (returning, returned)
1 to come back or go back to a place
He returned after the meeting.
2 to give or send something back
We returned the book to the library.

rhinoceros (rhino; rhinoceroses)
a big, wild animal with thick skin and one or two horns on its nose
There are rhinos in Africa and Asia.

rhinoceros

rhyme (rhyming, rhymed)
to end with the same sound as another word
Hat rhymes with cat.

ribbon (ribbons)
a narrow piece of material for tying up presents or decorating things
She's wearing ribbons in her hair.

rice
grains from a plant that are boiled and eaten as food
We had rice with our curry.

rice

rich
1 having a lot of money
Switzerland is a rich country.
2 food that has butter, cream and eggs is rich food
The cheese sauce is too rich for me!

riddle (riddles)
a difficult but funny question or puzzle
I know lots of jokes and riddles.

ride (riding, rode, ridden)
to travel on a bicycle or a horse and control it as it moves
My little sister can ride a bike.

right
correct, not having any mistakes
You got all the answers right!

a b c d e f g h i j k l m n o p q **r** s t u v w x y z

ring (rings)
1 a piece of jewellery worn on the
finger
That's a pretty silver ring.
2 a circle or something that is the
shape of a circle
We sat in a ring around the teacher.
3 the sound made by a bell
*The phone has a very loud
ring.*
4 a telephone call
Give me a ring tonight.
ring (ringing, rang, rung)
1 to make a sound like a bell
The doorbell rang.
2 to phone someone
Can you ring me later?

river (rivers)
a long line of water that flows to
the sea
Dad is fishing by the river.

road (roads)
a track for cars, buses and lorries
to travel on
The roads are very busy today.

roar (roars)
a loud noise like the sound a lion
makes
There was a roar outside the tent.

robin (robins)
a small bird with a patch of red
on its front
You often see robins in winter.

robot (robots)
a machine that can do things
that a person can do

robots

*I wish we had
a robot to do
the cleaning.*

rock
1 the hard,
stony part
of the Earth's surface
We drill through rock to find oil.
2 (rocks) a large stone
We sat on the rocks by the beach.
3 a type of music that has a
strong beat
My brother likes hard rock.

**rocket
(rockets)**
1 a space
vehicle shaped like
a tube

rocket

The rocket is going to the moon.
2 a firework in the shape of a
tube
Rockets were exploding in the sky.

roll (rolling, rolled)
to move by turning over and over
The ball rolled across the room.

roof (roofs)
the covering over the top of
a building or car
Rain leaked through the roof.

roofs

room (rooms)
part of a building that has its own
floor, walls and ceiling
There are four rooms in my house.

root (roots)
the part of a plant that is under
the ground
*Roots take water from the soil to
keep the plant alive.*

rope (ropes)
very thick string
Tie the rope tightly.

rose (roses)
a flower that grows
on a stem with thorns
The roses are blooming.

roots

rough
1 uneven, not smooth
We drove along the rough track.

2 not gentle
Don't be rough with the puppy.

**roundabout
(roundabouts)**
1 a round place where
roads meet
*Turn left at the next
roundabout.*

2 a round playground toy that
children spin and ride on
Let's ride on the roundabout.

rounders
a team game where players hit a
ball with a bat and run round the
four sides of the playing area
*We play rounders or cricket in the
summer in school.*

route (routes)
the way to go to a place
We took the quickest route home.

row (rowing, rowed)
to move a small boat
through water using oars
He rowed the boat across the lake.

royal
belonging to a queen or king
The royal coach car drove by.

a b c d e f g h i j k l m n o p q **r** s t u v w x y z

rubber
1 a strong, bouncy or stretchy material
Car tyres are made of rubber.
2 (rubbers) a small object that is used for taking pencil marks off paper
I've made a mistake in my homework. Can I use your rubber?

rubbish
1 paper and other things that are no longer needed
Put all the rubbish in the bin.
2 something that is wrong or silly
Don't talk rubbish!

ruby (rubies)
a red jewel
The queen was wearing a neckluce made out of rubies and diamonds.

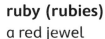
ruby

rude
speaking or acting in a way that is not polite
It's rude not to say 'please' and 'thank you'.

rug (rugs)
1 a small carpet
The cat is on the rug.
2 a blanket
Put the rug over your feet.

rule (rules)
a law or guide about how something must be done
It's wrong to break the rules at school.

ruler (rulers)
1 a long, flat piece of plastic or wood used to measure things or draw straight lines
I use a ruler in maths.
2 a person who has power over a country
The country didn't have a ruler when the king died.

run (running, ran, run)
1 to move your legs faster than when you are walking
Run as fast as you can!
2 to control
Mum runs her business from home.
3 to make a piece of equipment or a computer program work
Run the computer program.

run

How many things can you spot beginning with 's'?

S s

safe (safes)
a strong box with a lock where you can keep money or jewellery
We left our money and passports in the hotel safe when we went out.

safe
not dangerous
Home is where you feel good and safe.

sad (sadder, saddest)
unhappy
What's happened? You look so sad.

saddle (saddles)
a seat that you sit on when you are riding a horse or a bicycle
This saddle is hard and not very comfortable.

sail

sail (sails)
a big piece of strong material fixed to a pole on a boat, which catches the wind and makes the boat move
Let's raise the sail and go.

a b c d e f g h i j k l m n o p q r **s** t u v w x y z

sail (sailing, sailed)
to travel across water in a boat
or ship
We sailed to France on a ferry.

sailor (sailors)
someone who works on a ship
*Sailors in the navy wear dark blue
uniforms.*

salad (salads)
vegetables or fruit
mixed together,
usually eaten raw
*We'll put tomatoes and
cucumber in the salad.*

salt
very tiny grains that
come from sea water
and rocks, which are
put on food to make it
taste good
This needs a little more salt.

same
not different
or changed
*Look! Our
clothes are
exactly the
same.*

same

sand
tiny pieces of crushed rock
*The beach is covered in beautiful,
white sand.*

sandal (sandals)
one of a pair of light shoes with
straps that you wear in summer
I need a new pair of sandals.

Puzzle time
Can you put these
sandwich instructions in
the right order?
a. Next, spread one side
of each slice with butter.
b. Put the cheese on one
slice of bread.
c. Now put the other
slice on top.
d. First, take two slices
of bread.
e. Eat your sandwich

Answer: d, a, b, c, e

**sandwich
(sandwiches)**
two pieces of bread
with cheese, meat or
vegetables in
between
*We'll make some
sandwiches for the
picnic.*

sandwich

sari (saris)
a dress made from a
long piece of thin cloth
that Indian and South
Asian women wear
She was wearing a blue sari.

saucer (saucers)
a small dish that goes under a cup
We put some milk in a saucer for the kitten.

sausage (sausages)
a mixture of meat, cereal and spices inside a case shaped like a tube
We had sausages and chips for dinner.

scales
a machine that is used for weighing things
Weigh the ingredients on the scales.

scar (scars)
the mark left on your skin after a cut has healed
I have a scar above my left eye.

scare (scaring, scared)
to frighten
This film will really scare you!

scarecrow (scarecrows)
an object that is made to look like a person, which is put in fields to scare off birds
We made a scarecrow out of straw.

scared
feeling afraid, frightened
Please leave a light on. I'm scared of the dark.

scarf

scarf (scarves or scarfs)
a piece of material that you wear around your neck
I'm knitting a scarf.

school (schools)
the place where children go to learn things
I started school when I was five.

science (sciences)
the study of information about the world
Biology, physics and chemistry are all types of science.

scissors
a tool for cutting things that has two sharp blades and two handles with holes for your fingers
There's a pair of scissors in the drawer.

scarecrow

a b c d e f g h i j k l m n o p q r **s** t u v w x y z

a b c d e f g h i j k l m n o p q r s t u v w x y z

scooter (scooters)
1 a light motorbike with small wheels
Mum goes to work on her scooter.
2 a toy with two or three wheels and a long handle. You stand on it with one foot and use the other foot to push you along.
Riding a scooter is easier than riding a bike.

scooter

score (scores)
the number of points or goals each team or player has in a game
What's the score?

score (scoring, scored)
to get points in a game
They've scored another goal!

scorpion (scorpions)
a creature with eight legs, a curved tail and a poisonous sting
Scorpions live in warm and hot countries.

scorpion

scratch

scratch (scratching, scratched)
to rub or damage your skin with your nails or something hard
Don't scratch your face.

scream (screaming, screamed)
to make a loud noise when you are afraid, angry or hurt
The swimmers screamed when they saw the shark.

screen (screens)
a flat surface on a computer or television, or in the cinema that has words or pictures on
You're sitting too close to the screen.

scribble (scribbling, scribbled)
to write or draw quickly and untidily
The baby's scribbled all over my homework.

sea
a large area of salty water
Look! You can see the sea from here.

seal (seals)
1 a creature that lives in the sea and eats fish
Seals are good swimmers and can dive underwater for a long time.
2 wax, plastic or paper that you break to open a container
Do not buy this product if the seal is broken.

Seal

season (seasons)
the four parts of the year – spring, summer, autumn and winter
The weather is different in each season.

seaweed
a plant or plants that grow in or near to the sea
There was lots of seaweed floating in the water.

Seasons

secret
if something is secret only a few people are allowed to know about it
There's a secret passage in the house.

see (seeing, saw, seen)
1 to use your eyes to look, to watch
Did you see that programme on TV last night?
2 to understand
I've explained it to you. Now do you see?
3 to meet or visit someone
We went to see Chloe in hospital.

seed (seeds)
a small part of a plant that a new plant grows from
Put the seeds in the ground.

secret (secrets)
something that you do not want other people to know
Please don't tell anyone else – it's a secret.

seesaw (seesaws)
a long board that is balanced in the middle so that the ends go up and down
There's a seesaw in the playground.

a b c d e f g h i j k l m n o p q r **s** t u v w x y z

send (sending, sent)
to make something go or be
taken to another place
I sent her an email yesterday.

several
some, quite a few
I've seen that film several times.

**sew (sewing, sewed,
sewn)**
to join cloth together
with a needle and thread
I'll sew the button on for you.

shapes

shade
1 where the sun is not shining
Sit in the shade of the umbrella.
2 (shades) a thing to block out
light
*Can you pull the shade down,
please?*
3 (shades) a colour
That's a nice shade of green.

shadow (shadows)
a dark shape that
appears on the ground
when the something is
blocking the light
*You can see your shadow
on a sunny day.*

shake (shaking, shook, shaken)
to move something quickly up
and down or side to side
*Shake the bottle well before
opening.*

shampoo (shampoos)
liquid soap for washing your hair
Did you bring the shampoo?

shape (shapes)
the outline or
form of a thing
What shape is it?

shark (sharks)
a large fish that usually has
sharp teeth
*Some sharks can be dangerous to
humans.*

sheep (plural is the same)
a farm animal kept for wool and
meat
*There are sheep on
the hill.*

shadow

shelf (shelves)
a board, usually wooden, fixed on
a wall for putting things on
Can you reach that shelf?

shell (shells)
the hard covering of an egg, a
seed or an animal such as a turtle
or a crab
*Ostrich eggs are very big and have
thick shells.*

ship (ships)
a large boat
The ship sailed across the ocean.

shirt (shirts)
a piece of clothing with buttons
that you wear on the top half of
your body
Tuck your shirt in.

shiver (shivering, shivered)
to shake because you
are cold or scared
*You're shivering! Put
on your fleece.*

shock (shocks)
1 a bad surprise
*The bill was quite a
shock.*

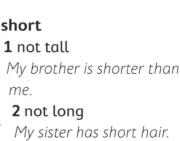
shivering

2 a pain you feel when electricity
goes through your body
I got a shock from that plug!

shoe (shoes)
one of two coverings for
your feet that are
usually made of
strong material
*Mum's wardrobe is
full of shoes.*

shoes

shoot (shooting, shot)
1 to fire a gun
Don't shoot!
2 to kick or throw a ball into a
goal or net in a game
*Shoot when you are closer to the
basket.*

shop (shops)
a place that sells things
What time does the shop open?

short
1 not tall
*My brother is shorter than
me.*
2 not long
My sister has short hair.
3 not lasting a long time
Let's take a short break.

a b c d e f g h i j k l m n o p q r **s** t u v w x y z

a
b
c
d
e
f
g
h
i
j
k
l
m
n
o
p
q
r
s
t
u
v
w
x
y
z

shorts
short trousers
We wear shorts in summer.

shoulder (shoulders)
the top of your arm where it joins
your body
Put the bag over your shoulder.

**shout (shouting,
shouted)**
to call out to someone
in a loud voice
*There's no need to shout
at me; I'm right here!*

shout

**show (showing,
showed, shown)**
1 to let someone see something
Show me your new game.
2 to guide someone somewhere
or help them to do something
The guide showed us around.

shower (showers)
1 something that you stand
under to wash your body
*Every room in the hotel has a
private shower.*
2 a light fall of rain
*There will be showers in the
afternoon.*

**shrink (shrinking, shrank,
shrunk)**
to become smaller
*My favourite jumper shrank in the
wash.*

shut (shutting, shut)
to close
Shut the door, please.

sideways
towards one side, not
forwards or backwards
*Turn sideways and then
you can get past.*

sign (signs)
1 a mark or symbol that means
something
The sign £ means pound or pounds.
2 a notice that tells you
something
*The sign says 'Danger
of avalanche'.*

**sign (signing,
signed)**
to write
your name
on something
*Sign your name at the
bottom of the form.*

DANGER
AVALANCHE

sign

silly (sillier, silliest)
stupid, not sensible
Don't be so silly!

similar
nearly the same as something
else
*My brother and I look similar and
we like similar things.*

**sing (singing, sang,
sung)**
to make music with
your voice
Sing us a song.

sink (sinks)
a bowl with taps in a kitchen or a
bathroom
Put the dirty dishes in the sink.

sink (sinking, sank, sunk)
to go down below the surface
of water
*The ship Titanic sank after it
hit an iceberg.*

sink

sister (sisters)
a girl or woman
who has the same
parents as you
Shannon is my younger sister.

sit (sitting, sat)
to put your bottom on a chair or
another type of seat
I must sit down; my feet ache.

size (sizes)
how big or small something is
These shoes come in all sizes.

skate (skates)
a boot with wheels or a blade
fixed to the bottom
*We're going to the park.
Don't forget your
skates.*

skate (skating, skated)
to move over ground or ice
wearing boots with wheels or
blades
*He skated over to us when he
saw us.*

**skateboard
(skateboards)**
a small board on wheels
that you can ride on
*He came down the
ramp on his
skateboard.*

skateboard

a
b
c
d
e
f
g
h
i
j
k
l
m
n
o
p
q
r
s
t
u
v
w
x
y
z

a
b
c
d
e
f
g
h
i
j
k
l
m
n
o
p
q
r
s
t
u
v
w
x
y
z

skeleton (skeletons)
the bones in your body
He wore a suit with a skeleton painted on it for Hallowe'en.

skeleton

sketch (sketching, sketched)
to draw quickly
Artists sketch a scene first.

ski (skis)
a long, flat piece of wood or plastic that you fix to special shoes for moving along on snow
We carried our skis to the top of the mountain.

ski (skiing, skied)
to move quickly over snow or water on long, narrow pieces of wood
Do you know how to ski?

skin (skins)
the outside layer covering your body, or covering fruits and vegetables
The skin is the body's largest organ.

skirt (skirts)
a piece of clothing worn by girls and women that hangs from the waist down
She was wearing a blue skirt and red jacket.

sky (skies)
the space above you where the sun, moon, stars and clouds are
The sky was full of stars.

slap (slapping, slapped)
to hit something with an open hand
She slapped his hand.

sledge (sledges)
a vehicle or toy for moving across ice or snow
We built a sledge out of an old wooden box.

sleep (sleeping, slept)
not to be awake
The baby is sleeping.

sleeping

slice (slices)
a thin piece of bread, cake, meat or other food that has been cut from a bigger piece
Can you eat another slice of meat?

slices

slide (slides)
1 a structure with steps and a slope that you climb then slide smoothly down
My favourite thing in the playground is the slide.
2 a small piece of metal or plastic that girls wear in their hair to keep it away from their face
My slide is shaped like a butterfly.

slide (sliding, slid)
to move across or down a smooth surface
The car slid across the ice.

slipper (slippers)
one of a pair of soft shoes that you wear indoors
Put your slippers on if your feet are cold.

slow
not fast, taking a long time
This is a slow train.

small
little or young
The jeans have a small pocket for coins.

smile (smiling, smiled)
to make your mouth curve up and look happy
The photographer asked us to smile.

smoke
the cloudy gas that is made when something burns
The room filled with smoke.

smooth
not rough or bumpy
You can skate on the pavement; it's smooth.

smoke

snack (snacks)
a small meal that you can prepare quickly
Let's just have a snack now because we're having a big meal this evening.

snail (snails)
a small creature with a soft, wet body and a shell on its back
Snails move very slowly.

snail

a b c d e f g h i j k l m n o p q r **s** t u v w x y z

snake (snakes)
a creature with a long body and no legs
I hope there aren't any snakes in the grass.

snake

sneeze (sneezing, sneezed)
to blow air out of your nose suddenly, with a loud noise
He's sneezing and coughing because he has a cold.

snow
small, soft pieces of ice that fall from the sky
The trees are covered in snow.

snow (snowing, snowed)
when it snows, small soft pieces of ice fall from the sky
Hurrah! It's snowing. Let's build a snowman.

snowing

soap
something that you use with water to wash your body
The soap is making lots of bubbles.

soccer
football, a game played by two teams that try to get a round ball between two posts
Do you prefer soccer or cricket?

sock (socks)
one of two pieces of clothing that you wear on your feet
Socks keep your feet warm.

sofa (sofas)
a long, soft seat for two or more people
Shall we sit on the sofa?

soft
1 not hard, smooth when you touch it
The rabbit has lovely, soft fur.
2 not loud
She has a soft voice.

software
the programs that run on a computer
He designs software.

soldier (soldiers)
a person in the army
The soldiers marched through the square.

soldier

solid
hard, firm
The front door is made of solid wood.

some
1 an amount of something that is not exact
Would you like some rice?
2 part of something, but not all
Some of these apples are rotten.

son (sons)
a male child
They have two sons.

song (songs)
a piece of music with words
The children sang songs in the school hall.

Space

sore
hurting or painful
Is the cut on your leg still sore?

sorry
feeling sad because something bad or unpleasant has happened
I'm sorry your mum is ill.

soup
a liquid food made from meat or vegetables and water
Have a bowl of tomato soup.

sour
having a taste like lemons, not sweet
This juice is a bit sour.

space
1 (spaces) an empty or open place
Is there any space left in the suitcase?
2 everything beyond the Earth's air
The rocket is travelling through space.

spade (spades)
a tool for digging
Turn the soil with a spade.

spaghetti
long, thin strips of pasta
Ellie likes spaghetti.

spaghetti

spare
extra, not needed at the moment
I've got a spare pencil if you need one.

a b c d e f g h i j k l m n o p q r s t u v w x y z

speed (speeds)
how fast something moves
At what speed are we travelling?

spell (spelling, spelt, spelled)
to write or say the letters of a
word in the correct order
How do you spell 'skateboard'?

spider

spider (spiders)
a small creature
with eight legs
that catches insects in a web
There's a spider in the bath.

spill (spilling, spilt, spilled)
to cause a liquid to fall to the
ground accidentally
I spilt the drink on the carpet.

spilt

Puzzle time
Can you unscramble the
names of these sports?

a. gruyb b. gsmwmin
c. cykeoh d. nintes

Answers: a. rugby
b. swimming c. hockey
d. tennis

spoon (spoons)
an object with a handle and
small bowl that is used
for eating
*We need knives,
forks and spoons
on the table.*

sport

sport
physical
activities such as
swimming and soccer
*Swimming is a sport the
whole family can enjoy.*

spring
the time of year
between winter and summer
The cherry tree flowers in spring.

squirrel (squirrels)
a small wild animal with a long,
bushy tail
*Squirrels are very good at climbing
trees.*

stadium (stadiums)
a big building where you can
watch sports matches or concerts
*Some stadiums have roofs and some
don't.*

stairs
a set of steps in a building that go from one floor to another
I'll take the stairs to the top floor.

stamp (stamps)
1 a piece of paper that you stick on a letter or postcard before you post it
I'd like a first class stamp.
2 a tool you put ink on and then press onto something to make a mark
There's a stamp on the library book showing the date you have to take it back.

stand (standing, stood)
to be on your feet
She's standing by the door.

star (stars)
1 a ball of burning gas that looks like a light in the sky
The stars are bright tonight
2 a famous person
She's a big star now.
3 a shape with five or six points
We baked biscuits shaped like stars.

statue

starfish (starfish or starfishes)
a star-shaped creature that lives in the sea
There's a starfish under the rock.

start (starting, started)
to begin
We started work at 10 o'clock this morning.

station (stations)
a place where trains and buses stop to let people on and off
My dad walks to the station every morning then gets the train.

statue (statues)
a model of a person or animal made out of stone or metal
There's a statue of a mermaid in the middle of the fountain.

stay (staying, stayed)
1 not to leave a place
You stay here; I'll be right back.
2 to live in a place for a short amount of time
When I was little, we stayed at my aunt's house every summer.
3 to continue to remain the same
He's never grumpy, his mood stays the same all the time.

a b c d e f g h i j k l m n o p q r **s** t u v w x y z

a
b
c
d
e
f
g
h
i
j
k
l
m
n
o
p
q
r
s
t
u
v
w
x
y
z

steal (stealing, stole, stolen)
to take something that doesn't
belong to you
Thieves stole my dad's car.

steam

steam
the hot gas that comes
off boiling water
*The kitchen is full of steam
because I forgot to put the
lid on the kettle.*

stick (sticks)
a long, thin piece of wood
*We made a fire by rubbing two
sticks together.*

stomach (stomachs)
the part inside your body where
food goes when you eat
*My stomach hurts; I've
eaten too much.*

stone
1 the hard solid
substance found in the
ground, rock
*The floor in the castle is
made out of stone.*
2 (stones) fourteen
pounds or 6.35 kilograms
What is your weight in stones?

3 (stones) the seed in some fruits
*Careful! The cherries have stones in
them.*

stool (stools)
a seat with no back
Sit on the stool.

stop (stopping, stopped)
1 to finish doing
something
Stop talking for a minute.
2 not to move any more
*You have to stop if the traffic lights
are red.*
3 to prevent something
happening
The referee stopped the fight.

storm (storms)
a time of very bad weather
with heavy rain, wind and
sometimes thunder and
lightning
*A lot of trees fell down in the
storm.*

storm

story (stories)
a description of events that
may be real or imaginary
*Everyone knows the story of Peter
Pan.*

straight
not crooked, bent or curly
She has straight hair.

strange
1 unusual
He looks a bit strange.
2 unfamiliar
There were a lot of strange faces at the party.

stranger (strangers)
someone you don't know
You must never get into a stranger's car.

strawberry (strawberries)
a soft, heart-shaped, red fruit
We sometimes have strawberries and cream in summer.

stream (streams)
a small river
We drank water from a mountain stream.

stretch (stretching, stretched)
1 to get longer or bigger
Tights can stretch quite a bit.

2 to straighten a part of your body
She stretched her legs out under the table.

string
thick thread or thin rope
Tie some string around the box.

strong
1 powerful, not weak
She must be very strong if she can carry this suitcase.
2 not easily broken or damaged
The window is made from very strong glass.

stupid
not sensible or clever
What a stupid idea!

submarine (submarines)
a ship that can travel underwater
Submarines can help us to find out about underwater life.

sudden
happening quickly and unexpectedly
Don't make any sudden movements.

strawberries

submarine

sugar
a sweet substance used to flavour food
Sugar can be white or brown.

suitcase (suitcases)
a case or bag to carry clothes in when you travel
Our suitcase has wheels.

summer (summers)
the time of year between spring and autumn
Are you going on holiday this summer?

sun (Sun)
the very bright star that the Earth travels around
All the planets in the solar system travel around the Sun.

sunflower (sunflowers)
a tall flower whose head is round and yellow like the sun
Sunflowers look like big, yellow daisies.

sunflowers

sunglasses
dark glasses that you wear to protect your eyes when it is sunny
Don't forget to pack your sunglasses.

suitcases

supermarket (supermarkets)
a large shop that sells food and other things
The supermarket stays open late on Fridays.

supper (suppers)
a meal you eat in the evening, or a snack you eat just before bedtime
For supper I usually have tea and toast.

surprise (surprises)
something that is completely unexpected
A bunch of flowers! What a lovely surprise!

swan (swans)
a white bird with a long neck that lives on rivers and lakes
Swans glide smoothly across the water.

a b c d e f g h i j k l m n o p q r **s** t u v w x y z

sweep (sweeping, swept)
to brush dirt from the floor or ground
Have you swept the floor?

sweet (sweets)
1 a small piece of sweet, sugary food such as a chocolate or toffee
Always clean your teeth after eating sweets.
2 a pudding or dessert
For sweet we could have strawberries and ice cream.

sweet
1 tasting sugary
These grapes are very sweet.
2 nice or pleasant
That's a sweet thing to say.

swim (swimming, swam, swum)
to move through or across water by using your arms and legs
I can swim a whole length of the pool.

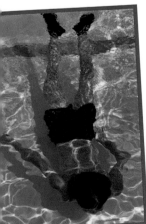

swim

sword

swimming pool (swimming pools)
a big, deep hole that contains water, where you can swim
There's an outdoor swimming pool in this town.

swing (swings)
a seat hanging from a bar or a tree that moves backwards and forwards
I'll sit on the swing first and you can push me.

swing (swinging, swung)
to move backwards, forwards or from side to side from a fixed point
The monkey swung from tree to tree.

sword (swords)
a very large knife that was used for fighting in the past
There are lots of old swords in the museum.

synagogue (synagogues)
a building where Jewish people go to pray
My uncle got married in a synagogue.

a b c d e f g h i j k l m n o p q r **s** t u v w x y z

How many things can you spot beginning with 't'?

T t

tadpole (tadpoles)
a very young frog or toad
Tadpoles have big heads and long tails and live in water.

tail (tails)
the part of an animal at the end of its back
The dog has a long, white tail.

— tail

table (tables)
1 a piece of furniture with legs and a flat top
Please clear the table.
2 a list of numbers or words written in rows and columns
We measured the height of everyone in the class and wrote the results in a table.

take (taking, took, taken)
1 to carry something
Take an umbrella with you.
2 to move something or someone to another place
Can you take us to the station?
3 to steal
The thieves took all the money.

a b c d e f g h i j k l m n o p q r s **t** u v w x y z

talent (talents)
the ability to do something very well without having to learn it
Maya has a talent for drawing.

talk (talking, talked)
to speak
We talked on the phone for ages.

tall
1 higher than normal
My grandad is tall, and I am short.
2 having a certain height
How tall are you?

tambourine (tambourines)
a small round musical instrument that you shake or hit
I played the tambourine in the school concert.

tank (tanks)
1 a container for liquids
There's a leak in the petrol tank.
2 a strong truck used by soldiers
Tanks have metal tracks or belts instead of wheels.

tap (taps)
something that controls the flow of a liquid or gas
Turn the tap off; don't waste water.

tape
a flat, narrow strip of plastic that is sticky on one side
Put some sticky tape on the envelope.

taste (tasting, tasted)
1 to have a flavour
What does the soup taste like?
2 to try a little food or drink to see what it is like
Have you tasted the pizza?

taxi (taxis)
a car that takes people to different places, for money
We'll take a taxi.

tea
1 a hot drink made from leaves
Do you take milk in your tea?
2 a meal you eat in the early evening
What's for tea?

teacher (teachers)
a person who gives lessons in a subject
Our teacher's name is Mrs Griffiths.

teacher

team (teams)
a group of people
who play a game or
work together
*There are eleven
players in a football
team.*

**tear (tears)
(rhymes with ear)**
a drop of water that
comes out of your eye
Tears ran down his face.

**tear (tearing, tore,
torn) (rhymes with fair)**
to rip, split or make a hole in
something
I tore the paper in half.

teddy bear (teddy bears)
a soft toy that looks like a bear
*I take my teddy bear to
bed with me.*

telephone (telephones)
a piece of equipment
that you use to speak to
someone in another place
Where's your telephone?

Puzzle time
Can you match these star
patterns to the names below?
1. Pegasus (the winged horse)
2. Ursa Major (Great Bear)
3. Hercules
4. Orion (the Hunter)

a

b

c

d

Answers: 1d 2b 3a 4c

**telescope
(telescopes)**
a piece of
equipment that
you use to look at
things that are
far away
*We looked at the
stars through the
telescope.*

**television (TV;
televisions)**
a machine with
a screen that shows programmes
*What's on television tomorrow
evening?*

tell (telling, told)
1 to pass on information
I told you that story yesterday.
2 to know or understand
I can't tell what it means.

temple (temples)
a building where
people of some
religions go to pray
*Hindus and
Buddhists
worship in a
temple.*

teddy bear

tennis

tennis
a game played by two or four people who hit a ball over a net to score points
Tennis is a summer game.

tent (tents)
a temporary shelter made of cloth or plastic.
The tent will keep us dry.

terrible
very bad
The film was terrible.

tent

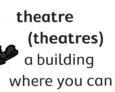

test (tests)
1 a set of questions to measure knowledge
We had a spelling test at school today.
2 a set of checks to find out if something is working properly
Cars must pass several tests.

text (texts)
1 a message you send by mobile phone
Send me a text when you are on the train.
2 the writing in a book or magazine, not the pictures
The book has fifty pages of text.

text (texting, texted)
to send someone a message by mobile phone
I'll text you later.

thank (thanking, thanked)
to tell someone you are pleased about something they have given you or have done for you
Remember to thank them for the present.

theatre (theatres)
a building where you can go and see plays
Shall we go to the theatre this weekend?

a b c d e f g h i j k l m n o p q r s **t** u v w x y z

thick

1 not thin

The furniture was covered with a thick sheet of plastic.

2 not watery

This pancake mixture is too thick.

thief (thieves)

a person who steals things

The police chased the thief.

thin (thinner, thinnest)

1 having not much distance from one side to the other

Cut the paper into thin strips.

2 slim, not fat

She's quite thin.

3 watery

It's a thin, clear soup.

throw

think (thinking, thought)

1 to use your mind to solve a problem or remember something

Think carefully before you answer.

2 to believe something is true, but not to know for sure

I think we break up next Wednesday.

thirsty (thirstier, thirstiest)

feeling that you need to drink something

Are you thirsty?

throat (throats)

the back of your mouth where food goes when you swallow

I've got a bone stuck in my throat.

through

from one side to the other

The cat came in through the cat flap.

throw (throwing, threw, thrown)

to make something go through the air

Throw the ball through the net.

thumb (thumbs)

the short, thick finger on the inside of your hand

I've cut my thumb.

thunder

the loud noise you can hear during a storm

There was thunder and lightning.

ticket (tickets)

a piece of paper that shows you have paid

I have tickets for the match on Saturday.

tickets

tidy (tidier, tidiest)
neat and organized
Leah's room is never tidy.

tie (ties)
a long strip of material that you
wear under a shirt collar and tie
at the front
We have to wear ties in our school.

tie (tying, tied)
to join pieces of string, rope or
thread together
Tie your shoelaces.

tiger (tigers)
a large, wild cat with
orange fur with
black stripes
*Tigers live in India and
Southeast Asia.*

tiger

tight
1 close-fitting
This shirt is a bit tight.
2 firmly in place
I can't undo the knot; it's too tight.

tights
clothing worn by girls and
women on the feet and legs
I always wear thick tights in winter.

timetable (timetables)
a list of times when things
happen or buses and trains leave
*Check the timetable to see when the
next train is.*

tiny (tinier, tiniest)
very small
Look at the tiny ladybird.

tired
feeling that you need to rest
The baby is tired.

toad (toads)
a creature like a big frog
Toads have dryer skin than frogs.

toast
bread that has been cooked in a
toaster or under a grill
*I have toast and marmalade for
breakfast.*

today
this day
What's the date today?

toe (toes)
one of the five parts of
your body at the end of your foot
Ouch! You stood on my toe.

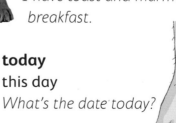

toes

a
b
c
d
e
f
g
h
i
j
k
l
m
n
o
p
q
r
s
t
u
v
w
x
y
z

a b c d e f g h i j k l m n o p q r s t u v w x y z

together
1 joined or mixed
Mix the eggs and milk together.
2 with each other
Shall we go together?

tomato (tomatoes)
a red fruit that you can eat raw
or cooked
Mum sliced a tomato for the salad.

tomorrow
the day after today
What shall we do tomorrow?

tool (tools)
a piece of equipment that you use
to do a job
Hammers and saws are tools.

tongue (tongues)
the part of your body inside your
mouth that you use to speak with
and to taste things
*The ice cream feels cold on my
tongue.*

tooth (teeth)
one of the hard, white
things in your mouth
*You should brush your
teeth twice a day.*

top (tops)
1 the highest part of something
*They reached the top of the
mountain.*
2 a piece of clothing for the
upper body
That's a pretty top.
3 a cover or lid for a container
Put the top back on the bottle.
4 a toy that spins round
The top is brightly coloured.

torch (torches)
a light that you
can carry around
with you
Shine the torch over here.

t o r c h

tortoise (tortoises)
a small animal with a thick, hard
shell that it can pull its legs and
head into
Tortoises move very slowly.

touch (touching, touched)
1 to put your
fingers or
hand on
something
*Please don't
touch the
paintings.*

teeth

2 to be so close to another thing that there is no space between the two
The wires are touching.

towel (towels)
a cloth that you use to dry things that are wet
Dry your hands on the towel.

tower (towers)
a tall, narrow building or part of a building
We climbed to the top of the tower.

town (towns)
a place with houses and other buildings where people live and work
There's a theatre in our town.

toy (toys)
something that children like to play with
The baby has lots of toys.

toys

tractor (tractors)
a big truck that farm workers drive
We were behind a tractor on the road so we had to drive slowly.

traffic
all the cars, buses, lorries and other vehicles that are travelling on a road
The traffic on this road is very heavy.

traffic jam (traffic jams)
a line of traffic that is moving very slowly or is not moving at all
We were stuck in a traffic jam for nearly an hour.

traffic lights

traffic lights
a set of red, orange and green lights where two or more roads meet
Turn left at the traffic lights.

train (trains)
a line of carriages pulled by an engine on a track
Mum goes to work on the train.

trainer (trainers)
a sports shoe
I bought some new trainers.

trampoline (trampolines)
a large piece of stretchy cloth attached to a metal frame that you can bounce up and down on
We all had a go on the trampoline.

a b c d e f g h i j k l m n o p q r s **t** u v w x y z

transport (transporting, transported)
to move people or things from one place to another
The tanker transports petrol.

trap (trapping, trapped)
to catch something in a piece of equipment
It traps mice.

trapeze (trapezes)
a bar hanging from two ropes that people swing from
I liked the acrobats on the trapeze best when we went to the circus.

travel (travelling, travelled)
to go from one place to another
They're travelling by car.

treasure
valuable things like gold or jewellery
The chest is filled with treasure.

tree (trees)
a large, tall plant with a trunk and branches
There's a big tree in our garden.

trick (tricks)
1 something clever that you do
The magician knows lots of tricks.
2 something that people do to fool or cheat someone
He played a mean trick on me.

trip (trips)
a journey
We've decided to go on a trip around the world.

trip (tripping, tripped)
to catch your foot on something and nearly fall
I tripped as I was coming down the steps.

trousers
a piece of clothing that covers the legs
He's wearing grey trousers.

truck (trucks)
a lorry
We were stuck behind a truck.

trunk (trunks)
1 the thick part of a tree
I sat on the grass with my back against the trunk of the tree.

tree

trunk

2 an elephant's nose
The elephant has a long trunk.
3 a box for storing things in
Where's the key for this trunk?

try (trying, tried)
1 to make an effort
I tried to open the window.
2 to test or sample something
Have you tried this cake?

T-shirt/t-shirt (T-shirts)
a piece of clothing like a vest with short sleeves
I love my purple T-shirt.

T-shirt

tunnel (tunnels)
a long hole under the ground
There is a tunnel under the sea between England and France.

turkey
1 (turkeys) a large bird that is kept on farms for its meat
There are hundreds of turkeys on the farm.
2 the meat from this bird
We usually have turkey for Christmas dinner.

turn (turns)
your time to play or to do something, your go in a game
Is it my turn yet?

turn (turning, turned)
1 to move so you are looking or going in a new direction
Turn round and face the door.
2 to move something to a different position
Turn the key.

turtle (turtles)
an animal that lives in water that looks like a tortoise
Turtles have thick shells covering their bodies.

twin (twins)
your brother or sister born at the same time as you
Tom and Dylan are twins.

twins

tyre (tyres)
a rubber ring that goes around the wheel of a car or bicycle
I think one of the tyres is flat.

a b c d e f g h i j k l m n o p q r s **t** u v w x y z

a b c d e f g h i j k l m n o p q r s t **u** v w x y z

How many things can you spot beginning with 'u'?

Uu

ugly (uglier, ugliest)
not nice to look at
What an ugly colour!

umbrella (umbrellas)
a piece of material stretched
over a frame with a handle, that
keeps the rain off
*It's raining
outside; I'll
take my
umbrella.*

umbrella

uncle (uncles)
the brother of your mother or
father, or the husband of your
aunt
*He looks like
his uncle.*

under
below
*Put your bag
under your seat.*

under

**understand (understanding,
understood)**
1 to know the meaning of words
or ideas
Does he understand English?
2 to know how something works
*I don't understand how the
machine works.*

3 to know how and why someone feels or acts a certain way
You don't understand.

underwear
pieces of clothing that you wear next to your body, under your other clothes
Vests and pants are items of underwear.

unhappy (unhappier, unhappiest)
not happy, sad
Cheer up! Try not to look so unhappy.

unicorn

unicorn (unicorns)
an animal in stories that looks like a white horse with a horn growing out of the front of its head
In the story, the prince searched for the unicorn in the forest.

uniform (uniforms)
a set of clothes worn by everyone in a group of people
In school we wear a uniform.

universe (universes)
all the planets, all the stars, the Sun and everything in space
Is there life anywhere else in the universe?

up
towards a higher position
Pass that brush up to me.

upset
1 feeling sad or worried
She was upset to hear the bad news.
2 feeling bad or sick
He's got an upset stomach.

upside-down

upside-down
turned over so that the top is at the bottom and the bottom is at the top
Turn the bottle upside-down and the sauce will come out.

upstairs
towards or on a higher floor of a building
I went upstairs to my bedroom.

urgent
needing attention immediately
Tell the headmistress it's urgent.

a b c d e f g h i j k l m n o p q r s t u v w x y z

a b c d e f g h i j k l m n o p q r s t u **v** w x y z

How many things can you spot beginning with 'v'?

V v

vanish (vanishing, vanished)
to disappear
The deer suddenly vanished.

vase (vases)
a container to put flowers in
Mum put the roses in a vase.

valley (valleys)
the low land between
two hills
There is a river in the valley.

vegetable (vegetables)
a plant grown for food
Carrots are my favourite vegetable.

vegetarian (vegetarians)
a person who doesn't eat meat
My best friend is a vegetarian.

van (vans)
a boxlike vehicle that
is bigger than a car
but smaller than a
lorry
*The plumber arrived
in a van.*

vehicle (vehicles)
a machine that moves people or
things from one place to another
Cars and trucks are vehicles.

vase

vest (vests)
a piece of clothing that you wear on your upper body under your other clothes
Put a vest on; it's cold today.

vet (veterinary surgeon; vets)
an animal doctor
The vet is treating our dog.

view (views)
everything you can see from a place
There's a lovely view from this window.

village (villages)
a group of houses and buildings in the country
It's a beautiful, old village.

vinegar
a sour liquid used to keep food fresh, or to give it a sharp taste
I like vinegar on chips.

violin (violins)
a musical instrument that you hold under your chin and play with a bow
My brother is learning to play the violin.

violin

virus (viruses)
1 a very tiny living thing that can make you ill if it gets inside your body
Flu is caused by a virus.
2 a computer program that damages information stored on a computer
The virus has damaged my files.

visit (visiting, visited)
to go to see a person or a place
We visit my grandparents every Sunday.

voice (voices)
the sound you make when you are speaking or singing
I didn't recognize your voice.

volcano (volcanoes)
a mountain with an opening that sprays out lava and ash
Mount Etna in Italy is an active volcano.

volcano

vote (voting, voted)
to show which idea or person you choose by raising your hand or writing on paper
Let's vote on this idea.

a b c d e f g h i j k l m n o p q r s t u **v** w x y z

a b c d e f g h i j k l m n o p q r s t u v **w** x y z

How many things can you spot beginning with 'w'?

Ww

waiter (waiters)
a man who serves food in a
restaurant or café
*The waiter gave each
of us a menu.*

waitress (waitresses)
a woman who serves
food in a restaurant
or café
*Ask the waitress
for the bill.*

waitress

wake (waking, woke, woken)
to stop sleeping
I woke up at eight o'clock.

walk (walking, walked)
to move along, putting one foot
in front of the other
I walk to school every day.

walk

wall (walls)
1 the side of a room or a building
There are some pictures on the wall.
2 a structure made of stone or
bricks that goes around a
garden or field
We climbed over the wall.

wand (wands)
a special stick used by fairies, witches and magicians to do magic
With a flick of her wand she turned the pumpkin into a coach.

wand

want (wanting, wanted)
if you want something you would like to have it or do it
Do you want a sandwich?

wardrobe (wardrobes)
a cupboard to hang clothes in
I have a wardrobe in my bedroom.

warm
slightly hot, not cool or cold
The water is lovely and warm.

wash (washing, washed)
to clean with water
I washed my hands.

wasp (wasps)
a black-and-yellow flying insect that stings
Wasps live in nests.

wasp

watch (watches)
a small clock that you wear on your wrist
I'd like a watch for my birthday.

watch (watching, watched)
to look at something and pay attention
We're watching the match.

water
a liquid that falls from the sky as rain
There is water in rivers and lakes.

H_2O

waterfall (waterfalls)
water from a stream or a river that falls straight down over rocks
There is a pool under the waterfall.

wave (waves)
1 a raised part of moving water on the sea
Waves crashed on the beach.
2 a movement of your hand from side to side to say hello or goodbye
Give them a wave.
3 the way light and sound move
Sound is carried on radio waves.

a b c d e f g h i j k l m n o p q r s t u v **w** x y z

wave (waving, waved)

1 to move your hand from side to side to say hello or goodbye

wave

She waved to me from the other side of the road.

2 to move from side to side

The children waved their flags.

weak

not strong

I feel weak and dizzy.

wear (wearing, wore, worn)

to have clothes on your body

What shall I wear to the party?

weather

the condition of the air – how hot it is, the wind, rain and clouds

What's the weather like today?

web

1 (webs) the very thin net a spider weaves

Spiders catch food in webs.

2 the World Wide Web on the Internet

You'll find the information on the web.

website (websites)

a place on the Internet where you can find out things

Please visit our website.

weed (weeds)

a plant that grows in a place where you do not want it to be

There are lots of weeds in our garden.

week (weeks)

seven days

We went to Spain for two weeks.

weekend (weekends)

Saturday and Sunday

We're going away for the weekend.

weigh (weighing, weighed)

1 to measure how heavy something is

The shop assistant weighed the fruit.

weigh

2 to be heavy or light

How much do you weigh?

well (wells)

a deep hole in the ground with water or oil at the bottom

People used to get water from wells.

well
1 in a good way
You played that tune very well.
2 healthy, not ill
Get well soon.

wet (wetter, wettest)
covered in water
Your hair's still wet.

whales

whale (whales)
a very large sea animal
Whales are mammals, not fish.

wheat
a cereal plant that is used to make flour
These fields are used to grow wheat.

wheel (wheels)
a round object that turns and moves a vehicle along
The wheel came off my bike.

whisker (whiskers)
one of the long, stiff hairs on an animal's face
My cat has long whiskers.

whisper (whispering, whispered)
to speak very quietly
Whisper the secret to me.

whistle (whistles)
a thing you blow into to make a loud, high sound
The referee blew his whistle.

whistle

whistle (whistling, whistled)
to blow air out through your lips and make a sound
Can you whistle?

wicked
very bad or evil
The wicked witch trapped them.

wife (wives)
the woman that a man is married to
His wife is very nice.

win (winning, won)
to be the first or the best in a race or other competition
He's won the race!

wind (winds)
air moving across the ground
There's a strong wind today.

a b c d e f g h i j k l m n o p q r s t u v **w** x y z

windmill (windmills)
a building with long blades,
called sails, that turn in the wind
*Windmills were used to generate
electricity.*

window (windows)
an opening in a wall that is
covered by glass
She looked out of the window.

wing (wings)
1 one of the parts of a
bird's or insect's body that
it uses for flying
The bird flapped its wings.
2 one of the flat parts of an
aeroplane that stick out at the
side and help the plane move
through the air
*I sat over the wing when I flew in a
plane.*

winter (winters)
the time of year between autumn
and spring
The weather is colder in winter.

wish (wishes)
a feeling of wanting something
very much
The fairy gave me three wishes.

wish (wishing, wished)
to hope for or want something
What did you wish for?

witch (witches)
a woman in stories who has
magic powers
The witch rode on a broomstick.

wizard

wizard (wizards)
a man in stories who has
magic powers
The wizard broke the spell.

wolf (wolves)
a wild animal
that looks like
a large dog
*Wolves hunt in
packs, or groups.*

woman (women)
a female adult
*Are there any women
in the team?*

wolf

**wonder (wondering,
wondered)**
to think about something and
why it is that way
I wonder why she said that?

wood
1 the hard material that a tree is made of
Put more wood on the fire.
2 (woods) an area of land where a lot of trees grow
We walked through the wood.

wool

wool
thick, soft hair that grows on sheep's bodies and that can be made into thread
I need four balls of wool to knit a scarf.

work (working, worked)
1 to do a job
She works in the hospital as a doctor.
2 to go or operate smoothly
This machine is working properly now.

world
our planet and everything that is on it
There are over six billion people in the world.

worm (worms)
a long, thin creature with no legs that lives in soil
Worms are good for the garden.

worry (worrying, worried)
to have the feeling that something bad might happen
Don't worry; I'll be all right.

worse (worst)
less good
My cold is worse today.

wrist (wrists)
the place where your arm and hand are joined
She was wearing a bracelet on her wrist.

write (writing, wrote, written)
to put words on paper using a pen or pencil
I wrote her a letter.

wrong
not right, incorrect
We've taken a wrong turn.

Puzzle time
Match the workers with the things they need to do their jobs

A	B
actor	paint
artist	theatre
pilot	menu
waiter	plane

Answers: actor/theatre
artist/paint pilot/plane
waiter/menu

a b c d e f g h i j k l m n o p q r s t u v **w** x y z

How many things can you spot beginning with 'x', 'y' and 'z'?

X-ray (X-rays)
1 a beam of energy that can go through solid things
X-rays are used at airports.
2 a photograph of the inside of the body
The X-ray shows that his hand may be broken.

xylophone (xylophones)
a musical instrument that you play by hitting wooden or metal bars with sticks
My baby sister has a toy xylophone.

yacht (yachts)
a sailing boat
They sailed around France in a yacht.

yawn (yawning, yawned)
to open your mouth and take a deep breath, usually when you are tired
You're yawning. It must be bedtime.

year (years)
a period of 12 months, especially from January to December
We've lived here for five years.

yell (yelling, yelled)
to shout very loudly
The teacher told us not to yell in the classroom.

a
b
c
d
e
f
g
h
i
j
k
l
m
n
o
p
q
r
s
t
u
v
w
x
y
z

yes
a word that you say when you
agree with something or when
something is true
Yes, you're right.

yesterday
the day before today
I phoned you yesterday.

yoga
exercises for your body and mind
My mum does yoga on a mat.

yoghurt (or yogurt)
a thick liquid food made from milk
I'd like a strawberry yoghurt, please.

yolk (yolks)
the yellow part of an egg
I like dipping my toast into the yolk.

young
not old, not yet an adult
*You're too young to walk
to school on your own.*

yo-yo (yo-yos)
a toy that moves up
and down on a string
that you hold in your hand
This yo-yo glows in the dark.

zebra (zebras)
a wild, black-
and-white
striped animal
*Zebras look like
horses.*

zebra

**zebra crossing
(zebra
crossings)**
part of a road painted with
black-and-white stripes where
you can cross the road safely
*The driver stopped at the zebra
crossing so the children could cross
the road.*

zero
nothing, 0
The temperature is zero degrees.

zip (zips)
a fastener made of two rows
of teeth that lock together
*Some of my skirts have zips
and some have buttons.*

zoo (zoos)
a place where wild animals are
kept so that people can go to
look at them
We went to the zoo.

a b c d e f g h i j k l m n o p q r s t u v w x y z

How to use your thesaurus

Keywords and synonyms
*Each keyword is in large, coloured type. Above it is a list of synonyms in **bold** type. Each synonym is in alphabetical order.*

Alphabetical order
All of the entries are in alphabetical order. The alphabet is listed down the side of each page. Use the highlighted letters to help you find your way around.

Cartoons
These illustrate many of the entries in a fun way. Each cartoon has its own label to tell you exactly what it is.

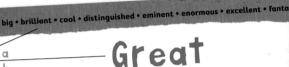

big • brilliant • cool • distinguished • eminent • enormous • excellent • fantas

Great

a b c d e f **g** h i j k l m n o p q r s t u v w x y z

• very good

brilliant (informal)
very good
I thought the book was brilliant.

cool (informal)
very good, excellent
The party was really cool.

excellent
extremely good
The food was excellent.

fantastic (informal)
extremely good
You look fantastic in that hat!

first-class
excellent
You've done a first-class job by picking up all the litter.

magnificent
beautiful, wonderful
They live in a magnificent house on the hill.

super (informal)
extremely good
I've had a super time.

terrific (informal)
very good
The restaurant gives terrific value for money.

fantastic

Did you know?
The word **cool** is also used to descibe a fairly low temperature –
The afternoon felt cool.

Entries

Each synonym is explained and placed in an example sentence to show you how it could be used.

In other words

An idiom is a phrasing of words that gives a different meaning from each of the words on their own. Idioms are fun ways to say things. We use them more in speech than when we are writing. Look for the speech bubbles to find more idioms.

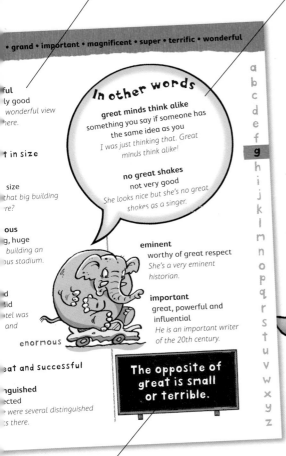

• grand • important • magnificent • super • terrific • wonderful

ful
ly good
wonderful view
here.

t in size

size
that big building
re?

ous
g, huge
building an
us stadium.

d
lid
tel was
and

enormous

at and successful

nguished
ected
were several distinguished
s there.

In other words

great minds think alike
something you say if someone has the same idea as you
I was just thinking that. Great minds think alike!

no great shakes
not very good
She looks nice but she's no great shakes as a singer.

eminent
worthy of great respect
She's a very eminent historian.

important
great, powerful and influential
He is an important writer of the 20th century.

The opposite of great is small or terrible.

a b c d e f **g** h i j k l m n o p q r s t u v w x y z

Did you know?

These panels give interesting information about words such as where they came from and how old they are.

Opposites

There are small chalkboard panels throughout this section. These give the opposites of the keywords.

Look for the green picture frames to have some fun! You can play games, solve puzzles and take part in quizzes.

a
b
c
d
e
f
g
h
i
j
k
l
m
n
o
p
q
r
s
t
u
v
w
x
y
z

Angry

• feeling a little angry

annoyed
feeling slightly angry or impatient
Arran will be annoyed if we forget his birthday.

cross
feeling a little annoyed or angry
Our teacher gets cross when the class keeps talking.

irritable
getting annoyed easily
He gets very irritable after having a fizzy drink.

irritated
feeling annoyed or impatient about something that keeps happening
I'm really irritated. This game keeps crashing.

• angry or very angry

fuming
feeling very angry inside
We had an argument yesterday and I'm still fuming.

furious
extremely angry
There was a furious row going on between the two teams.

incensed
very angry
Some people in the audience were so incensed at what they heard that they walked out of the theatre.

irate
angry because something has upset you
The company received a lot of complaints from irate customers about the poor level of service.

cross

livid
so angry that you
can't think
Angry? She was livid!

mad (informal)
feeling angry
*This DVD player
makes me so mad!*

seething
feeling angry but not
saying a word
*He was so tense, you
could tell he was
seething.*

In other words

to fly off the handle
to respond in a very angry way to
something someone says or does
*Be careful! She will fly off the handle if
you make a mess.*

steam coming out of your ears
to be really angry about something
*You could almost see
the steam coming
out of his ears!*

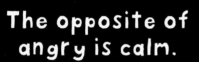

The opposite of angry is calm.

• **angry and upset because something is wrong or not fair**

indignant
angry because something is
wrong, unfair or insulting
*Many parents wrote indignant
letters when the playgroup closed.*

Put these words in order,
from very angry to just
a little bit angry:
a. annoyed b. furious
c. mad
Answer: b c a

resentful
angry about something that is
unfair and that you cannot
change
*She feels resentful because she has
had a very difficult life.*

a b c d e f g h i j k l m n o p q r s t u v w x y z

a
b
c
d
e
f
g
h
i
j
k
l
m
n
o
p
q
r
s
t
u
v
w
x
y
z

Argue

• **to argue**

bicker
to argue about small things
They bickered over whose turn it was next.

clash
to fight or argue in public
The rioters clashed with police.

disagree
to think differently from someone else
I disagree with you. I think she's very nice.

fight
to argue very noisily
What are you two fighting about now?

quarrel
to argue with a friend or someone in your family
My brother and I often quarrel.

Can you unscramble these words that mean to argue?
wor
ickber
shalc
Answers: row bicker clash

squabble

row
to argue loudly
They're always rowing about money.

squabble
to argue about something that isn't important
Stop squabbling over those sweets!

• an argument

debate
an argument where
opposite views are
discussed
*There was a debate on
the subject in
Parliament.*

ding-dong (informal)
a noisy argument
*There was a real ding-dong
happening in the apartment
next door.*

dispute
an official argument between
groups or countries
*The dispute was between the council
and the farmer.*

feud
a long fight between two groups
or families
*Why did the feud between the two
families start?*

spat (informal)
a small argument
*They had a spat about whose turn
it was to do the washing up.*

In other words

to fight like cat and dog
to argue all the time
My sister and brother fight like cat and dog.

tiff (informal)
a little argument between friends
*It was just a little tiff. We're good
friends again now.*

Did you know?

William Shakespeare's
famous play *Romeo and
Juliet* is about two
feuding families.

a
b
c
d
e
f
g
h
i
j
k
l
m
n
o
p
q
r
s
t
u
v
w
x
y
z

a b c d e f g h i j k l m n o p q r s t u v w x y z

Ask

beg
to ask strongly for something you really want or need
The prisoner begged to be released.

consult
to ask for advice or information from an expert
Consult your doctor first.

cross-examine
to ask someone a lot of questions to check they are telling the truth
The police officer cross-examined the witness.

enquire
to ask for information
Tourists can enquire at the information centre.

grill
to ask someone a lot of questions
My mum grilled my sister about where she'd been.

interrogate
to ask someone a lot of questions about a crime
The police interrogated the suspect for several hours.

interview
to ask someone questions for a newspaper or TV programme, or to find out if they are right for a job
The manager interviewed everyone who applied for the job.

plead
to ask someone for something that you really want
The children pleaded with their mother for some more chocolate.

plead

pump (informal)
to ask someone a lot of questions to get as much information as possible
We pumped them for all the information they knew about the new campsite.

query
to ask because you have not understood something or do not think it is right
They queried the bill.

question
to ask someone a lot of questions
The headmaster questioned each pupil about who had broken the window.

quiz
to ask questions about something, usually in an annoying way
They quizzed us about the new teacher.

In other words

a loaded question
a question that is asked in a certain way to get a certain answer
That's not fair. That's a loaded question!

request
to ask politely for something you want
He requested an appointment with the boss.

sound out
to find out what someone thinks or is planning to do
Could you sound out your members and let me know if anyone is free.

survey
to ask people a set of questions
We surveyed the school pupils and found that most children have a mobile phone.

> **The opposite of ask is answer.**

a
b
c
d
e
f
g
h
i
j
k
l
m
n
o
p
q
r
s
t
u
v
w
x
y
z

a
b
c
d
e
f
g
h
i
j
k
l
m
n
o
p
q
r
s
t
u
v
w
x
y
z

Bad

- **describing something that is bad**

appalling
bad in a shocking way
The animals were kept in appalling conditions.

dreadful
very unpleasant or of poor quality
It was a dreadful film. Don't bother to go and see it.

ghastly
very unpleasant or shocking
It was a ghastly accident.

horrible

horrible
very bad
What's that horrible smell?

inferior
not as good as something else
These trainers are cheaper because they're of inferior quality.

nasty
unkind or unpleasant
Pulling Claire's chair away was a nasty thing to do.

In other words

to have a bad hair day
a funny way to say that your hair is a mess and everything is going wrong
I'm having a really bad hair day!

> ## The opposite of bad is good.

poor
of low quality
Your marks this term have been quite poor.

serious
bad or worrying
There was a serious accident earlier.

terrible
very unpleasant or sad
Have you heard the terrible news?

inept
not skilled
The goalkeeper was so inept he let in six goals.

Did you know?

The great scientist Albert Einstein was **useless** at maths when he was young.

• badly behaved

mischievous
causing trouble in a playful way, not meant to be harmful
He has a very mischievous sense of humour.

• bad at doing something

hopeless/useless (informal)
not very good at doing something
I'm hopeless at maths, I can't even do simple sums.

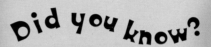

hopeless/useless

naughty
badly behaved, usually when talking about a child
It's very naughty to hit someone.

a b c d e f g h i j k l m n o p q r s t u v w x y z

a
b
c
d
e
f
g
h
i
j
k
l
m
n
o
p
q
r
s
t
u
v
w
x
y
z

Big

• **big in size**

bulky
big and heavy
The sofa is too bulky to go through the door.

colossal
of huge size
The blue whale is the most colossal animal.

enormous
unusually large
What an enormous bag!

gigantic
big, like a giant
Some dinosaurs were gigantic.

great
big and important
There are a few great houses in this area.

huge
very big
They live in a huge house.

large
big in size or amount
There was a large number of people there.

massive
big in size or weight
The castle had massive stone walls.

sizeable
fairly big
The school has a sizeable number of Jewish pupils.

gigantic

The opposite of
big is small
or little.

a **b** c d e f g h i j k l m n o p q r s t u v w x y z

In other words

to be a big fish in a small pond
to have an important job or position in a small company or organization
I'd rather be a big fish in a small pond than have a boring job in a big company.

bigwig
an important person
All the local bigwigs were at the ceremony.

too big for your boots
thinking you are more important than you really are
She's getting far too big for her boots these days.

• **big in importance**

important
serious, where the result matters
There's an important meeting at the club tonight.

major
more important or more serious
There are some major problems with his spelling.

vast
covering a very big area
The Sahara is a vast desert in northern Africa.

whopping (informal)
very big
The bike costs a whopping £500.

Did you know?

The word **colossal** originally comes from the Greek *kolossos*, which means giant statue.

Bit

chunk
a bit of something that has been cut unevenly
I bought a tin of pineapple chunks.

component
a part or piece of a machine or system
The hard disk is a component of a computer.

crumb
a tiny piece of bread or cake
Who ate all the cake? There are only crumbs left!

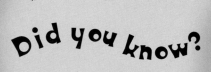
crumbs

dash
a tiny amount of one thing added to something else
I'll add a dash of lemon juice to the sauce.

drop
a tiny amount of a liquid
Could I have a drop more milk in my tea, please?

fraction
a small amount of the total
We've only raised a fraction of the money we need.

fragment
a small bit broken off from something
Pick up all the fragments of glass.

morsel
a bit of food
They ate every last morsel.

part
a separate part or bit
In biology we learnt about the different parts of a plant.

Did you know?

Fraction and **fragment** are related to the word 'fracture', which means to crack or break a bone.

a
b
c
d
e
f
g
h
i
j
k
l
m
n
o
p
q
r
s
t
u
v
w
x
y
z

piece
a bit or part of something
The puzzle has two pieces missing.

pinch
a bit of powder, the amount you can hold between your thumb and first finger
The recipe says to add a pinch of salt.

portion
a piece of something larger
A portion of the profit goes to charity.

section
a part of something that is separate from something else
Which section of the school is your classroom in?

segment
a part from a whole thing, especially a round object
Divide the orange into segments before you put it in the fruit salad.

slice
a piece of food that has been cut from a larger piece
Would you like a slice of pizza?

sliver
a very thin slice
I'm not very hungry so I'll just have a sliver of cake, please.

wedge

wedge
a bit of food that is shaped like a triangle
I bought a wedge of cheese in the supermarket.

slice

a b c d e f g h i j k l m n o p q r s t u v w x y z

a b c d e f g h i j k l m n o p q r s t u v w x y z

Box

bin
a large container for storing things
Put the loaf in the bread bin.

carton
a small or large box made from cardboard
Mum bought two cartons of orange juice.

case
a container for storing or showing things
The Queen's jewels were displayed in a glass case.

casket
a small box that looks pretty
She kept her jewellery in a casket.

chest
a strong wooden box
The pirate stored his treasure in a chest.

crate
a box made of wood, plastic or metal
There are crates of milk bottles outside the door.

drum
a round container
Oil is stored in drums.

pack/ packet
a small container made of paper or cardboard
We bought a packet of biscuits at the supermarket.

chest

packing case
a big strong box for sending things to another place
The removal men carried out all the packing cases.

packing cases

Did you know?

Trunk is also the word for an elephant's long nose, and the thick, woody stem of a tree.

trunk
a big strong container for carrying clothes and personal things
We packed all our things in the trunk.

safe
a strong box or cupboard where you keep money and valuable things
She kept her jewellery in a locked safe.

In other words
to box someone up
to confine someone in a small area
We were boxed up in a very small elevator.

tea chest
a large wooden box that was once used for storing tea, but is now used when packing things to move house
The paintings were discovered in an old tea chest.

a b c d e f g h i j k l m n o p q r s t u v w x y z

Break

- **to cause to break**

crack
to nearly break, but not quite separate into two pieces
During the earthquake the ground cracked open.

fracture
to break (of something hard, like a bone)
I've fractured my wrist.

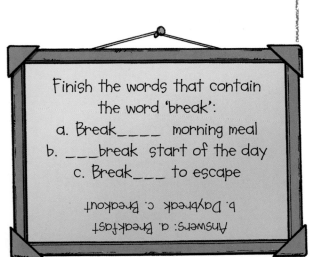

crack

smash
to cause something to break noisily
The thieves smashed the windows of the jewellery shop.

- **to separate into two or more pieces**

snap
to break with a cracking sound
My ruler snapped in two when I accidentally stood on it.

split
to break along a line
The tree trunk had split down the middle.

- **to break into lots of pieces**

disintegrate
to break into lots of small pieces
The wallpaper had disintegrated and you could see the plaster underneath.

Finish the words that contain the word 'break':
a. Break____ morning meal
b. ___break start of the day
c. Break___ to escape

Answers: a. Breakfast
b. Daybreak c. Breakout

fall apart
to break into pieces
My shoes are falling apart.

fragment
to break into tiny pieces
The meteor fragmented when it entered the Earth's atmosphere.

shatter
to break suddenly into lots of tiny pieces
The lady sang a very high note and the glass shattered into pieces.

shatter

splinter
to break into small, sharp pieces
The floorboards had splintered because they were old.

In other words

to give up the ghost
to stop working (of a machine)
Our washing machine has finally given up the ghost.

• to stop working

break down
to stop working (of a machine or car)
Our car broke down on the motorway.

break down

a b c d e f g h i j k l m n o p q r s t u v w x y z

a
b
c
d
e
f
g
h
i
j
k
l
m
n
o
p
q
r
s
t
u
v
w
x
y
z

Call

• to say something loudly

bellow
to speak in a very loud or very deep voice
The headmaster bellowed at the class to be quiet.

cry
to speak in a loud voice because something is wrong
"Get a doctor!" they cried.

scream
to cry out loudly because you are excited, frightened or angry
The witch came on stage and all the children in the audience screamed.

shout
to speak as loudly as you can
There's no need to shout! I can hear you.

shriek
to give a short, high cry
We all shrieked and clapped when our team won the game.

yell
to speak in a loud voice, usually because you are angry
The player was yelling at the referee.

• to order someone to come to a place

page
to call someone over a loudspeaker in a public place
The woman at the information desk paged the passenger who had lost his ticket.

send for
to ask someone to come and see you
Do you think we need to send for the doctor?

scream

In other words

to call a spade a spade
to tell the truth about something, even if it is not very polite
She is very direct and just calls a spade a spade.

• **to call someone or something a name**

christen
to give someone a name in a Christian church, or to give someone a nickname
We christened her 'Bubbles' because she has curly hair.

name
to give someone a name
What are you going to name the kitten?

summon
to order someone to be at a certain place
The Foreign Office summoned the ambassador back to London.

• **to telephone**

phone/ring
to telephone
I'll ring you later.

Can you understand this text message?

Call me L8R–K8

Answer:
Call me later –
Kate

a b c d e f g h i j k l m n o p q r s t u v w x y z

Carry

bear (formal or old-fashioned)
to carry something to a place
The Wise Men arrived at the stable bearing gifts for the newborn baby boy.

bring
to take something in the direction of the person speaking
Bring your homework to my house and we'll work on the essay together.

cart (informal)
to carry something heavy
We had to cart all the rubbish down to the dump.

convey
to take or carry something to a particular place
This pipe conveys gas into the kitchen.

deliver
to take something to a house or building
The postman delivered a big parcel this morning.

fetch

fetch
to go to get something and then bring it back
Throw a stick and the dog will fetch it.

haul
to drag or pull something heavy
Four men hauled the box around the corner.

haul

lift
to raise something in the air
We lifted the baby out of his pram.

lug (informal)
to carry something, especially something heavy
We lugged a big bag of newspapers around all the houses.

support
to hold something up
They supported the stone blocks on wooden logs and rolled them along.

take
to carry something in a direction away from the person speaking
Take your jacket with you. It's going to rain.

tote
to carry something, especially something awkward or large
You can take your bag with you if you want, but you'll have to tote it around all day.

transport
to take goods from one place to another
Brand new cars are usually transported from the factory on special lorries.

In other words

to carry the weight of the world on your shoulders
to feel worried or sad about things
She looks so worried – as if she is carrying the weight of the world on her shoulders.

a
b
c
d
e
f
g
h
i
j
k
l
m
n
o
p
q
r
s
t
u
v
w
x
y
z

a
b
c
d
e
f
g
h
i
j
k
l
m
n
o
p
q
r
s
t
u
v
w
x
y
z

Clever

- **good at learning or thinking**

brainy
intelligent and good at studying
Our last teacher liked brainy kids who got all the answers right.

bright
clever and quick to learn
My little brother is really bright. He's always asking questions.

bright

brilliant
very, very clever
His mother is a brilliant scientist.

intelligent
good at learning and understanding things
You need to be intelligent to be a doctor.

quick
able to understand things quickly
She has a very quick mind.

smart
able to solve problems or learn things easily
That's a great idea! You're so smart!

- **having a lot of knowledge or information**

gifted
naturally very clever, having a natural ability at something
My whole family is gifted except me!

Did you know?

The word **clever** comes from the Norwegian word *klover* – meaning ready or skilful.

> # The opposite of clever is foolish or unintelligent.

intellectual
educated in subjects that need to be studied for a long time
A very intellectual group of people took part in the discussion.

knowledgeable
knowing a lot about a subject
The librarian is knowledgeable about ancient history.

talented
being skilled at something naturally
He's a talented musician.

wise
having a lot of experience of life
A wise person saves money and doesn't spend it all.

• good at using your brain to get along

cunning
able to think and plan secretly so that you get what you want
She was very cunning and pretended to be too sick to work.

streetwise
experienced in living in a city
The kids in that neighbourhood are pretty streetwise.

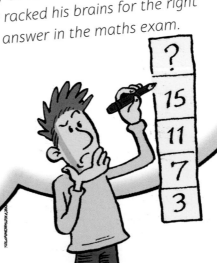

In other words

to rack your brains
to think very hard about something, usually to find a solution to a problem
He racked his brains for the right answer in the maths exam.

a b c d e f g h i j k l m n o p q r s t u v w x y z

a
b
c
d
e
f
g
h
i
j
k
l
m
n
o
p
q
r
s
t
u
v
w
x
y
z

Cold

• **a bit cold**

chilly
quite cold
Autumn is here and it's starting to get chilly at night.

chilly

cool
slightly cold
There's a nice, cool breeze down on the beach.

crisp
cold, dry and bright
It was a lovely crisp morning.

draughty
a draughty place has cold air blowing through it
My room is cold and draughty.

> **The opposite of cold is hot.**

nippy (informal)
quite cold
It's a bit nippy today, so make sure you take a coat.

2 very cold

bitter
so cold that it causes pain
The weather was bitter and I could hardly feel my fingers.

freezing
below the temperature at which water freezes
Polar bears live in freezing conditions.

frosty
extremely cold, enough for frost to form
It was a clear, frosty morning.

icy
extremely cold
The water was icy.

wintry
cold, like winter
I don't like these cold, wintry mornings.

• **cold, of a person or animal**

have goose pimples (or goosebumps)
to be so cold (or frightened) that your skin raises up in little bumps
By the end of the walk we had goose pimples on our arms and legs.

goose pimples

shivering
so cold that you tremble
The puppies were wet and shivering.

In other words

as cool as a cucumber
very relaxed under pressure
Dominic is always as cool as a cucumber during exam time.

to pour cold water on
to be negative about someone's idea or suggestion
She poured cold water on our suggestions for activities for fun day.

Did you know?

Goose pimples get their name because the little bumps look like those on a goose's skin after it's been plucked.

a b c d e f g h i j k l m n o p q r s t u v w x y z

a b **c** d e f g h i j k l m n o p q r s t u v w x y z

Come

appear
to become visible
The Sun appeared from behind the clouds.

approach
to come near to something
The explorer approached the giraffe very quietly.

approach

arrive
to get to a place
The train arrives in London at 9:30 a.m.

draw near
to get closer to something
As the figure drew near I could see it was my teacher.

The opposite of come is go.

enter
to come or go into a place
We entered the building through the side door.

move closer/nearer
to go towards something
I moved closer to the fire because I was cold.

Did you know?

Proceed as a verb means to move forwards.
Proceeds as a noun is an amount of money raised by an activity.

show up (informal)
to come to a party or place where there are other people
He didn't show up until nine o'clock.

In other words

come what may
whatever happens
I'll be at the concert to watch you tonight come what may.

till the cows come home
for a very long time
I could eat chocolates till the cows come home. I love them!

proceed (formal)
to go in a particular direction
Passengers should proceed to gate 49.

reach
to get to a place, or get as far as a place
We reached our hotel late in the evening.

turn up
to come, especially when you are not expected
So many people turned up that some of them had to stand.

visit
to come or go to see a person or a place
Please visit us again next week.

a b c d e f g h i j k l m n o p q r s t u v w x y z

a b c **d** e f g h i j k l m n o p q r s t u v w x y z

Different

assorted
made up of different things mixed together
We bought a box of assorted biscuits.

contrasting
very different
Blue and yellow are contrasting colours.

dissimilar
not similar, not like (usually in the form 'not dissimilar')
Our new house is not dissimilar to our old one.

distinctive
different, which makes it easy to recognize
The owl has a distinctive call.

diverse
used to talk about many things being different from each other
Our pupils come from diverse backgrounds.

individual
having your own way of doing something
He has an individual style of dressing.

opposite
completely different
If you're a boy or man, then girls and women are the opposite sex.

sundry
several different
The secretary found letters, invoices and sundry bills in the drawer.

individual

Did you know?

The word **sundry** comes from the Old English *sundrig* – meaning separate or apart.

> ## The opposite of different is the same.

various
many, and all different
We didn't go on holiday this year for various reasons.

unalike
not the same
The three sisters are quite unalike.

unlike
different from
I like jazz, unlike most people in my class.

unique
not like anything else in the world
Every person's fingerprints are unique.

In other words

to be like chalk and cheese
if two people are like chalk and cheese they are completely different from each other
Georgie and Katie are sisters but they're like chalk and cheese.

varied
of different types
Insects are a very varied group of creatures.

varied

a b c **d** e f g h i j k l m n o p q r s t u v w x y z

Difficult

a
b
c
d
e
f
g
h
i
j
k
l
m
n
o
p
q
r
s
t
u
v
w
x
y
z

• **not easy**

awkward
difficult in a way that makes people uncomfortable
My little sister is always asking awkward questions.

challenging
not easy but interesting or fun to work on
Writing a page for our school website is challenging.

complicated
difficult because there are a lot of different parts
The book is complicated.

demanding
needing hard work or a big effort
Being at school all day can be demanding for young children.

fiddly
full of lots of small things or problems
This jigsaw is really fiddly.

hard
not easy to understand or do
These sums are really hard to solve.

impossible
so difficult that it can't be done
It's impossible for me to get there in half an hour.

In other words

to be no picnic
to be in a difficult or unpleasant situation
Being in Mr Harrison's class is no picnic, I can tell you! $(4+2+11)-7 =$

easier said than done
if something is easier said than done, it sounds like a good idea, but would be difficult to do in reality
Asking my dad for money is easier said than done.

tough
needing a lot of thought or work
*The exams I am taking are
very tough.*

• **not easy to do because it
is physically hard**

arduous
needing a lot of effort and energy
*He began the long, arduous climb
to the top of the hill.*

back-breaking
needing a lot of
physical work,
especially lifting
heavy things
*Gardening can be
back-breaking work.*

tricky

gruelling
tiring and difficult
because it lasts a long time
*In Victorian times children
worked long, gruelling hours in
factories.*

tricky
needing your full attention
*Decorating a birthday cake can
be quite tricky.*

laborious
needing a lot of time and effort
*Printing books and newspapers used
to be a laborious process.*

**The opposite of
difficult is easy.**

strenuous
needing a lot of physical effort
*Cross-country skiing is a strenuous
sport.*

a b c **d** e f g h i j k l m n o p q r s t u v w x y z

a
b
c
d
e
f
g
h
i
j
k
l
m
n
o
p
q
r
s
t
u
v
w
x
y
z

Drink

down
to drink something very quickly
He downed three glasses of lemonade in one minute.

drain
to drink the last drop of something
Louise drained her glass before going to bed.

drain

gargle
to move liquid around in your mouth without swallowing it
If you have a sore throat, gargle with salt and water.

gulp
to drink something very quickly in large mouthfuls
We were so thirsty after the race that we gulped down lots of water.

guzzle
to drink a lot of something very greedily
If you guzzle too much fizzy orange you will get a tummyache.

imbibe (formal)
to drink, especially alcohol
He attended the mayor's party and imbibed far too much wine.

knock back (informal)
to drink something very quickly, especially alcohol
The guests were knocking back the champagne at the wedding reception.

lap up
to drink using the tongue, as animals do
The puppies are old enough to lap water now.

Did you know?

The words **lap**, **sip** and **drink** all come from Old English.

swallow
to make something such as food or drink go down your throat
This milk tastes so sour that it's hard for me to swallow.

swallow

polish off
to finish drinking something that you like
Hannah polished off all the apple juice.

quench (your thirst)
to drink something so that you stop being thirsty
A glass of water is the best way to quench your thirst.

sip
to drink small mouthfuls of something
Just sip water slowly after you've been running.

slurp
to drink noisily
Please don't slurp your juice.

swig
to drink something in large mouthfuls
We walked around the funfair and swigged our lemonade.

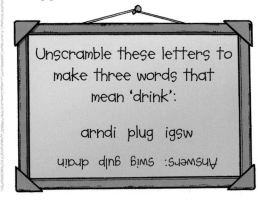

Unscramble these letters to make three words that mean 'drink':

arndi   plug   igsw

Answers: swig gulp drain

a b c **d** e f g h i j k l m n o p q r s t u v w x y z

a
b
c
d
e
f
g
h
i
j
k
l
m
n
o
p
q
r
s
t
u
v
w
x
y
z

Easy

• easy to do or understand

basic
easy and not at all complicated
I just need the basic information, not all the small details.

a breeze (informal)
very easy to do
Sarah was faster than Peter so she found it a breeze to beat him in the race.

a doddle (informal)
very easy to do (especially things such as tests)
The spelling test wus a doddle.

easy peasy (very informal)
very easy
I thought ice skating would be difficult but I tried it and it was easy peasy.

effortless
not easy, but made to look easy because someone does it well
Ballet dancers make dancing look so effortless.

elementary
basic, easy to deal with
There are three levels – elementary, intermediate and advanced.

a breeze

simple
easy to understand
Can you explain it to me using simple English.

The opposite of easy is difficult.

straightforward
easy to understand or to do
*Painting walls is pretty
straightforward.*

uncomplicated
easy to understand
or to do
*I suggest you make
something simple and
uncomplicated for your
first attempt at cooking.*

In other words

a piece of cake
if something is a piece of
cake it is easy to do
That puzzle was a piece of cake!

money for old rope
money you get for doing
something that is easy
*I'd like to be a TV presenter –
their job is money for old rope!*

• easy to use

idiot-proof (informal)
extremely easy to use
*You can buy digital cameras that
are idiot-proof.*

painless
not needing a lot of effort
*Applying for a passport
online was pretty painless.*

user-friendly

user-friendly
clear and easy to use
(especially electronic
things)
*The new television is very
user-friendly.*

a b c d **e** f g h i j k l m n o p q r s t u v w x y z

a
b
c
d
e
f
g
h
i
j
k
l
m
n
o
p
q
r
s
t
u
v
w
x
y
z

Eat

• **to eat food**

chew
to grind food with your teeth so
that you can swallow it
This meat is hard to chew.

consume (formal)
to eat
*Once opened, this product should
be consumed within two days.*

dine (formal)
to eat the main meal of the day
*Her parents usually dine at
eight o'clock.*

feed
to eat (talking about animals)
The panda feeds on bamboo.

munch
to eat noisily
*The people behind us
were munching crisps
all through the film.*

munch

tuck in/tuck into (informal)
to start eating
*There are plenty of sandwiches so
please tuck in.*

• **to eat quickly**

bolt
to eat food quickly because you
are in a hurry
*We bolted down our lunch so we
could get back to the game.*

devour
to eat something quickly because
you are very hungry
*He devoured the whole loaf when he
came home from school.*

gobble
to eat quickly
We gobbled our breakfast as we ran to catch the bus.

scoff
to eat something quickly and greedily
What! You scoffed the lot?

wolf (informal)
to eat a lot of food, usually too quickly
They wolfed down the sandwiches, then started on the jelly.

In other words

could eat a horse
to be very hungry
What's for dinner? I could eat a horse!

• **to eat a lot**

• **to eat a little**

nibble
to take small bites
Our rabbit nibbles at carrots and lettuce.

nibble

gorge
to eat until you cannot possibly eat any more
If you gorge yourself on chocolate, you'll make yourself ill.

snack
to eat a small meal
It's better to have three meals a day than to snack all afternoon and evening.

overeat
to eat too much
I think I must have overeaten because I have a tummyache.

a b c d **e** f g h i j k l m n o p q r s t u v w x y z

Fast

brisk
fast and energetic
We had a brisk walk along the seafront.

express
moving fast
If we catch an express train we'll be there in an hour.

nippy (informal)
easy to drive
and handle
(of a vehicle)
*This is a nippy
little scooter.*

quick
fast, lasting
only a short time
I had a quick look in the drawer.

rapid
very fast
The team made rapid progress.

speedy
fast and successful
Wishing you a speedy recovery.

swift
fast and happening smoothly
The man's life was saved thanks to swift action by the ambulance driver.

• **moving fast**

in a flash
quickly or suddenly
It was all over in a flash.

quickly
at a fast speed
You'll have to walk quickly if you're going to catch the train.

quickly

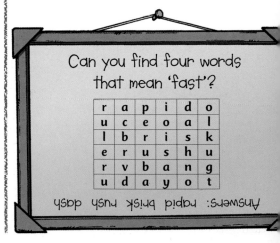

Can you find four words
that mean 'fast'?

r	a	p	i	d	o
u	c	e	o	a	l
l	b	r	i	s	k
e	r	u	s	h	u
r	v	b	a	n	g
u	d	a	y	o	t

Answers: rapid brisk rush dash

dash

a b c d e **f** g h i j k l m n o p q r s t u v w x y z

• to go fast

accelerate
to go more quickly, usually in a vehicle
The driver accelerated on the motorway.

dash
to move quickly
They dashed out of the house when they saw the bus coming.

rush
to move quickly because you are in a hurry
She rushed off to pick up her daughter from school.

• capable of going fast

high-speed
moving very fast
The dentist uses a high-speed drill.

supersonic
able to move faster than the speed of sound
The RAF has supersonic jets.

> # The opposite of fast is slow.

Friend

a b c d e f g h i j k l m n o p q r s t u v w x y z

• **a friend**

ally
a person or country who helps or supports you
Russia was one of Britain's allies in the Second World War.

buddy (informal)
a friend
We've been buddies for years.

chum (old-fashioned and informal)
a friend
They're old school chums.

companion
someone you spend a lot of time with or go travelling with
They are travelling companions.

comrade (old-fashioned)
a friend, especially in the army or in a tough situation
The old comrades laid a wreath on the war memorial.

crony (informal)
a close friend (used in a negative or disapproving sense)
I'm not going to vote for the minister or his cronies.

mate (informal)
a friend
I go to the swimming pool with my mates.

In other words

to have friends in high places
to know important people who can help you get what you want
The prisoner had friends in high places so was quickly released.

The opposite of friend is enemy.

pal (informal)
a friend
I enjoy spending time with all my pals.

playmate

playmate
a friend a child plays with
Lisa and Archie are playmates.

• a group of friends

circle
the people you know
We have a big circle of friends.

clique (negative)
a group of people who won't let other people join their group
There's a clique of parents who always stand together in the playground.

crowd
a group of friends you go out and do things with
A crowd of us are going out tonight. Do you want to come?

gang (informal)
a group of friends that meet often
He goes out with a gang from the office every Friday.

gang

set
a group of people who have similar interests
She started mixing with the wealthy jet set.

a b c d e **f** g h i j k l m n o p q r s t u v w x y z

a
b
c
d
e
f
g
h
i
j
k
l
m
n
o
p
q
r
s
t
u
v
w
x
y
z

Frightened

• frightened

afraid
nervous or frightened of something
Dad has never been on a plane because he is afraid of flying.

fearful
frightened or worried
She was fearful of her parents' reaction.

petrified
so frightened that you can't even move
We were absolutely petrified when we went on the ghost train.

scared
frightened or worried
I'm scared of spiders.

startled
worried or frightened by something that happens suddenly
She was startled when he spoke to her.

terrified
very frightened
Our dog is terrified of thunder and lightning.

scared

• to be frightened

dread
to be afraid or worried that something bad might happen
I'm really dreading the school play.

fear
to be afraid of something unpleasant
Many older people fear losing their job.

panic
to suddenly feel so frightened that you can't think clearly
The crowd panicked when the lights went out.

• **frightening**

hair-raising
frightening because something is dangerous
He read a hair-raising story about their escape.

In other words

to get cold feet
to get frightened suddenly before an important event
She got cold feet on the morning of her wedding.

to give someone the creeps
to frighten or worry someone
Walking down this dark alley gives me the creeps.

scary

scary
frightening
That Hallowe'en mask is just too scary.

hair-raising

spooky
frightening in a strange way that makes you feel uneasy
The castle is really spooky in the middle of the night.

a b c d e **f** g h i j k l m n o p q r s t u v w x y z

Funny

a
b
c
d
e
f
g
h
i
j
k
l
m
n
o
p
q
r
s
t
u
v
w
x
y
z

• **making you laugh**

amusing
funny and entertaining
Her stories are always amusing.

comical
funny in an unexpected or
silly way
*My dad looked really comical trying
to catch the dog.*

hilarious
extremely funny
*The jokes on that website are
hilarious.*

humorous
funny and entertaining
*I am reading a humorous book
about a trip around the world.*

jokey (informal)
funny and containing lots of jokes
*The politician made a jokey speech
to the members of the club.*

light-hearted
funny and not at all serious
*The programme takes a light-
hearted look at living on a farm.*

rib-tickling (informal)
very funny (of a joke or story)
*The pantomime was full of
rib-tickling songs and jokes.*

comical

satirical
criticizing people or things in
a way that makes you laugh
*The programme is a
satirical news quiz.*

slapstick
a type of acting where actors behave in a silly way – throwing things at each other or falling over, for instance
There was a lot of slapstick humour in the show.

witty
using words in a funny and entertaining way
Uncle Derek made a very witty speech.

clown

• a person who is funny
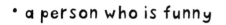

buffoon
a person who does silly things to make other people laugh
Harry is the class buffoon.

clown
a person whose job it is to act silly and make people laugh
The clown at the circus had spotty trousers and a big red nose.

comedian
a person whose job it is to make people laugh
I want to be a comedian when I grow up.

stand-up/stand-up comedian
a person who stands in front of an audience telling jokes
I don't know how stand-ups manage to remember all their jokes.

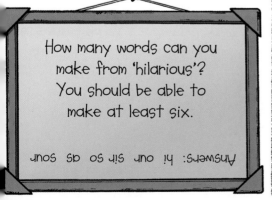
How many words can you make from 'hilarious'? You should be able to make at least six.

Answers: hi our sir so as sour

a b c d e **f** g h i j k l m n o p q r s t u v w x y z

a
b
c
d
e
f
g
h
i
j
k
l
m
n
o
p
q
r
s
t
u
v
w
x
y
z

Get

• to get or have something

accept
to take something that is offered to you
She went to the town hall to accept her prize.

Did you know?

Some dogs like to play **fetch** – they chase and bring back a stick or ball you have thown.

acquire
to get or gain something
They acquired the company ten years ago.

buy
to give money to get something
What did you buy at the shops?

collect
to go to a place and get something or someone
I need to collect my dry cleaning today.

earn

earn
to get money after working
He earned a fortune last year.

fetch
to go to get something and then bring it back
Will you please fetch my glasses?

obtain
to get, earn or gain something
She obtained a university degree last year.

purchase

purchase
to buy
Sam purchased an ice cream with his pocket money.

receive
to get or be given something
I received his letter in the post.

• **to get a joke**

follow
to keep up and understand something
The story was very difficult to follow.

understand
to know what something means
I didn't understand the last line.

• **to be**

become
to start to be
It has become very dark all of a sudden.

grow
to gradually change
I grew bored of it in the end.

turn
to change into or come to be
It has turned cold.

a b c d e f g h i j k l m n o p q r s t u v w x y z

a
b
c
d
e
f
g
h
i
j
k
l
m
n
o
p
q
r
s
t
u
v
w
x
y
z

Give

- **to give something to someone**

bequeath
to arrange to give someone something after your death
She bequeathed her jewellery to her granddaughter.

contribute
to give with other people to a person or cause
We all contributed to Mr Brown's leaving present.

grant (formal)
to agree to give or allow
She granted their request.

hand
to pass something to another person
Hand me that book, will you?

lend
to give something to someone for a short time and get it back later
I'll lend you my pen if you can't find yours.

The opposite of give is take.

pass on
to give someone information from another person
I'll pass your message on to the manager.

slip

slip
to give someone something secretly
She slipped me a note as I walked past.

- **to give someone something because of what they've done**

award
to give someone a prize officially
They awarded the medals after the competition.

present
to give someone something as part of a ceremony
The headmaster presented the prizes.

reward
to give someone something for being helpful
We rewarded the person who found our cat.

- **to give something to a group**

distribute
to give something to a lot of people
She stood outside the supermarket and distributed leaflets.

In other words

give and take
a situation between two groups or two people when each is allowed some of the things they want
Brothers and sisters have to give and take.

dole out
to give something to several people
She doled out soup and bread in the canteen.

donate
to give something to an organization or group
We donated our unwanted books to charity.

share
to divide something into portions to give to others
We won some sweets and shared them out among the team.

a b c d e f **g** h i j k l m n o p q r s t u v w x y z

a
b
c
d
e
f
g
h
i
j
k
l
m
n
o
p
q
r
s
t
u
v
w
x
y
z

Go

• to go by vehicle

commute
to regularly go to and from a place, such as work
Dad commutes to his office every day.

cycle
to go by bike
I usually cycle to school if the weather's fine.

drive
to go by car
Do you drive to school or walk?

fly
to move through the air, such as in an aeroplane
I'm flying to Germany tomorrow.

go on a trip
to go somewhere and then come back
We went on a trip to the zoo last year.

sail

sail
to go by ship or boat
The ship is about to set sail.

travel
to go from one place to another
He's travelled all over the world.

fly

The opposite of go is come.

• a trip

crossing
a trip in a boat or a ship across water from one side to the other
It was a rough crossing because of the storm.

cruise
a trip on a ship going to visit different places
My grandparents are going on a cruise down the Nile.

Did you know?

Cruise ships are hotels on water, with cinemas, gyms, swimming pools and restaurants.

excursion
a short trip to visit a place
We have an excursion every term.

expedition
a trip for a particular purpose
The Scouts are going on an expedition to Wales.

globetrotting
travelling around the world or lots of different countries
A lot of students enjoy globetrotting in the summer holidays.

journey
a trip from one place to another
The journey to Edinburgh was long but interesting.

outing
a short trip or visit to a place, usually nearby
There is a class outing on Friday to the castle.

tour
a visit to and around a place
We went on a tour of the city.

voyage
a long journey in a ship or spacecraft
We set out on our voyage to the Moon.

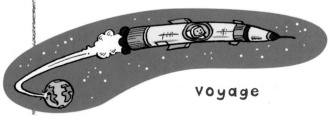

voyage

a b c d e f **g** h i j k l m n o p q r s t u v w x y z

a
b
c
d
e
f
g
h
i
j
k
l
m
n
o
p
q
r
s
t
u
v
w
x
y
z

Good

amazing (informal)
really good
The film was amazing.

awesome (informal)
extremely good
The view is awesome.

brilliant (informal)
very, very good
This website is brilliant!

decent
morally good and honest
Giving the money to charity was the decent thing to do.

enjoyable
fun, pleasant
I've had a very enjoyable evening.

In other words

as good as gold
well behaved
Kira has been as good as gold today.

to be in someone's good books
someone is pleased with you
I've done all my homework so I'm in the teacher's good books.

too good to be true
so good that you can't believe it, or
so good that it can't be true
There's a job advertised in the newspaper, but it sounds too good to be true.

excellent
very good
Your homework is excellent.

fantastic
extremely good
The view from the top of the mountain is fantastic.

fine
good
I'm fine, thank you.

great (informal)
very good
This is a great book.

outstanding

The opposite of good is bad.

impressive
of a high standard and something that you admire
That last goal was really impressive.

outstanding
better than other things or than what is usual
That was an outstanding performance.

splendid
beautiful and very good
The weather was splendid.

superb
of very good quality
That was a superb meal.

talented

talented
naturally good at doing something
She's a very talented musician.

a b c d e f **g** h i j k l m n o p q r s t u v w x y z

a b c d e f **g** h i j k l m n o p q r s t u v w x y z

Great

• very good

brilliant (informal)
very good
I thought the book was brilliant.

cool (informal)
very good, excellent
The party was really cool.

excellent
extremely good
The food was excellent.

fantastic (informal)
extremely good
You look fantastic in that hat!

first-class
excellent
You've done a first-class job by picking up all the litter.

magnificent
beautiful, wonderful
They live in a magnificent house on the hill.

super (informal)
extremely good
I've had a super time.

terrific (informal)
very good
The restaurant gives terrific value for money.

fantastic

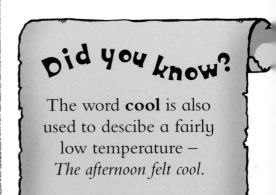

Did you know?

The word **cool** is also used to descibe a fairly low temperature –
The afternoon felt cool.

wonderful
extremely good
There's a wonderful view from up here.

• **great in size**

big
large in size
What's that big building over there?

enormous
very big, huge
They're building an enormous stadium.

grand
big and splendid
The hotel was grand and posh.

enormous

• **great and successful**

distinguished
respected
There were several distinguished guests there.

In other words

great minds think alike
something you say if someone has the same idea as you
I was just thinking that. Great minds think alike!

no great shakes
not very good
She looks nice but she's no great shakes as a singer.

eminent
worthy of great respect
She's a very eminent historian.

important
great, powerful and influential
He is an important writer of the 20th century.

The opposite of great is small or terrible.

a b c d e f **g** h i j k l m n o p q r s t u v w x y z

a b c d e f g **h** i j k l m n o p q r s t u v w x y z

Happy

cheerful
happy and in a good mood
She's usually such a cheerful person to have around.

content
happy and satisfied in a quiet way
On a rainy day, I'm content sitting inside with a cup of tea.

delighted
very pleased
We're delighted to be here.

ecstatic
extremely happy and very excited
He was ecstatic when he discovered he had won the prize draw.

glad
pleased and happy
I'm so glad I found my mobile phone.

in high spirits
happy and enjoying yourself
We set off for the picnic in high spirits.

jolly
happy and smiling
There was a jolly lady serving the tea.

joyful
full of great happiness
The Christmas concert was a very joyful occasion.

content

Did you know?
The word **happy** probably comes from an old Norse word, meaning chance or luck.

overjoyed

The opposite of happy is sad.

overjoyed
very happy
He was overjoyed to find the treasure.

thrilled
very excited and happy
She was thrilled with the presents.

pleased
happy and satisfied
Our teachers were pleased with the art exhibition.

satisfied
feeling happy and pleased because of something
The players were satisfied with the result of the match.

sunny
happy and cheerful
The little girl had a lovely smile and a sunny personality.

In other words

over the moon
very pleased about something
Mum got the job and she's over the moon.

on cloud nine
overjoyed and excited
He's been on cloud nine since winning the race.

a b c d e f g **h** i j k l m n o p q r s t u v w x y z

Hate

abhor (formal)
to hate or find something disgusting and immoral
They abhor violence.

can't bear
to be unable to accept or tolerate something
She can't bear scary movies.

can't stand
to be unable to accept or tolerate something that is unpleasant
I can't stand the sight of blood.

despise
to dislike someone or something very much
She despised him for the way he spoke to her.

The opposite of hate is love.

detest
to hate something or someone very much
The queen detested Snow White.

can't bear

disapprove of
to think that something is wrong
I disapprove of swearing on the television.

dislike
not to like someone or something
Why do you dislike me so much?

loathe
to hate something
Some people loathe cabbage.

loathe

- **hatred for something or someone**

animosity
a feeling of dislike
There is a great deal of animosity between the two teams.

contempt
a feeling of hatred about something that you think is worthless
The school has nothing but contempt for bullies.

disdain
a feeling of dislike because you cannot respect someone or something
The team treat their fans with disdain.

disgust
a strong feeling of dislike because of someone's behaviour
She walked out of the meeting in disgust.

In other words

a pet hate
something that you don't like because it annoys you
Mobile phones are my teacher's pet hate.

a b c d e f g **h** i j k l m n o p q r s t u v w x y z

a
b
c
d
e
f
g
h
i
j
k
l
m
n
o
p
q
r
s
t
u
v
w
x
y
z

Hit

bash (informal)
to hit hard
He bashed his enemy in the eye.

bash

batter (informal)
to hit lots of times
She battered on the door.

belt (informal)
to hit hard
He belted three goals into the net.

bump
to hit firmly
I bumped my head on the ceiling.

clobber (informal)
to hit hard
I'll clobber you if you do that again!

clout (informal)
to hit with your fist or open hand
She clouted him around the face.

Did you know?

A mixture called **batter** is used to make pancakes. It includes flour, eggs and milk.

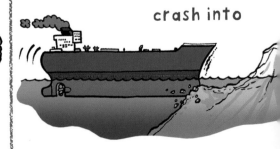

crash into

crash into
to hit something hard
The ship crashed into an iceberg.

knock
to hit hard
Someone's knocking at the door.

pound
to hit hard lots of times
He pounded the door with his fists.

pummel
to hit someone or something lots
of times using your fists
The boxer pummelled his opponent.

punch
to hit with your fist
He punched his attacker.

slap
to hit someone or
something with an
open hand
He slapped his thighs.

smack
to slap or hit
*I was so angry I could have
smacked you.*

strike
to hit hard
*I wish I could strike the
ball that hard.*

thrash
to hit hard with something, such
as a stick or whip
*He wouldn't thrash the horse with
his whip.*

thump
to hit with your fist
*He thumped his pillow because he
was so angry.*

whack (informal)
to hit noisily
*He whacked the railings with a stick
as he walked along.*

Strike

a b c d e f g **h** i j k l m n o p q r s t u v w x y z

a
b
c
d
e
f
g
h
i
j
k
l
m
n
o
p
q
r
s
t
u
v
w
x
y
z

Horrible

disagreeable (formal)
unpleasant, not nice
I had the disagreeable task of telling him we didn't need him.

disgusting
horrible and unacceptable
This soup is disgusting.

dreadful
very bad or of low quality
The service in this restaurant is dreadful.

ghastly (formal)
unpleasant or shocking
Don't give me all the ghastly details.

hideous

hideous
horrible to look at
What a hideous coat!

> ## The opposite of horrible is lovely or nice.

horrid (informal)
unpleasant, unkind
That was a horrid thing to do.

mean
unpleasant, not nice
Don't be mean!

nasty
horrible, unpleasant
There's a nasty smell in here.

obnoxious
very unpleasant in manner
He's so rude and obnoxious.

repulsive
horrible and disgusting
The princess was captured by a repulsive monster.

In other words

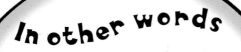

a nasty piece of work
a horrible or unpleasant person
Keep away from him! He's a nasty piece of work.

shocking
causing a sudden feeling of disgust
The spider's long legs and big body were shocking.

shocking

revolting
horrible and vile
Don't cut your toenails in here. It's revolting!

Did you know?

A lot of people think that spiders are **nasty**. Yet most spiders are harmless to humans.

unpleasant
not nice
What an unpleasant waitress!

vile
extremely unpleasant
Mrs Robinson's in a vile mood today.

a b c d e f g **h** i j k l m n o p q r s t u v w x y z

Hot

• hot to the touch

lukewarm
only slightly warm (liquid or food)
The water in the sink is only lukewarm.

scalding
very hot (liquid or steam)
Careful! That water is scalding!

toasty
comfortably warm
My hands feel lovely and toasty in these mittens.

warm
between hot and cool
I think I'll have a nice warm bath.

• hot (weather or places)

baking (informal)
very hot and dry
It's baking outside today.

balmy
pleasantly warm
The weather is surprisingly balmy for this time of year.

boiling
very hot and uncomfortable
It's boiling in here. Let's open a window.

muggy
unpleasantly hot and damp
Muggy weather makes you feel tired.

roasting
very hot and uncomfortable
It was roasting in there! I was glad to get out.

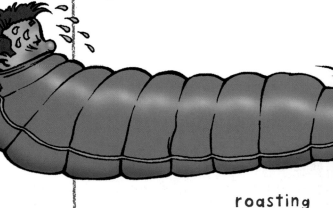

roasting

scorching
very hot
It was a scorching summer's day.

sultry
uncomfortably warm and damp
It was a hot, sultry evening.

sweltering
uncomfortably hot
It was sweltering in the sports hall.

In other words

hot air
when someone is full of hot air, they don't mean what they say and talk about things that aren't going to happen
Their promises turned out to be just hot air.

sweltering

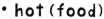

• **hot (food)**

piping hot
very hot food or drink
We sipped the piping hot coffee.

spicy
tasting hot and with a strong flavour
I like very spicy curry.

The opposite of hot is cold.

a b c d e f g **h** i j k l m n o p q r s t u v w x y z

Job

- **work that you are given to do or have to do**

assignment
a piece of work that someone gives you to do
Our assignment is to write a short essay.

chore
a boring job you have to do often
I do all the chores at home

duty
something that you have a responsibility to do
At Scout camp, everyone has duties.

errand
a small job
Will you run some errands for me?

mission
an important job that someone is given to do
In the movie their mission was to bring back the secret formula.

assignment

project
an important piece of work that needs a lot of planning
This is a long-term project.

responsibility
a job or duty to deal with
Selling tickets for the concert is your responsibility.

role
a person's job or duty in a bigger project
A receptionist's role is to greet visitors.

a
b
c
d
e
f
g
h
i
j
k
l
m
n
o
p
q
r
s
t
u
v
w
x
y
z

task
a job or piece of work to do
Each person is given a task so that the work gets done more quickly.

undertaking
a big and important job
Raising money for a new sports hall is a huge undertaking.

- **jobs that people do to earn money**

career
a job that someone does for a long time
I'd like a career in the theatre.

occupation
a person's full-time job
Write your occupation on the form.

Did you know?

A person who has a **profession** is a professional. A person who teaches at a high level in a college or university is a professor.

post
a job in a company
He has held the post of sales director for five years.

profession
a job for which you need special training
He's a doctor by profession.

trade
a skilled job that you use your hands to do
He chose carpentry as his trade.

vocation
a job that you do because you feel strongly about doing it
She wanted to become a nurse because she felt it was her vocation.

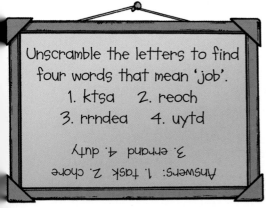

Unscramble the letters to find four words that mean 'job'.
1. ktsa   2. reoch
3. rrndea   4. uytd

Answers: 1. task 2. chore
3. errand 4. duty

a b c d e f g h i **j** k l m n o p q r s t u v w x y z

Joke

• something funny

anecdote
a short, funny story
He told us an anecdote about the time he tried to sell his car.

banter
conversation that is funny and not serious
We were only having a bit of banter.

gag
a short joke
The comedian had some good gags.

in jest
said to make people laugh
It was said in jest; he didn't really mean it!

one-liner
a short joke
There are some very funny one-liners in the book.

practical joke
a carefully planned joke
My brother played a practical joke by filling the sugar bowl with salt.

prank
a silly trick that isn't supposed to hurt anyone
We played a few pranks at Hallowe'en.

pun

pun
a play on words that sound the same but mean something else
This is a pun: Why was six scared of seven? Because seven eight nine!

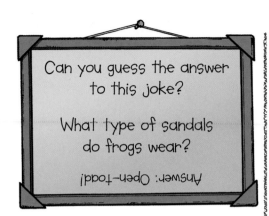

Can you guess the answer to this joke?

What type of sandals do frogs wear?

Answer: Open-toad!

punchline
the last line of a joke that makes it funny
Sam loves to tell jokes but he always forgets the punchline.

riddle
a strange or difficult question that usually has a funny answer
If you can solve the riddle you will win a prize.

wisecrack
a funny, clever remark
He's full of wisecracks!

wisecrack

- **to joke or say funny things**

be joking
to say something that you know is not true
Mrs Davies is leaving? Are you joking?

be kidding
to say something as a joke
I didn't really forget your birthday; I was only kidding.

quip
to say something short and funny
"A schoolboy's work is never done," he quipped.

tease
to laugh at someone or say something that is not true
Don't get upset! I was only teasing.

a b c d e f g h i **j** k l m n o p q r s t u v w x y z

a b c d e f g h i **j** k l m n o p q r s t u v w x y z

Jump

bob
to move up or down quickly
*She bobbed down behind the wall
when she saw us coming.*

bound
to move quickly with big jumps
A deer bounded across the field.

clear
to jump over something without
touching it
*The horse cleared all
the fences.*

gambol
to jump in a
playful way
*The lambs
gambolled in the field.*

hop
to jump on one leg
Can you hop across the room?

hurdle
to jump over something while you
are running
They hurdled the fence.

leap
to jump a long way
*They leapt across the ditch to the
other side.*

lunge
to move forward quickly
and suddenly
*The old man lunged at them with
his stick.*

pounce
to jump to catch something
*The cat pounced on
the mouse.*

pounce

recoil
to give a little jump backwards
because you're afraid of
something or don't like it
*He recoiled in horror when I showed
him the spider.*

In other words

to jump the gun
to do something too soon
Now, don't jump the gun. Let's just think about this a bit more.

to jump to conclusions
to decide what you think about something before you know all the facts
I'm not to blame! Why do you always jump to conclusions about me?

skip
to go forward with small, quick jumps
We tried to skip all the way to school but we grew too tired.

spring

spring
to jump suddenly and quickly
The cheetah seemed to spring from nowhere.

start
to give a little jump when something surprises you
He started at the sound of the bell.

vault
to jump over something
The thief vaulted over the wall.

vault

a b c d e f g h i **j** k l m n o p q r s t u v w x y z

a b c d e f g h i j k l m n o p q r s t u v w x y z

Laugh

• to laugh in a loud way

burst out laughing
to laugh loudly
and suddenly
*We looked at
her and burst
out laughing.*

crease up (informal)
to laugh a lot
*I creased up when he
fell off his chair.*

fall about (informal)
to laugh loudly and in a way that
is out of control
*We all fell about when we saw
his disguise.*

guffaw
to laugh very loudly
*We guffawed when she told us
the joke.*

hoot with laughter
to suddenly laugh loudly
*They all hooted with laughter when
the clown's trousers fell down.*

roar with laughter
to laugh noisily and hard
The children roared with laughter.

roar with laughter

snort with laughter (informal)
to laugh loudly and a lot
*When my dad saw me on stage in
my funny costume he snorted
with laughter.*

• to laugh in a quiet way

chuckle
to laugh quietly or to yourself
*My grandad was chuckling in his
armchair as he watched the
baby play.*

In other words

to be in stitches
to be laughing so hard that you can't stop
We were in stitches all through the clowns' performance.

titter
to laugh nervously or to giggle
The girls were tittering in the back row of the cinema.

• to laugh in an unpleasant way

cackle
to laugh loudly in a high voice
The witches cackled as they cast their spell.

cackle

giggle
to laugh in a silly, quiet way because something is funny or you are embarrassed
We were all giggling at our teacher's tie.

chortle
to laugh in a satisfied way, usually at or about someone else
They chortled as they played their trick on him.

snigger
to laugh at someone in an unkind way
Stop sniggering behind my back! Let's see if you can do any better than me!

The opposite of laugh is cry.

a b c d e f g h i j k **l** m n o p q r s t u v w x y z

Like

admire
to like and respect someone
I admire people who speak their mind.

adore
to really love someone or something
Molly adores chocolate.

adore

appreciate
to like something and understand its value or importance
I really appreciate your gift.

The opposite of like is dislike.

approve of
to like someone or something and have a positive opinion about them
My mother doesn't approve of my friends.

be devoted to
to love and be loyal to someone
My grandparents are devoted to each other.

be fond of
to like someone or something very much
Sam and Laura are very fond of each other.

be keen on
to like or to be interested in someone or something
I'm very keen on tennis.

dote on
to love someone very much and give them lots of attention
They dote on their new baby daughter.

a
b
c
d
e
f
g
h
i
j
k
l
m
n
o
p
q
r
s
t
u
v
w
x
y
z

In other words

to have a soft spot for
to like someone or something very much
I've always had a soft spot for Teri.

to think the world of
to like someone and have a high opinion of them
Our children think the world of their grandparents.

fancy (informal)
to find a person of the opposite sex attractive
Do you think she fancies me?

idolize
to like someone very much, sometimes too much
He's such an attractive, popular singer and a lot of young people idolize him.

love

enjoy
to like or get pleasure from something
I enjoy our little conversations.

love
to like very much
I love my cat so much.

be partial to (old-fashioned)
to like, be fond of
I'm partial to a bit of chocolate cake occasionally.

worship
to love or admire someone or something very much, without noticing any faults
My Dad worships our local football team even though they never win!

Did you know?

Famous movie stars and singers who are **loved** and **admired** by lots of people are called idols.

Look

• to look at something quickly

glance
to look at something or someone for a short time
She glanced at her watch.

• to look at something

observe
to look at something or someone in order to learn something
The scientists observed the gorillas to find out how they lived.

squint
to look at something or someone through partly closed eyes because you can't see very well
I squinted at the funny squiggles on the page.

peep

watch
to look at something or someone, especially if they are changing or moving
Did you watch the match last night?

• to look at someone or something secretly

peek
to look at something quickly, hoping that no one will see you
They peeked at the presents under the Christmas tree.

peep
to look at something secretly for a short time, usually through a narrow opening
Rebecca peeped around the corner see if her friends were still trying to find her hiding place.

spy on
to watch someone secretly to get information about them
The maid spied on the family through the keyhole.

• to look at something for a long time

gaze
to look at someone or something for a long time, usually with a good feeling
We gazed up at the stars in the sky.

glare
to stare angrily at someone or something
Emma and Robert glared at each other.   **glare**

stare
to look directly at someone or something without moving your eyes away
It's rude to stare.

• to look at something or someone carefully

examine
to look at something very carefully, usually to discover something
They examined the fossils closely.

inspect
to look at something carefully, to make sure it is safe or correct
The mechanic inspected all the tyres.

peer
to look carefully at something, because you can't see it very well
They peered into the cave.

scrutinize
to look very carefully at something to find out information
He scrutinized their faces to see if anyone was lying.

study
to look at something carefully, to learn or understand something
Study the map closely.

view
to look at something carefully and thoroughly
We're going to view the new flat this evening.

a b c d e f g h i j k l m n o p q r s t u v w x y z

a
b
c
d
e
f
g
h
i
j
k
l
m
n
o
p
q
r
s
t
u
v
w
x
y
z

Lovely

adorable
lovely, cute
The baby is so adorable.

angelic
as lovely and as pure as an angel
She's got an angelic face.

attractive
lovely to look at
The new museum is an attractive building.

beautiful
lovely to look at
What a beautiful view of the countryside!

charming
lovely in manner or lovely to look at
They're a charming young couple.

cute

cute
lovely and often small
The baby elephant is really cute.

delightful
very pleasant or very enjoyable
Thank you. We've had a delightful time tonight.

enchanting
very pleasant, lovely
The town has an enchanting toy museum.

In other words

the beautiful game
another term for 'football'
He wrote a poem about 'the beautiful game'.

drop-dead gorgeous
very attractive to look at
She's quite pretty, but I wouldn't say she was drop-dead gorgeous.

good-looking
nice to look at (of men or women)
The prince is very good-looking.

gorgeous
lovely, beautiful
What a gorgeous dress you are wearing!

> The opposite of lovely is horrible or ugly.

gorgeous

pretty
nice to look at
The seeds I planted have grown into pretty flowers.

picturesque
lovely to look at (of a view or place)
We stayed in a picturesque little village.

pretty

stunning
extremely lovely to look at
You look stunning with that new hairstyle.

pleasant
very nice
We spent a pleasant day on the beach.

sweet
pleasant, cute
What a sweet little puppy!

a b c d e f g h i j k l m n o p q r s t u v w x y z

a
b
c
d
e
f
g
h
i
j
k
l
m
n
o
p
q
r
s
t
u
v
w
x
y
z

Make

assemble
to put together the parts of something
We have to assemble the desk from a kit.

build
to make something by putting parts together
They're building new houses at the edge of town.

concoct
to make something strange to eat or drink
The wizard concocted a magic potion.

construct
to build or make out of different parts
The builders who constructed this block of flats have gone out of business.

create
to make something that wasn't there before
Our class created a sculpture.

erect
to build or make a structure
We don't know who erected Stonehenge.

fashion
to make something to do a particular job
The castaway fashioned a sail for the raft out of palm leaves.

form
to make, or to be a part of, something
These lessons form the first term of a two-year course.

concoct

a
b
c
d
e
f
g
h
i
j
k
l
m
n
o
p
q
r
s
t
u
v
w
x
y
z

generate
to make something by using
a process
The power station generates
electricity.

invent
to make something that has
never been made before
Does anyone know who invented
the bicycle?

knock together (informal)
to make very quickly to be used
for a short time
Dad knocked a sledge together from
a few pieces of wood.

manufacture
to make something, especially in
a factory
They manufacture toys.

The opposite of
make is destroy.

mould
to shape a substance, such as
clay or wax
Wax is moulded into candles.

produce
to make something or bring
something into existence
I produced a
vase at my first
pottery class.

put
together
to make
something by putting smaller
parts together
The models come in small pieces
and you have to put them together.

put up
to build
They're planning to put up a new
hospital where the school used
to be.

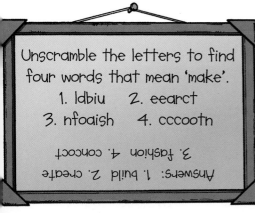

Unscramble the letters to find
four words that mean 'make'.
1. ldbiu   2. eearct
3. nfoaish   4. cccootn

Answers: 1. build 2. create
3. fashion 4. concoct

Mistake

a • b • c • d • e • f • g • h • i • j • k • l • m • n • o • p • q • r • s • t • u • v • w • x • y • z

• a mistake

blunder
a stupid or clumsy mistake
It was a foolish blunder.

error
a mistake you don't know you're making
They made an error when they charged us for the meal.

fault
a mistake, usually that someone or something is to blame for
I think there is a fault in the system.

gaffe
an embarrassing mistake
Putting sugar on your eggs in the restaurant was a real gaffe.

howler
a stupid mistake in something you write or say
His essay was full of howlers.

mix-up
a mistake that confuses things
We were supposed to play yesterday but there was a mix-up with the dates.

In other words

to drop a clanger
to say something that you shouldn't have said and that makes you feel embarrassed
I dropped a clanger when I asked him about his job. I didn't know he'd been sacked.

to put your foot in it
to say something stupid or secret that you shouldn't have said
You really put your foot in it when you mentioned the surprise party!

oversight
a mistake you make by forgetting or not noticing something
Everyone should have been invited. Leaving their names off was an oversight.

slip
a small mistake that is easy to correct
It was just a slip of the tongue.

• to make a mistake

goof (informal)
to make a silly mistake
If you hadn't goofed, we'd have won the match.

goof

misjudge
to make a mistake by deciding to do the wrong thing
They misjudged the situation.

slip

typo (informal)
a spelling mistake in a text made when it was being typed or written
There are a lot of typos in this letter.

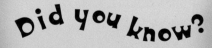

Did you know?
Fault is also the name for a crack in the Earth's crust.

a b c d e f g h i j k l **m** n o p q r s t u v w x y z

Money

cash
notes and coins used as money
Do you have any cash with you?

change
money that you get back when you pay for something
Make sure you check your change is correct.

change

coins
small pieces of metal used as money
Some vending machines take only coins, not notes.

currency
the type of money that is used in a country
The dollar is the currency of Canada, the USA and Australia.

dosh (informal)
a slang word for money
I'd like to go on holiday but I haven't got the dosh.

legal tender
the lawful currency of a country
The French franc stopped being legal tender in France in 2002.

• a lot of money

a fortune
a very large amount of money
What a fantastic idea! We should be able to make a fortune.

wealth
a large amount of money
The king had great wealth.

• amounts of money

figure
an exact amount of money
The figure we have decided on is £34.98.

a b c d e f g h i j k l m n o p q r s t u v w x y z

grant
money given to someone that must be used for a special purpose
My grandparents received a grant to repair their roof.

income
money that people receive, usually from working
Our joint income means we can afford to go on holiday.

pocket money
money that children receive from their parents each week
I work for my dad on Saturdays to earn pocket money.

In other words

money doesn't grow on trees
often used if money is in short supply, or to explain that you should spend money wisely
No, you can't have a new bike. Money doesn't grow on trees you know!

sum
an amount of money
It added up to a large sum.

• **money that someone gives to another person**

allowance
money someone receives regularly, not for working
She gets an allowance from her parents to buy clothes.

Did you know?
The word **money** probably comes from *Moneta*, a name given to the Roman goddess Juno, whose temple was used to store valuable things.

a b c d e f g h i j k l **m** n o p q r s t u v w x y z

Move

a b c d e f g h i j k l **m** n o p q r s t u v w x y z

budge
to move a little way
This window is stuck. It won't budge.

change position
to move into another position
If you're not comfortable, change your position.

edge
to move slowly and in stages
The hunters edged nearer to the animals.

emigrate
to move to another country permanently
They emigrated to Australia recently.

fidget
to move and wriggle about
Please don't fidget during my lessons.

In other words

to move heaven and earth
to do everything that you possibly can to make something happen
I moved heaven and earth to get you tickets.

inch
to move very slowly
He inched his way along the rooftop.

relocate
to move permanently to another place
We're moving house because my dad's firm has relocated to another city.

shift
to move something from one place to another
We shifted the sofa out of the way.

squirm
to move your body from side to side because you are uncomfortable
Stop squirming and sit still.

stir
to move slightly
She stirred slightly in her sleep but didn't wake up.

swing
to move through the air
Monkeys swing from tree to tree.

transfer
to move from one place to another
The player transferred to another team

transport
to take people or goods from one place to another
Many goods are transported by rail.

wiggle
to make small movements from side to side or up and down
The baby wiggled her toes.

stir

wriggle
to move your body this way and that way to get yourself through a small space
He wriggled through the crack in the rock and into the cave.

writhe
to move and twist your body in big, sudden movements
She was writhing in agony.

a b c d e f g h i j k l **m** n o p q r s t u v w x y z

New

brand new
completely new, never been used before
We've just bought a brand new car.

just out
very new
Have you seen his new film? It's just out on DVD.

latest
the newest or most recent
I've just bought the latest version of the game.

modern
new, made using today's ideas
The new art gallery is a modern building.

brand new

current
not old, relating to now
It's a quiz on current events.

fresh
new or different
I've put fresh sheets on the bed.

innovative
new, different and better
The skateboard is of an innovative design.

newcomer
a person who has recently arrived in a place
The family are newcomers to the town.

The opposite of new is old.

a b c d e f g h i j k l m n o p q r s t u v w x y z

In other words

hot off the press
the latest news
This is the news from the Olympics – hot off the press.

recent
made or done a short time ago
We are looking for recent articles about the zoo.

state-of-the-art
using the latest technology and design
We've just bought a state-of-the-art computer.

novel
new and not seen or done before
We've come up with a novel idea for raising money.

original
new, not done before and not a copy
The original doors and fireplace are still in the house.

pioneering
using new ideas
Marie Curie carried out pioneering research in the science world.

state-of-the-art

up to date
recent or containing the latest information
We must keep the register up to date.

a b c d e f g h i j k l m **n** o p q r s t u v w x y z

a b c d e f g h i j k l m **n** o p q r s t u v w x y z

Nice

• **nice, of people**

charming
nice, pleasing
She's a charming girl.

friendly
nice and behaving kindly
towards someone
Our dogs are really friendly.

friendly

good-natured
pleasant, having a nice nature
They were a good-natured crowd.

kind
helpful and nice to others
*Our neighbours were really kind to
us when mum was ill.*

Did you know?

Prince **Charming** is a
male character that
appears in many
famous fairy tales.

The opposite of
nice is horrible
or nasty.

likeable
nice and easy to like
He's a very likeable bloke.

• nice, of times, things or events

enjoyable
giving you pleasure
That was a very enjoyable film.

fine
nice, of weather
If it's fine, we'll go to the park.

pleasing
satisfying, giving pleasure
It's pleasing to hear that they've arrived safely.

sunny
nice and warm with blue skies
It is a sunny day, perfect for gardening.

• nice, of places

attractive
nice to look at
They live in a very attractive house.

beautiful
very nice to look at
There's a beautiful view of the lake from this window.

• nice, of people or events

delightful
nice, lovely, pleasant
They're a delightful couple.

lovely
beautiful, attractive
The people we met tonight were really lovely.

pleasant
nice, enjoyable, friendly
It has been a very pleasant day.

sunny

a
b
c
d
e
f
g
h
i
j
k
l
m
n
o
p
q
r
s
t
u
v
w
x
y
z

Old

• old, of things

ancient
extremely old, existing many years ago
There are a lot of ancient objects in the museum.

ancient

bygone
belonging to a much older era
His hairstyle and whiskers looked like something out of a bygone age.

antique
old and valuable
My grandfather gave me an antique pocket watch.

dated
old-fashioned
These shoes my mum used to wear look very dated now.

second-hand
owned by someone else before you
Charity shops sell second-hand clothes.

used
not new, or owned by someone else before
We bought a used car.

vintage
old and of high quality
He has a wonderful collection of vintage cars.

The opposite of old is new or young.

In other words

as old as the hills
very old
That joke is as old as the hills!

no spring chicken
not young any more
Who are you calling old?
You're no spring chicken yourself!

over the hill
old and no longer useful
Some employers think you're over
the hill at the age of 40!

getting on (informal)
getting older
Grandad is
getting on a bit.

mature
middle-aged or
older than is
normal or typical
My mum's a
mature student.

senior
older
It only costs £2 for senior
citizens to get in.

veteran
old and experienced
He's a veteran sports reporter.

• **old, of people**

ageing
becoming older
The UK has an ageing
population.

elderly
old
Gran is elderly but she still likes to
go cycling with us.

elderly

a b c d e f g h i j k l m n **o** p q r s t u v w x y z

a
b
c
d
e
f
g
h
i
j
k
l
m
n
o
p
q
r
s
t
u
v
w
x
y
z

Open

• to open

force
to open something that is stuck
or locked by pushing hard on it
*The firefighters had to force the
door.*

pick a lock
to open a lock with something
that is not a key
*Car locks are extra safe so thieves
can't pick the locks.*

prise
to force something apart to
open it
*We had to prise the trunk open
because we had lost the key.*

prise

unbolt
to open a door or gate by sliding
a metal bar across
*He carefully unbolted the door and
led the pony out.*

unbutton
to open a piece of clothing that
has buttons
*You can unbutton your jacket if
you're too hot.*

The opposite of open is close or closed.

unfasten
to open or undo something,
usually a piece of clothing
She unfastened her seat belt.

unfold
to open paper or cloth and
spread it out
*Unfold the map and try to find out
where we are.*

a b c d e f g h i j k l m n **o** p q r s t u v w x y z

unlock
to open a lock using a key
Can you unlock the door?
My hands are full.

unscrew
to take the top off a
container by turning it
Can you unscrew this jar
of coffee? I'm not strong
enough.

unwrap
to open a parcel by taking
paper off it
We can't wait to unwrap our
presents on Christmas morning.

unzip
to open something that has a zip
Can you help me unzip my kit bag?

• open

ajar
slightly open
If the door is
ajar, just go
straight in.

a jar

gaping
wide open, of a hole
There were gaping holes in the road.

off the latch
closed, but not locked
Come in! The door's off the latch.

wide open
completely open
We left the garage door wide open
by mistake.

yawning
wide open, of a hole
We looked into the yawning mouth
of the cave.

Did you know?

We sometimes use **open**
to describe people who
are honest and happy to
talk about things.

a b c d e f g h i j k l m n **o** p q r s t u v w x y z

Ordinary

average
typical, like most others of the same type
An average lesson lasts 45 minutes.

bland
boring, dull or not tasty
Baby food is usually bland.

commonplace
happening or seen often
Red buses are commonplace in this city.

conventional
ordinary and traditional
They wear conventional clothes even though they are art students.

> **The opposite of ordinary is special or extraordinary.**

everyday
ordinary, not unusual
The supermarket sells food and everyday items you need.

mundane
ordinary and dull
Mum finds mopping the floor a very mundane task.

conventional

In other words

nothing to write home about
nothing special, not very exciting
The new restaurant is okay, but nothing to write home about.

neutral
plain, without strong colours, flavours or opinions
I've painted the entire house in neutral colours.

normal
like other people or things of the same type
His height and weight are normal for his age.

routine
usual and done frequently
It's just a routine dental check-up.

run-of-the-mill
ordinary, not exciting
My job is fairly run-of-the-mill.

standard
something basic without extra features
Our car is the standard model.

typical
like other things of the same type
Dad dresses like a typical tourist when we go on holiday.

unremarkable
ordinary, not interesting
The houses in this street are unremarkable.

typical

usual
normal, happening most often
My usual bedtime is 8 o'clock, but as it's Christmas Mum says I can stay up late.

Unscramble the letters to find four words that mean 'ordinary'.

1. treiuon   2. ldnab
3. aolnmr   4. geaaevr

Answers: 1. routine 2. bland 3. normal 4. average

a b c d e f g h i j k l m n o p q r s t u v w x y z

Poor

badly off (informal)
not having much money
My father's family was badly off when he was a boy.

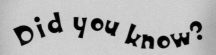

Did you know?

The word **broke** is also the past tense of the verb (doing word) 'break'.
He broke his leg.

broke (informal)
not having any money temporarily
I can't come out tonight; I'm broke until Friday.

deprived
not having the things you need for a normal life
My grandad had a deprived childhood.

destitute
so poor that you do not have basic things such as enough food
The man was destitute and couldn't afford to buy new clothes.

destitute

disadvantaged
not having the same opportunities as other people
The charity helps disadvantaged families.

The opposite of poor is rich.

hard up (informal)
not having much money
I can't come with you to the cinema tonight as I'm a bit hard up at the moment.

impoverished (formal)
very poor
The country was impoverished after many years of drought.

needy
not having enough money
Anyone who is needy is welcome to come for a free meal.

poverty-stricken
extremely poor
Parts of the country are rich and parts are poverty-stricken.

skint (informal)
having no money
I can't lend you any money, I'm afraid. I'm skint.

underprivileged
poor and with fewer opportunities than other people
We collect aluminium cans to raise money for underprivileged families.

penniless

penniless
without any money
The winning lottery ticket was found by a penniless beggar.

Unscramble these words that mean 'poor'.
a. erbok b. eyedn
c. nlinessp

Answers: a. broke b. needy c. penniless

a b c d e f g h i j k l m n o **p** q r s t u v w x y z

a
b
c
d
e
f
g
h
i
j
k
l
m
n
o
p
q
r
s
t
u
v
w
x
y
z

Pretend

• to pretend

bluff
to pretend that you know something
Do you really know the answer or are you just bluffing?

impersonate
to pretend you are someone else
Someone impersonated the team captain and gave an interview to a radio station.

masquerade as
to dress up as someone else
He masqueraded as a doctor.

play-act
to put on an act
Don't take any notice of him; he's only play-acting.

pose as
to pretend to be someone else
She was posing as the head of the committee.

In other words

crocodile tears
tears that you pretend to cry but you are not really sad or sorry.
Your crocodile tears don't fool me.

put it on
to pretend to have a certain feeling
I can't tell if he's really ill or if he's just putting it on.

• not real

artificial
not real or not natural
The vase contains artificial flowers.

fake
not real, although it looks real
The coat was made of fake fur.

false
not real, but made to look real
Are you wearing false eyelashes?

false

insincere
not really meaning what you say
His apology sounded very insincere.

made-up
invented, not true
I think most of the stories in the newspapers are made-up.

make-believe
not real
The film is just make-believe.

sham
something that isn't real and is intended to trick people
We bought tickets for the raffle but it turned out to be a sham.

• people who pretend

impostor (or imposter)
a person who pretends to be someone else
The king was really an impostor.

quack
a person who pretends to be a doctor or to have medical knowledge
Don't listen to her; she's just a quack trying to sell you things.

Did you know?

Masquerade is also the word for a party or dance where the guests wear masks and costumes. A masquerade is sometimes called a 'masked ball'.

a b c d e f g h i j k l m n o **p** q r s t u v w x y z

a b c d e f g h i j k l m n o **p** q r s t u v w x y z

Problem

catch
a hidden problem
This seems so easy that there must be a catch somewhere.

In other words

stumbling block
a problem that is likely to stop someone from doing what they want to do
We could sell lots of our products to China, but language is the main stumbling block.

tight spot
a difficult situation
I'm in a bit of a tight spot; I left my wallet at home.

你好

complication
a problem that makes a situation more difficult
I will be on time unless there are complications.

difficulty
a problem that is not easy to deal with
I'm having difficulty choosing which car to buy.

dilemma
a very difficult choice between two things
We have a dilemma – the cricket match is on one channel and the Cup Final is on another.

glitch
a small mistake or fault in the workings of something
There were a few glitches in the first couple of weeks, but things are going smoothly now.

gremlin (informal)
an imaginary little creature that gets into a machine and stops it from working
We must have gremlins in the computer; it won't work.

headache (informal)
a problem that causes you worry
Several players are injured, which is a big headache for the manager.

hiccup
a small problem that is quickly solved
There was a minor hiccup but nothing serious to worry about.

hitch
a small problem
The performance went off without a hitch.

hurdle
a problem that you have to solve so that you can do what you are trying to do
The team has had to overcome several hurdles: injuries, player transfers and a lack of funds.

snag
a difficulty
I'd love to go to the concert. The only snag is that tickets cost £30.

Did you know?

Hiccup also refers to the noise you sometimes make if you eat or drink too quickly!

hindrance
something that stops you from doing something easily
I was trying to wash our car but the rain was a real hindrance.

hindrance

a
b
c
d
e
f
g
h
i
j
k
l
m
n
o
p
q
r
s
t
u
v
w
x
y
z

Put

a
b
c
d
e
f
g
h
i
j
k
l
m
n
o
p
q
r
s
t
u
v
w
x
y
z

apply
to put a liquid such as paint
on something
*Apply a thin layer and allow to dry
completely.*

arrange
to put something in order
*She arranged the
flowers in a vase.*

deposit
to put something
somewhere
*He deposited the
book on the table
with a thump.*

deposit

dump (informal)
to drop or put something down in
a careless way
*Don't just dump your bag in the
middle of the floor.*

lay
to put something down gently,
flat on a surface
*Can you take the coats upstairs and
lay them on the bed, please?*

place
to put something somewhere
carefully
Place the stencil on the paper.

plonk (informal)
to put something down heavily
and in a careless way
She plonked her bag on the table.

pop (informal)
to put something somewhere
quickly
*Just pop your credit card in the
machine.*

position
to carefully move something into
a certain position
Position the prism at an angle.

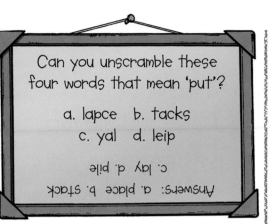

Can you unscramble these four words that mean 'put'?

a. lapce   b. tacks
c. yal   d. leip

Answers: a. place b. stack c. lay d. pile

• to put something against something else

lean
to stand something against a wall or another vertical surface
The window cleaner leant the ladder against the wall.

prop
to lean something against something else for support
I'll prop my bike against the wall.

rest
to lean something on something else for support
She rested her head on my shoulder.

stand
to lean something up so that it is nearly vertical
Stand the picture over there.

• to put things on top of one another

heap
to throw or drop things on top of each other in an untidy way
His room is so messy because he just heaps his clothes on the floor.

heap

pile
to put things on top of each other
He piled potatoes onto his plate.

stack
to put things carefully on top of one another
Stack the CDs in the cupboard.

a b c d e f g h i j k l m n o **p** q r s t u v w x y z

a
b
c
d
e
f
g
h
i
j
k
l
m
n
o
p
q
r
s
t
u
v
w
x
y
z

Quiet

calm
quiet and peaceful
Everything's calm after the storm.

hushed
quiet on purpose
They spoke in hushed voices.

inaudible
so quiet that you cannot hear it
He spoke in an inaudible whisper.

low
quiet and deep
*There was a low hum coming from
the machine.*

muffled
quiet and unclear
or blurred
*Their speech is
muffled by the
helmets they are
wearing.*

muted
quieter than usual
*We could hear muted
voices in the corridor.*

noiseless
silent
Electric cars are almost noiseless.

peaceful
quiet and calm
*We found a peaceful place to have
our picnic.*

silent
with no sound
*Please be absolutely silent while we
are recording.*

soft
quiet and pleasant
*There is soft music
playing in the
background.*

muffled

speechless
unable to speak because you are shocked or angry
He was almost speechless with anger when he was told the news.

still
calm and silent
The night was still and the sky was full of stars.

subdued
quieter than usual because you are sad or worried
You seem a bit subdued today – are you okay?

taciturn
saying very little
He plays the part of a stern, taciturn man.

The opposite of quiet is noisy or loud.

tight-lipped
refusing to speak
The journalist asked lots of questions, but the politician remained tight-lipped.

In other words

keep mum
to keep quiet because something is a secret
The manager is keeping mum on the goalkeeper's injury.

as quiet as a mouse
very quiet
I didn't hear you come in; you were as quiet as a mouse.

a b c d e f g h i j k l m n o p q r s t u v w x y z

a b c d e f g h i j k l m n o p q **r** s t u v w x y z

Real

• not false

authentic
real or true
This is an authentic antique map.

factual
based on facts
The article gave a lot of factual information about the chemicals in our food.

genuine
not fake
Genuine leather lasts a long time.

lifelike
like the real person or thing
The trees and flowers in the painting look so lifelike.

proper
real, correct or appropriate
A sandwich and a packet of crisps is not a proper meal.

real-life
real, that actually happened
The story is based on real-life events.

tangible
real, easy to see
The police need more tangible evidence before they can arrest him.

true

true
not a lie
It's true! The dog really did eat my homework!

• **real, of feelings**

heartfelt
strong and truly meant
*Please accept our
heartfelt thanks.*

sincere
real and truly felt
*I trust her and think
she is being completely
sincere.*

• **existing, not
imaginary**

actual
real, existing in fact
*They said that about
3000 people were at
the demonstration,
but the actual
figure might be
much higher.*

concrete
based on facts
*Do the police have
any concrete
evidence to
identify the suspect?*

In other words

the Real McCoy
the real thing, not a copy
*Is that Chinese vase made out of
plastic or is it the real McCoy?*

*This comes from an American boxer, Kid McCoy,
who was called the Real McCoy.*

concrete

solid
based on real facts
*There is solid evidence that
smoking is bad for you.*

**The opposite of
real is artificial
or imaginary.**

a
b
c
d
e
f
g
h
i
j
k
l
m
n
o
p
q
r
s
t
u
v
w
x
y
z

a b c d e f g h i j k l m n o p q r s t u v w x y z

Rich

affluent
having a lot of money to buy things with
This is an affluent neighbourhood.

comfortable
having enough money
My grandparents aren't millionaires, but they're comfortable.

flush

flush
having more money than you usually have
I'll treat you – I'm flush right now.

loaded (informal)
rich
Look at his car! He must be loaded.

In other words

rolling in money
very rich
You gave him a £20 tip! You must be rolling in money!

prosperous
successful and having a lot of money
The town has become prosperous since the factory was built.

wealthy
rich
They are a wealthy family and they're very generous.

well-heeled
having a lot of money and nice clothes
They look well-heeled.

a b c d e f g h i j k l m n o p q **r** s t u v w x y z

well-off
having more money than most people
They're quite a well-off couple.

well-to-do
having enough money to live well
It's a story about a well-to-do family in Pakistan.

Did you know?
The word **rich** comes from an Old English word *rice*, which meant wealthy, powerful or mighty.

1 people who are rich

billionaire
a person who has at least a billion pounds
He owned four businesses and was a billionaire by the age of thirty.

millionaire
a person who has at least a million pounds
The farmer became a millionaire after he discovered buried treasure in his field.

magnate
a wealthy person who works in business
He's a well-known newspaper magnate.

millionaire

The opposite of rich is poor.

tycoon
a rich and powerful person in business or industry
She married a wealthy shipping tycoon.

Right

a b c d e f g h i j k l m n o p q **r** s t u v w x y z

accepted
approved or agreed that
something is right
*It is an accepted fact that the world
is round.*

accurate
completely correct and without
any mistakes
*I don't have enough accurate
information to make a decision yet.*

appropriate
right for a certain situation
*It's not appropriate to wear
pyjamas to school.*

apt
exactly right or suitable for
a situation
*Several pupils made apt remarks
during the discussion.*

**The opposite of
right is wrong.**

correct
right, and with no mistakes
*Use a calculator to check that your
answers are correct.*

exact
completely right
Have you got the exact time?

fair
correct and reasonable
*He didn't do his fair share of the
work.*

fitting
suitable or right for a particular
situation
*The poem was fitting for the
ceremony.*

ideal
perfect, exactly right
*My ideal house would have a
swimming pool and cinema.*

just
fair, morally right
*It was a just punishment for the
crime.*

perfect
completely correct in every way, ideal
I've found the perfect job.

precise
completely correct
There were several people there – eight to be precise.

proper
right or correct
Put the books in the proper order.

In other words

as right as rain
fit and healthy, especially after having been ill
Take this tablet and by tomorrow you'll be as right as rain.

in the right place at the right time
in a place or a position where something good is offered
She's so lucky; she's always in the right place at the right time.

Suitable

spot on (informal)
exactly right
If you want to get top marks for your essay the spelling has to be spot on.

suitable
right for a particular situation or time
Trainers aren't suitable shoes to wear to a wedding.

true
real, correct
His story is only partly true.

a b c d e f g h i j k l m n o p q **r** s t u v w x y z

a b c d e f g h i j k l m n o p q **r** s t u v w x y z

Run

bolt
to run or move quickly because you are frightened
The horse bolted when the bell rang.

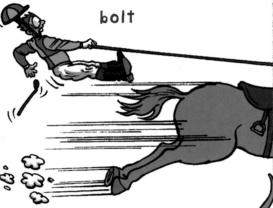

bolt

dart
to move quickly or suddenly
I darted into the kitchen to hide.

dash
to run fast for a short distance
It was raining so we dashed to the car.

flee
to run away from danger
The children were fleeing from the monsters.

gallop
to run quickly with big steps
He galloped around the house.

hare
to run very quickly
She hared off down the road.

jog
to run slowly for quite a long way
Mum jogs three times a week.

flee

leg it (informal)
to run away from something
They legged it as soon as they saw a teacher coming.

lope
to run with long, relaxed strides
The animal loped off through the grass.

race
to run fast, especially against someone in a competition
We raced around the school field as fast as we could.

rush
to move quickly to get somewhere or do something in a hurry
Mum was rushing around the house looking for her keys.

scamper
to run with small, quick steps
The children scampered on ahead.

scurry
to move quickly with short steps
She scurried out of the room like a frightened mouse.

scuttle
to move quickly with small, short steps
The crab scuttled across the sand towards the sea.

race

sprint
to run as fast as you can
The athletes sprinted around the track.

tear
to run fast without watching where you're going
He tore around the corner of the building and straight into the teacher.

zip (informal)
to move or go quickly
The motorbike zipped past us on the motorway.

a b c d e f g h i j k l m n o p q **r** s t u v w x y z

a
b
c
d
e
f
g
h
i
j
k
l
m
n
o
p
q
r
s
t
u
v
w
x
y
z

Sad

disappointed
sad that something did not
happen, or did not turn out as
well as you had expected
*We were disappointed at the team's
performance.*

down/low
sad and without energy
*You might feel a little bit down after
you've had flu.*

fed up
unhappy and annoyed or bored
I'm fed up waiting for you.

glum
sad-looking
*You're looking
very glum today.
What's the matter?*

homesick
sad because you
are away from
home and miss
the people there
*You'll be homesick
for the first few days at university.*

glum

unhappy
sad because of something that
has happened
What's wrong? You look unhappy.

The opposite of sad is happy.

upset
sad or worried
*I was upset when we had to cancel
the holiday.*

• very sad

dejected
sad and without hope
*We felt dejected when we
lost the game.*

depressed
feeling sad, usually for a
long time
*I was quite depressed when we first
moved here but now I really like it.*

desolate
extremely sad and lonely
She felt desolate on the first day in her new school.

despondent
very sad and not hopeful about the future
The team is despondent – they haven't won a match all year.

distressed
very sad or worried
My little brother gets very distressed when my mum goes out of the room.

miserable
extremely sad
I felt miserable because no one talked to me.

• **sad, of things**

distressing
worrying, making you feel sad
There were some distressing scenes in the programme.

In other words

down in the dumps
sad and fed up
The caveman was feeling down in the dumps because he ran out of food to eat.

tragic
sad, of news or a story, often because someone suffers
We heard the tragic news earlier.

Did you know?

A **tragic** event or a play that deals with sad events is called a tragedy.

a b c d e f g h i j k l m n o p q r s t u v w x y z

a b c d e f g h i j k l m n o p q r **s** t u v w x y z

Same

alike
not quite the same, but looking similar
My brothers and I look alike.

consistent
staying the same, not changing
We did the experiment six times and got consistent results.

identical
exactly the same
That jacket is identical to mine.

similar
almost the same but not quite
We have similar hobbies and interests.

uniform
the same for everyone
The workers are paid a uniform rate per hour.

word for word
using exactly the same words
She repeated his speech, word for word.

• **something that is the same as something else**

carbon copy
a thing that is exactly like another thing
The puppies are carbon copies of their mother.

clone
something that is exactly the same as something else because it has the same genes
In the film the scientist made a clone of the monster.

carbon copy

counterpart
someone who has the same position or job as someone else
The British minister met her French counterpart.

duplicate
something that is an exact copy of something else
Please keep a duplicate of the letter.

equivalent
something that has the same amount, size or value as something else
Do you know what the equivalent of £10 is in euros?

synonym
a word that means the same as another word
Big and large are synonyms.

match

The opposite of same is different.

In other words

like two peas in a pod
exactly the same, especially in appearance
The twins are like two peas in a pod.

• **to be the same**

match
to go together
Make sure you wear socks that match on your first day in your new job.

resemble
to look like something or someone else
The playing field resembles a building site at the moment.

tally
to match, be the same as something else
We both did the same sum but our results don't tally.

a b c d e f g h i j k l m n o p q r **s** t u v w x y z

a
b
c
d
e
f
g
h
i
j
k
l
m
n
o
p
q
r
s
t
u
v
w
x
y
z

Say

announce
to say something in public or formally
The headmistress announced that the school would close early because of the snow.

blurt out
to say something without thinking
He blurted out the answer.

groan
to complain
"Not mashed potato again!" he groaned.

hint
to say something indirectly so people know what you mean
Mr Hunt hinted that there would be a test.

blurt out

comment
to give an opinion
The captain commented on each player's performance.

exclaim
to say something loudly or suddenly
"This ride is fantastic!" she exclaimed.

mention
to say a little bit about something
The head mentioned that there would be new pupils this term.

mumble
to say something unclearly
Don't mumble when you're on stage. Speak clearly.

mutter
to say something quietly, especially if you are complaining
One of the players muttered something about the referee.

pronounce
to say an individual sound or word
The word 'February' is hard to pronounce.

remark
to say what you think about something
The reporter remarked on how good our school's website is.

shout
to say something loudly
"I'm over here", she shouted.

snarl
to say something angrily
"Clear off!" he snarled.

speak
to say words, to talk
I was speaking to the headmaster earlier.

In other words

it goes without saying
to be so obvious that something does not actually have to be said
It goes without saying that he'll do a good job.

whisper

tell
to say something to someone
Can I tell you a secret?

whisper
to say something very softly
She whispered the answer in my ear.

a b c d e f g h i j k l m n o p q r **s** t u v w x y z

Secret

abcdefghijklmnopqrstuvwxyz

cagey
not willing to tell other people about your plans
Dad's being a bit cagey about where we're going on holiday. He wants it to be a surprise.

classified
kept secret for reasons of security, and not to be shown to anyone
This envelope contains classified documents.

cloak-and-dagger
concerned with secrecy and spying
What's all this cloak-and-dagger stuff? Why won't you tell me what you're doing?

concealed
not showing
He's wearing a concealed microphone.

confidential
private, not for other people
The report is highly confidential.

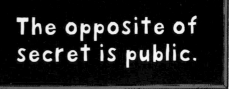

The opposite of secret is public.

covert
done in a secret way
Spies are involved in covert operations.

covert

furtive
done secretly, and in a guilty way
He made a couple of furtive telephone calls.

hidden
not shown or visible
There's a message hidden in the book.

hush-hush
(informal)
very secret
The plans are all very hush-hush so you mustn't say a word.

personal
private or to do with your private life
You are not allowed to read my diary; it's personal.

In other words

between you, me and the gatepost
what you say when you tell someone something you don't want anyone else to know
Now, this is just between you, me and the gatepost.

in private
done where other people cannot see or hear
They will discuss it in private.

top secret
extremely secret and not to be shown or mentioned to anyone
This mission is top secret.

undercover
working secretly
He's an undercover agent for the government.

Did you know?
The opposite of **covert** is overt, which means open and not secret or hidden.

a b c d e f g h i j k l m n o p q r s t u v w x y z

a
b
c
d
e
f
g
h
i
j
k
l
m
n
o
p
q
r
s
t
u
v
w
x
y
z

See

• to see in front of you

catch sight of
to see something or someone
suddenly
*She suddenly caught sight of Simon
and their eyes met.*

spy

glimpse
to see something or someone for
a short time
*I glimpsed some bluebells from the
train window.*

make out
to see something that is difficult
to see
*I can't make out this word as the ink
has smudged.*

notice
to be aware of something
I noticed a hole in my jumper.

spot
to see something or someone
suddenly
*I've just spotted Hannah. There she
is – over there.*

spy (old-fashioned)
to see something or
someone, usually from a
distance
*The captain spied dry land
through his telescope.*

witness
to see something happen
*The police want to speak to anyone
who witnessed the accident.*

Did you know?

The word **picture** is also
used to mean a painting
or drawing, a photograph
and a movie.

• to see in your mind

daydream
to spend time thinking of nice things so that you forget about what you are doing or where you are now
I was daydreaming about ice creams and didn't hear what the teacher said.

daydream

dream
to see things in your mind when you are asleep
I dreamt I was sailing across the ocean in a big yacht.

imagine
to make a picture of something in your mind
Imagine you are lying on a sandy beach under a palm tree.

picture
to have a picture of something in your mind
I know who you mean but I can't picture his face.

visualize
to get a clear picture of something in your mind
I'm sorry, I can't visualize what you mean.

• to go and see someone

drop in (informal)
to call in and see someone for a short time
I'll drop in on Grandma on my way home from school.

visit
to go and see a person or place
I visited the doctor on Tuesday for a health check.

visit

a b c d e f g h i j k l m n o p q r **s** t u v w x y z

a
b
c
d
e
f
g
h
i
j
k
l
m
n
o
p
q
r
s
t
u
v
w
x
y
z

Sleep

• a sleep, time spent asleep

catnap
a very short sleep, usually not very deep
Why don't you have a quick catnap before we leave for the airport?

forty winks (informal)
a short sleep
I'll feel better after I've had my forty winks.

kip
a short sleep
It's a long journey, why don't you have a kip in the car?

nap
a short sleep, usually in the afternoon
Grandma usually has a nap after lunch.

siesta
a sleep in the afternoon, especially in hot countries
The shops are closed because everyone's having a siesta.

slumber
a sleep, often said in stories
The princess ate the apple and fell into a deep slumber.

snooze (informal)
a short, light sleep
Dad had a snooze on the sofa while we went out for a walk.

The opposite of asleep is awake.

• to sleep

crash out (informal)
to go to sleep very quickly
I got home after running the marathon and just crashed out.

doze
to sleep lightly
I was just dozing in front of the TV.

drift off
to go to sleep slowly
Be quiet, we're hoping the baby will drift off.

drop off
to go to sleep easily
I dropped off as soon as my head hit the pillow.

drift off

In other words

to hit the hay/hit the sack
to go to bed
I think I'll hit the hay now; I'm exhausted.

to sleep like a log
to sleep very well
"Did you manage to get some sleep?"
"Yes, I slept like a log!"

hibernate
to go to sleep during the winter (of animals)
Bears sometimes hibernate in caves.

nod off (informal)
to fall asleep, often when you don't want to
Dad's nodded off in the armchair again.

retire (formal)
to go to bed
It's time for us to retire to bed now; thank you for a lovely evening.

a
b
c
d
e
f
g
h
i
j
k
l
m
n
o
p
q
r
s
t
u
v
w
x
y
z

a b c d e f g h i j k l m n o p q r **s** t u v w x y z

Small

dainty
small and delicate
The doll has dainty hands.

dinky (informal)
small and cute
What a dinky little room you have.

little
small, not big
They live in a sweet little cottage.

meagre
not enough, too little
The farmer had to try to survive on his meagre harvest.

miniature
much smaller than normal
The doll's house had miniature tables and chairs inside.

In other words

what a small world!
something you say when you meet someone who knows a person or a place you know, and you are surprised
I don't believe you know Sally too – what a small world!

The opposite of small is large or big.

minor
not important
Don't worry about the minor details.

minuscule
very small
A newborn panda is minuscule compared to its mother.

minute
extremely small
The picture shows the inside of your body in minute detail.

petite
small and dainty
This shop sells clothes for petite women.

petty
not important
There are too many petty rules in this office.

puny
small and weak
He's a champion tennis player now, but he was puny when he was a boy.

tiny
very small
Coral reefs are made up of thousands of tiny creatures.

puny

titchy (informal)
very small
You've got really titchy hands!

trivial
very unimportant
Stop worrying about such a trivial thing.

• **become smaller**

shrink
to get smaller, often because of the effects of water or heat
My T-shirt shrank in the wash and it's too small now.

shrink

shrivel (up)
to get smaller and drier
Tomatoes shrivel up in very hot sun.

a b c d e f g h i j k l m n o p q r s t u v w x y z

a
b
c
d
e
f
g
h
i
j
k
l
m
n
o
p
q
r
s
t
u
v
w
x
y
z

Smile

• to smile because you are happy

beam
to smile a big smile for a long time, usually because you are proud of something or someone
The parents beamed as their children went up to receive their prizes.

break into a smile
to suddenly start smiling
She broke into a smile when she heard the good news.

face lights up
to look happy suddenly
The children's faces lit up as soon as they saw the fireworks blast into the sky.

grin
to suddenly break into a wide, happy smile
He grinned so widely that you could see nearly all of his teeth!

look amused
to show you are pleased or happy by giving a small smile
He didn't say he found it funny but he looked amused.

Did you know?

In Old English, **smirk** was the word for **smile**, but not in the unpleasant way that we understand it now.

smile/beam/grin from ear to ear
to give a big smile
The little girl beamed from ear to ear during the circus performance.

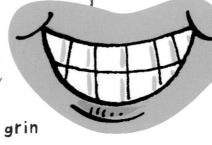

grin

In other words

to grin like a Cheshire cat
to smile very widely because you're pleased about something
He was grinning like a Cheshire cat.
This comes from a character in Lewis Carroll's book Alice's Adventures in Wonderland. Alice goes to a land where nothing is normal and meets many strange characters. The Cheshire cat is one of these. He fades away as Alice is talking to him. The only thing left is his grin, floating in the air.

smirk
to smile in a nasty way because you are pleased about someone else's bad luck
She smirked when she saw him fall over during the hurdles race.

sneer
to smile in an unpleasant way that shows that you don't respect someone or something
He sneered at his sister's attempt to play football.

• to smile in an unpleasant or insincere way

simper
to smile in a silly, annoying way
The student simpered at the teacher.

The opposite of smile is frown.

a b c d e f g h i j k l m n o p q r **s** t u v w x y z

a b c d e f g h i j k l m n o p q r **s** t u v w x y z

Start

• **to start**

activate
to start something happening or working
The machine is activated by pressing this button.

begin
to start something or to start doing something
You should begin the letter with 'Dear Sir'.

commence (formal)
to start or begin
The ceremony will now commence.

embark on
to start a big, important job or a journey
It was announced that the ship was going to embark on its long journey.

get cracking (informal)
to start something immediately
The teacher will be back soon. We'd better get cracking on the project!

get going (informal)
to start to go
We'd better get going, otherwise we'll miss the train.

initiate
to start something such as a discussion about something
A neighbouring country initiated the peace talks.

launch
to start something publicly
The company is launching a new product.

embark on

The opposite of start is finish or end.

open
to begin to be shown, of a film or show
We want to see the film when it opens.

set in motion
to start something like a process, that will take a long time
The plan has been set in motion.

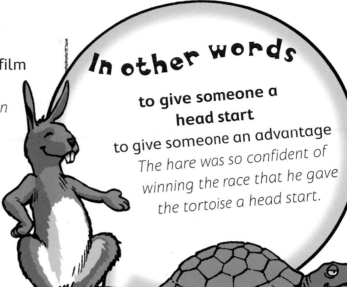

In other words

to give someone a head start
to give someone an advantage
The hare was so confident of winning the race that he gave the tortoise a head start.

• to start something in an organization

establish
to start something permanent
Oxford University was established more than 800 years ago.

found
to start something such as a company or city
The company was founded in 2007.

set up
to make all the plans to start something
We've set up everything for the experiment.

• a start

beginning
the start of something
At the beginning of the story the princess is living in a big palace.

dawn (formal)
the start or beginning of something new
We hope that this agreement will mark the dawn of a new era.

outset
the start or beginning
We need to make the rules clear from the outset.

a b c d e f g h i j k l m n o p q r **s** t u v w x y z

Steal

a b c d e f g h i j k l m n o p q r s t u v w x y z

• to steal

burgle
to steal things from a place such as a house or office
Our house was burgled last night.

burgle

loot
to steal things from shops during a riot
Hooligans looted shops in the centre of town during the protest.

> ## Did you know?
> The word **poach** also means to cook an egg without its shell in boiling water.

mug
to attack and steal from someone in the street
The man was mugged as he walked home from work.

nick (informal)
to steal something
He left his bike in the garden and someone nicked it.

pilfer
to steal small or cheap things
It's wrong to pilfer stationery from your place of work.

pinch (informal)
to steal something
Who's pinched my ruler?

poach
to catch and steal animals without permission
The farmer said the men were poaching on his land.

rob
to steal something from a person or place
An armed gang robbed the bank.

• people who steal

burglar
a person who steals things from a building
The burglar must have entered the house through a window.

cat burglar
a burglar who climbs up the sides of buildings
The actor plays the role of a cat burglar in his latest film.

pickpocket
a person who steals things from people's pockets
The pickpocket targeted people in a large crowd.

In other words

daylight robbery
very expensive
The price of this shirt is daylight robbery, but I really like the style.

robber
a person who steals things from a public place
The robbers wore masks when they broke in to hide their faces.

shoplifter
a person who steals from shops
The security cameras caught the shoplifter stealing.

thief
a general word for a person who steals things
Car thieves can steal a car very quickly.

a b c d e f g h i j k l m n o p q r **s** t u v w x y z

Stop

a b c d e f g h i j k l m n o p q r **s** t u v w x y z

abandon
to stop doing something before it is finished because it is difficult
The team abandoned the search.

break
to stop for a short time
Shall we break for lunch now?

break off
to suddenly stop doing something
He broke off to see what the noise was outside the window.

cease (formal)
to stop happening
The fighting has ceased.

In other words

to call it a day
to stop what you are doing
You're looking tired. Shall we call it a day now?

to stop someone in their tracks
to surprise someone suddenly so they stop what they are doing
A loud noise stopped me in my tracks.

The opposite of stop is start or begin.

come to a standstill
to stop moving
Traffic has come to a standstill.

conclude
to finish a speech or a piece of writing
To conclude, I will just remind you of the most important points.

drop
to stop doing something because it does not seem like a good thing to do
We've decided to drop plans for a concert until after the holidays.

end
to finish or stop
How does the story end?

finish
to stop doing something because it is complete
When you finish the test you may leave.

halt
to stop moving
The procession halted.

pause
to stop for a short time
I paused the movie so that I could make a sandwich.

quit
to stop doing something
Quit running! Walk!

retire
to stop working
Grandma retired when she was 60.

stall
to stop, of an engine in a car or plane, because there is not enough power
Dad stalled the car going up a hill.

halt

a
b
c
d
e
f
g
h
i
j
k
l
m
n
o
p
q
r
s
t
u
v
w
x
y
z

a b c d e f g h i j k l m n o p q r **s** t u v w x y z

Story

anecdote
a short, usually funny, story
He told an anecdote about his first day at school.

epic
a very long story about past times, told in a poem, book or film
The film is an epic set in ancient Rome.

fable
a story with a moral message, usually with animal characters
Aesop wrote a fable about a tortoise and a hare.

fairy tale
a story for children about magical beings and events
I like reading fairy tales about witches and princesses.

legend
a very old magical story
The legend of William Tell is about a man who had to shoot an apple off his son's head.

myth
an ancient story
Pandora's Box is a myth from ancient Greece.

novel
a book about imaginary people and events
Would you like to borrow this novel? It's a great story!

novel

parable
a story that teaches you something about morality or religion
The play is based on the parable of the Good Samaritan.

a b c d e f g h i j k l m n o p q r s t u v w x y z

In other words

to cut a long story short
to tell the main facts of a story leaving out most of the details
Anyway, to cut a long story short, we decided to come home early.

a shaggy-dog story
a very long joke or story that is hard to believe
I can't believe I wasted my time listening to that shaggy-dog story.

saga
a story about a long period of time
It's a saga about three generations of a family.

tale
an exciting story
My uncle always tells us tales about his adventures in Antarctica.

thriller
a very exciting story in a book or film, especially one about a crime
I've just read a thriller about spies and secret agents.

whodunnit (informal)
a detective or murder story
Hercule Poirot is the name of the detective in Agatha Christie's whodunnits.

yarn
a long story about exciting things that are hard to believe
My dad is always spinning yarns.

a
b
c
d
e
f
g
h
i
j
k
l
m
n
o
p
q
r
s
t
u
v
w
x
y
z

Strong

• strong, of people

beefy (informal)
large and strong
Most of the rugby players in the team are beefy men.

brawny

brawny
strong physically and having big muscles
The Spartan warriors of ancient Greece were big and brawny.

burly
big and strong
A big, burly policeman approached the gang.

muscular
having well-developed muscles
Everyone in the weightlifting team is very muscular.

• strong, of things

durable
lasting a long time
Leather is a durable material.

hard-wearing
remaining in a good condition for a long time
The carpet on the staircase needs to be hard-wearing.

heavy-duty
stronger than usual or normal
The workers' overalls are made of heavy-duty cotton.

The opposite of strong is weak.

Did you know?

The word tuff (said the same as **tough**) is a type of rock formed by compacted volcanic ash.

sturdy
strong and well made
Don't forget to pack some sturdy shoes, as we'll be doing a lot of walking.

tough
strong and difficult to break
Children's toys are often made of very tough plastic.

indestructible
impossible to break
We guarantee that our plastic storage boxes are indestructible.

mighty
strong and powerful
The mighty elephant is strong enough to flip a car over onto its side.

mighty

powerful
very strong
Kangaroos use their powerful back legs to jump along.

robust
strong and well built
The front door needs to be more robust than doors inside the house.

• **strong-tasting**

hot
making your mouth burn, of food
This curry is so hot.

pungent
strong, of food or smells
This salad dressing has a pungent smell, but tastes delicious.

spicy
strong because spices are in the food
I've added chilli powder to make the sauce more spicy.

a b c d e f g h i j k l m n o p q r **s** t u v w x y z

Stupid

• **words for describing ideas or other things that are stupid or not sensible**

absurd
completely stupid
The plan is absurd.
It will never work.

daft

daft
childishly stupid but
sometimes funny
Michael is very bright but
sometimes he has daft ideas.

dopey
silly or stupid
The dopey thief took his mask off
right in front of the CCTV camera.

foolish
stupid in a way that could cause
problems in the future
I think it would be foolish to plant
the seeds this early.

hare-brained
silly, not thinking carefully
about something
He had this hare-brained
idea of going to live on a
desert island.

idiotic
very stupid, sometimes risky
The game seems idiotic to me. All
you do is run around shouting.

irresponsible
doing something stupid because
you didn't think carefully
It was irresponsible to leave the
back door open when the postman
came, as the dogs escaped.

pointless
silly and a waste of time
It's pointless arguing with him. He
won't change his mind.

ridiculous
unbelievably stupid
That's a ridiculous idea! We can't be in two places at the same time.

silly
childishly stupid, sometimes in a funny way
We played a few silly games but they were fun.

unwise
stupid in a way that could cause problems, not sensible
It is unwise to exercise without drinking plenty of water.

wacky (informal)
silly but fun
We laughed at all the wacky characters in the film.

The opposite of stupid is sensible.

In other words

as thick as two short planks
very stupid and unintelligent
Don't expect me to answer the question. I'm as thick as two short planks!

to play the fool
to act in a silly way to make people laugh
Sam is always playing the fool.

• **not intelligent**

dim
slow to understand or learn
Now I get what you mean. Sorry to be so dim!

thick (informal)
not intelligent at all
You'll probably think I'm thick, but I can't understand a word of these instructions.

a b c d e f g h i j k l m n o p q r s t u v w x y z

a b c d e f g h i j k l m n o p q r **s** t u v w x y z

Surprised

• surprised

amazed
so surprised you can't quite believe what has happened
We were amazed by some of the card tricks.

astonished amazed
very surprised that something has happened
I'm astonished he won the race.

astounded
very surprised or shocked
We were astounded by the news.

flabbergasted (informal)
very surprised, shocked
Our neighbours were flabbergasted when the elderly lady was arrested for spying.

gobsmacked (very informal)
so shocked that you cannot speak
I was gobsmacked when they told me I'd won the award.

open-mouthed
with an open mouth because you are so surprised
Fans were left open-mouthed when the striker suddenly announced his retirement.

shocked
very surprised by something bad
We were shocked by their behaviour.

speechless
so surprised that you can't talk
When they told us the price we were speechless.

speechless

startled
surprised or worried
She looked startled when she heard the sound of a key in the lock.

stunned
very surprised or shocked
Viewers were stunned by the violence in the television programme.

• **surprising**

breathtaking
surprisingly beautiful or exciting
The views from the top of the hill are breathtaking.

incredible
so surprising you can hardly believe it
It's incredible that no one realized the two men were robbers.

staggering

In other words

you could have knocked me down with a feather!
something you say when you are really surprised
You could have knocked me down with a feather when the lights came on and everybody shouted "Surprise!"

staggering
extremely surprising and shocking
The rocket launch cost a staggering amount of money.

unexpected
surprising because you didn't expect it
The player made several unexpected moves, which helped him win the match.

a b c d e f g h i j k l m n o p q r **s** t u v w x y z

a b c d e f g h i j k l m n o p q r s **t** u v w x y z

Take

• to take hold of

clutch
to take hold of something tightly, often out of fear
The little girl clutched her mother's arm.

grab/seize
to take hold of something suddenly and with force
She suddenly grabbed my hand.

snatch
to take something quickly and roughly
He snatched the book out of my hand.

withdraw
to remove or take something away from somewhere
I withdrew £50 from my bank account.

The opposite of take is give.

• to take something somewhere

bring
to take something in the direction of the person speaking
Please bring some food to share when you come to the party.

carry
to take something from one place to another
The helicopter carried fresh supplies of food and water to the stranded campers.

convey
to carry something such as liquid, electricity or gas from one place to another
Blood is conveyed from the heart through the body's arteries.

deliver
to take something, such as letters, parcels and newspapers, to a place
We had to deliver all of the Christmas cards on foot.

In other words

to take something in your stride
to be able to deal easily with problems and difficulties and not to let them bother you
He has lots of things to do but he just takes it in his stride.

• to take someone somewhere

accompany
to go somewhere with someone
Would you like me to accompany you to the dentist?

guide
to take someone to or around a place you know well
A young woman guided us around the modern art exhibition.

lead
to guide someone somewhere by going in front of them
The rescue team led us out of the cave and to safety.

fetch
to go to get something and then take it back
Could you fetch my glasses if you go upstairs?

shepherd
to guide or direct a group of people somewhere
Police shepherded shoppers away from the shopping centre and towards the green.

transport
to take lots of people or things from one place to another
Oil is transported in tankers.

a b c d e f g h i j k l m n o p q r s **t** u v w x y z

a b c d e f g h i j k l m n o p q r s t u v w x y z

Talk

• to talk

chat
to talk in a friendly way
We were chatting about what we did in the summer holidays.

chatter
to talk about things that are not important
They were chattering away in the corner.

converse (formal)
to talk to or have a conversation with someone
Parents' evening is a time when teachers and parents meet and converse.

discuss
to talk about something with other people, and hear their opinion on the matter
We need to discuss the plans for the new sports hall.

gossip
to talk about other people's lives
I could tell they were gossiping about something when I walked in.

natter (informal)
to talk about things for fun
We sat and nattered about our favourite bands all afternoon.

gossip

Did you know?

The word **talk** dates back to the 12th century. It is related to the Middle English word 'tale', which means 'story'.

rabbit on (informal)
to keep talking about something that is
usually boring
He's always rabbiting on about the goal he scored in the final.

waffle
to talk about something without saying anything useful
He waffled on for ages but he still didn't answer my question.

In other words

can talk the hind legs off a donkey
to be able to talk a lot
My Aunt Jo can talk the hind legs off a donkey.

witter (informal)
to talk for a long time without saying much
Jamie wittered on for hours about what we all should be doing.

• a talk

chat
a friendly talk
Let's go for coffee tomorrow. It would be nice to have a chat.

conversation
a talk between two or more people
We were just having a conversation about the new cinema in town.

discussion
a talk where people consider all sides of a topic or subject
The workers are having discussions with the bosses about salary and working conditions.

small talk
polite conversation about nothing in particular
The taxi driver made small talk as he drove us to the station.

speech
a formal talk to an audience
He gave a very long and boring speech.

speech

a b c d e f g h i j k l m n o p q r s **t** u v w x y z

a
b
c
d
e
f
g
h
i
j
k
l
m
n
o
p
q
r
s
t
u
v
w
x
y
z

Tell

• **to tell someone about something**

announce
to say something in public or formally
The boss announced that he would be retiring soon.

explain
to tell someone what something means or why it has happened
Abbie explained the rules to us.

inform
to give information about something to someone
This letter informs parents about the events going on this term.

keep posted
to tell someone what is happening as it happens
Keep me posted on how the team's training programme is going.

let know
to tell someone something
Let me know if you need any help.

narrate
to tell a story or to say what happened
The book is narrated by a famous actor.

notify
to tell someone officially about someone
Please make sure you notify us if you change your address or phone number.

relate (formal)
to tell someone what happened
He related the story of losing his passport.

Did you know?

'Barn' and 'yarn' have the same ending as **warn**, but are pronounced differently.

report
to give information about something to someone
We'll report on the results of our survey tomorrow.

• **to tell someone to do something**

advise
to tell, to give advice to someone
They advised us to avoid the high street because of all the roadworks.

brief
to give someone instructions
The soldiers were briefed for their next mission.

command
to tell someone firmly to do something
The officer commanded his soldiers to break down the door.

instruct
to tell someone to do something officially
They instructed us to move behind the line.

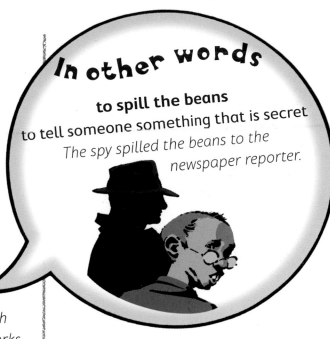

In other words

to spill the beans
to tell someone something that is secret
The spy spilled the beans to the newspaper reporter.

order
to tell someone to do something firmly
Jack was ordered to sweep the kitchen floor.

order

warn
to tell someone that there might be danger or problems ahead
He warned us not to go into the room at the end of the corridor.

a b c d e f g h i j k l m n o p q r s **t** u v w x y z

a b c d e f g h i j k l m n o p q r s t u v w x y z

Think

believe
to think that something is correct
I believe she used to live in Leeds.

brood
to keep thinking about something that upsets you
Don't just sit there brooding. Do something about it!

brood

concentrate
to think hard about something and pay attention
I can't concentrate on my work with all that noise outside.

consider
to think about something that you might do
We're considering going to France.

contemplate
to think seriously or deeply about something
We're contemplating major changes in the department.

imagine
to believe that something is probably true
I imagine he has had a very hard life.

meditate
to think deeply about something for a long time
I meditate for twenty minutes every morning.

meditate

In other words

to put your thinking cap on
To consider something seriously and come up with solutions or answers
I'll put my thinking cap on and come up with some ideas.

muse
to think carefully about something for a long time
I mused about what children's lives must have been like in Victorian times.

ponder
to think carefully about a difficult question or a problem
He pondered over the meaning of the words in the sentence.

reckon (informal)
to think or suppose
I reckon it'll cost about £5.

reflect
to think carefully about something
We need time to reflect on what has happened.

regard
to have an opinion of someone or something
I've always regarded you as a very clever and sensible person.

suppose
to think that something is probably true
I suppose you'll be going to the match on Saturday.

suspect
to think that something is probably true
I suspect there will be a question about gravity in the test.

weigh up
to think carefully about the advantages and disadvantages of something before making a decision
We have to weigh up what facilities people would like compared to what they will cost.

a b c d e f g h i j k l m n o p q r s **t** u v w x y z

Throw

cast (formal)
to throw off or get rid of something
The club has cast off its old reputation and is a much better place now.

catapult
to throw something forward with great force
The passengers were catapulted out of their seats when the train suddenly stopped.

chuck

chuck
(informal)
to throw something carelessly
Don't chuck litter on the ground.

fling
to throw or move something with great force
She flung herself down on the sofa.

flip
to throw something a little way up in the air so that it turns over
Can I try to flip the next pancake?

heave
to throw something heavy
They heaved the sacks onto the back of the truck.

hurl
to throw something with great force
He hurled the spear at the target.

lob
to throw something high into the air
We lobbed the ball over the fence.

pass
to throw the ball to another player on the same team
Quick! Pass it over here!

pass

pelt

pelt
to throw things at someone
or something repeatedly
*The clowns pelted each
other with tomatoes.*

In other words

to throw a wobbly
to get very angry or upset
*My sister threw a wobbly when she
found out that I'd borrowed her new dress
without asking her.*

to throw in the towel
to stop doing something because you
don't think you can succeed
*The boxer grew tired of fighting and
threw in the towel.*

scatter
to throw or sprinkle things
around in different places
*She scattered the seeds on
the ground.*

sling (informal)
to throw something carelessly
*Don't just sling the book on
the table.*

strew
to throw things around
untidily
*The bedroom floor was strewn
with her clothes.*

toss
to throw something with a
quick, small movement
Toss me that cushion, will you?

a b c d e f g h i j k l m n o p q r s **t** u v w x y z

Tired

dead beat (informal)
very tired
Sorry, I've got to rest. I'm dead beat.

dog-tired
extremely tired
I'm dog-tired and hungry after my long day.

drained
tired, without any energy left
I felt drained after my karate class.

drowsy
tired and sleepy
The heat made us drowsy so we went up to bed.

exhausted
very tired after doing something that used up your energy
You walked all the way? You must be exhausted.

fed up
tired of doing something
I'm fed up of playing this game. It's been going on too long.

flagging
starting to lose energy
You could see she was flagging after staying up late the night before.

jet-lagged
tired after a long flight from a place in a different time zone
I can hardly keep awake, as I'm still jet-lagged.

shattered (informal)
very tired
I'm absolutely shattered. Is it okay if we stay at home tonight?

drained

flagging

a b c d e f g h i j k l m n o p q r s **t** u v w x y z

a b c d e f g h i j k l m n o p q r s **t** u v w x y z

sleepy
ready to go to sleep
*Go on up to bed. You
look sleepy.*

sluggish
tired and lazy
*I feel very sluggish
after that heavy meal.*

In other words

to be sick and tired of something
to feel angry or bored because
something has been happening
for a long time
I'm sick and tired of all this ironing.

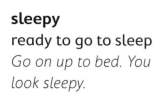

sleepy

weary
to feel tired after doing
something for a long period
of time
*We had been walking all day and
felt very weary.*

tired out
very tired after a lot of
physical effort
*That's it! We have to stop running.
I'm tired out.*

worn out
extremely tired
*Dad's been working in the garden
all day. He must be worn out.*

Try

a b c d e f g h i j k l m n o p q r s t u v w x y z

attempt
to try to do something
I attempted to speak to him in the corridor but he turned away and walked off.

do your best
to try as hard as you can
Don't worry if you don't get every question correct. Just do your best.

endeavour
to try to do something
The manager endeavoured to get all the workers to attend the meeting.

make an effort
to try hard
I made a big effort to meet new people when I moved to another town.

persevere
to keep trying and never give up
She persevered to row the boat across the lake.

persist
to continue to do something even if it's the wrong thing to do
If you persist with this behaviour, I shall have to ask you to leave.

sample

sample
to try or taste a small amount of food or drink
I asked Grandma to sample the sauce to see if it had enough salt.

seek (formal)
to try
The supermarket sought to reassure customers that the food was safe.

persevere

Did you know?

Words that rhyme with **struggle** include juggle, smuggle and snuggle.

strive
to try to do something difficult
We must strive to eliminate poverty in the world.

struggle

struggle
to try very hard to do something you find difficult
I struggled home in the snow and ice.

taste
to try a small amount of food or drink
Taste this soup and tell me what you think.

test
to try something out to see if it works or if it is safe
Doctors tested the new drug on volunteers.

In other words

to bend over backwards
to try really hard, even when it is inconvenient for you
She bent over backwards to be helpful to new members of staff.

to pull out all the stops
to try as hard as you can to make something a success
The children and teachers pulled out all the stops to make Open Day a success.

a b c d e f g h i j k l m n o p q r s **t** u v w x y z

a b c d e f g h i j k l m n o p q r s t u v w x y z

Very

absolutely
very, as much as possible
You look absolutely fantastic.

completely
in every way
There's no point in coming to the lesson completely unprepared.

decidedly
very much, in an obvious way
The results this year are decidedly better than those last year.

Did you know?

We don't use **very** with words that already have a strong meaning. For example, we don't say "I was very astounded." Instead we say something such as, "I was completely astounded."

exceedingly
extremely, to a very great degree
I have always found maths exceedingly difficult.

exceptionally
very, much more than usual
He's an exceptionally talented musician.

exceptionally

extremely
very
The book about dinosaurs is extremely interesting.

highly
very
Computer programmers are highly skilled people.

noticeably
very, in a way that is easy for people to see
The sports centre is noticeably busier in the school holidays.

particularly
especially
The judges were particularly impressed with her gymnastic routine.

quite
very much
They are twins but their personalities are quite different.

really

really
very
It's really hot in here – may I open the window?

remarkably
very much so, in a surprising way
The results were remarkably good this year.

super (prefix)
very, or more than usual
Only the super-rich can afford to buy a yacht.

terribly (informal)
very
I'm terribly sorry I'm late; I overslept.

truly
very, truthfully
I'm truly sorry about the broken window.

ultra (prefix)
very
The gallery is in an ultra-modern building.

truly

> **The opposite of very is slightly or fairly.**

a
b
c
d
e
f
g
h
i
j
k
l
m
n
o
p
q
r
s
t
u
v
w
x
y
z

a b c d e f g h i j k l m n o p q r s t u v w x y z

Walk

amble
to walk slowly and in a leisurely way
He was ambling along the street.

creep
to walk quietly, slowly and secretly
Let's creep up on Dad and surprise him.

hike
to walk a long way, usually in the country
We hiked up the hill and found a good place to have our picnic.

limp
to walk dragging one foot because it hurts
The injured player limped slowly off the football pitch.

march
to walk together using strong, regular steps
The group of soldiers marched proudly past the flag.

plod
to walk slowly and with difficulty
We plodded through the muddy fields for more than an hour.

creep

Did you know?

Limp as a verb means to walk dragging one leg. **Limp** as an adjective means soft or floppy.

roam

to walk about not having any firm plans about where you want to go

There is nothing to do in this town so we just roam around the streets in the evening.

saunter

to walk slowly and in a relaxed way

I sauntered down the road, looking in the shop windows.

tiptoe

stride

to walk confidently with big steps
He strode into the room.

stroll

to walk slowly and comfortably
We strolled through the park.

swagger

to walk very confidently, and in a way that shows you think you are important

The young man swaggered into the room grinning from ear to ear.

tiptoe

to walk on your toes, trying not to make a noise

I tiptoed past their bedroom door.

trek

to walk a long way, especially in hills or mountains

I'd like to trek in the Himalayas.

wade

to walk through water

I waded into the pond to retrieve the ball.

wander

to walk without a purpose or because you are lost

They wandered in the forest for hours before they found the camp.

a
b
c
d
e
f
g
h
i
j
k
l
m
n
o
p
q
r
s
t
u
v
w
x
y
z

Want

aspire to
to want or hope to do something or be something, and work towards it
The story is about a girl who aspired to stardom.

crave
to want something so much that you can't think about anything else
I woke up craving chocolate.

crave

desire
to want something very much
You can have whatever you desire. There's something for everyone.

fancy (informal)
to want something
Do you fancy going for a walk?

feel like
to want to do something
I don't feel like going for a walk just now.

hanker after

hanker after
to think about something that you want but can't have
After a week at school, we were hankering after Mum's cooking.

hope
to want or expect something to happen
I hope our team wins.

long for
to want something very much
She longed for some peace and quiet.

a
b
c
d
e
f
g
h
i
j
k
l
m
n
o
p
q
r
s
t
u
v
w
x
y
z

wish
to want something to happen
I wish they'd hurry up and get here.

would like
to want
I would like a cup of tea.

yearn for

yearn for
to want something so much that you feel sad without it
The prisoner yearned for freedom.

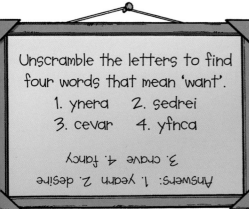

Unscramble the letters to find four words that mean 'want'.

1. ynera   2. sedrei
3. cevar   4. yfnca

Answers: 1. yearn 2. desire
3. crave 4. fancy

• a feeling of wanting something

ambition
a wish to do something in your life
My ambition is to be in a pop band.

dream
something that you want to happen very much
My dream is to play for England.

impulse
a sudden feeling that you want to do or have something, without thinking first whether it is a good idea
I bought this bag on impulse.

target
an aim or goal that you want to achieve
Our target is to raise £500 for new equipment.

whim
a sudden feeling that you want to do or have something
He bought a sports car on a sudden whim.

a
b
c
d
e
f
g
h
i
j
k
l
m
n
o
p
q
r
s
t
u
v
w
x
y
z

Win

a b c d e f g h i j k l m n o p q r s t u v **w** x y z

• a win

achievement
something that you succeed
in doing
*Setting a new school record was an
outstanding achievement.*

conquest
a victory over a country or place,
usually after winning a battle
*The Norman Conquest was led by
William the Conqueror.*

conquest

landslide
when one side or candidate gets
many more votes than another
*The voting revealed that we had
won by a landslide.*

success
a win, especially in a series of
games, matches or fights
I'm so proud at the team's success.

triumph
a very great win in something
difficult or important
*It was a great triumph for their
team.*

walkover

victory
a win in a
game,
competition
or battle
*The streets were full
of people celebrating
the army's victory.*

walkover (informal)
a very easy win,
especially in sport
*The third set was a
walkover for her.*

gain
to get or win something
*Our company gained several
  awards for our new designs.*

win easily
  to win a race or game without
  a lot of difficulty
  *They won the first few events
  easily.*

In other words

to sweep the board
to win every prize or all the points
*Our class swept the board at the
lower school sports day, winning
the football, rugby and
hockey tournaments.*

win hands down

• to win

beat
to do better than someone else
Josh beat me at draughts.

defeat
to win a victory over someone
*We need to defeat the French team
in order to go through to the next
round.*

come/finish first
to win a race or competition
*Whoever comes first will recieve the
gold medal.*

win hands down
to win easily
Imogen won the race hands down!

The opposite of win is lose.

a b c d e f g h i j k l m n o p q r s t u v **w** x y z

a b c d e f g h i j k l m n o p q r s t u v w x y z

Work

beaver away (informal)
to work hard at something
You've been beavering away at your homework for ages.

beaver away

be employed
to have a job or work somewhere
My mum is employed by the local council.

Did you know?

Like **beaver away**, animals appear in other phrases. 'Horse around' means to fool about.

be industrious
to work very hard and get lots of things done
The workers here are industrious and efficient.

operate
to work a machine
Does anyone know how to operate the washing machine?

push yourself

push yourself
to force yourself to work hard
If I push myself, I will finish this job by midday.

run
to work or go, of a machine
The machine isn't running. Is it switched on?

slave away (informal)
to work extremely hard at
something that you do not enjoy
*I've been slaving away in the kitchen
all day.*

slog (away) (informal)
to work hard at something
difficult or boring
*I've been slogging away at my
geography project for weeks.*

toil (away)
to do boring work for
a long time
*A hard-working team
of volunteers toiled
away in the garden
all afternoon.*

grind
difficult and boring work
*Memorizing your times tables is a
bit of a grind, but it's worth it.*

grind

• work you do

drudgery
work that is physically hard and
boring
My job is nothing but drudgery.

duties
things that you have to do as part
of your job
I have lots of duties to do each day.

job
the work that a person does to
get money
Mum is looking for a new job.

labour
work, particularly hard
physical work
*Building a new garage will involve
five days of difficult labour.*

a b c d e f g h i j k l m n o p q r s t u v **w** x y z

a
b
c
d
e
f
g
h
i
j
k
l
m
n
o
p
q
r
s
t
u
v
w
x
y
z

Wrong

at fault
having done something wrong
*The owner is at fault. He should
have kept the dog on a lead.*

false
not right or true
*She gave the
policeman a false
name and
address.*

faulty
not working
correctly
*The exhaust on your car must be
faulty, it's blowing out smoke.*

foolish
not right, silly
*That was a foolish thing to say.
Now she's upset.*

illegal
wrong because it is against
the law
*It is illegal to drop litter from
your car.*

faulty

immoral
morally wrong
Stealing is immoral.

inaccurate
not correct or exactly right
*The figures in this chart are
inaccurate.*

inappropriate
not right for the time or place
*Jeans are inappropriate for a
wedding.*

The opposite of wrong is right.

a
b
c
d
e
f
g
h
i
j
k
l
m
n
o
p
q
r
s
t
u
v
w
x
y
z

incorrect
wrong, not correct
Some of your spellings are incorrect.

mistaken
wrong in what you think
You must be mistaken if you think you saw me. I was away on holiday.

out of order (informal)
wrong, unsuitable
Your behaviour at the meeting was completely out of order.

sinful
morally wrong, against the teachings of God and your religion
Do you think stealing is sinful?

In other words

two wrongs don't make a right
just because someone has done something bad to you, doesn't mean that you should do something bad to them
Even if your sister did pull your hair, it was wrong to pull hers. Two wrongs don't make a right, you know.

Did you know?

Words with negative meanings often have a 'un–' or 'in–' prefix, such as **untrue** and **inappropriate**.

unacceptable
wrong and not acceptable to people
Shouting in the classroom is unacceptable behaviour.

untrue
wrong, not true
It's untrue to say that I'm not making an effort.

wicked
morally wrong
Pinching your brother for no reason was a wicked thing to do.

a b c d e f g h i j k l m n o p q r s t u v w x **y** z

Young

• a young person

adolescent
a young person who is developing into an adult
The club puts on activities for adolescents.

bairn
a Scottish word for a child
Bring the bairns with you next time.

infant
a baby or young child
The flight attendants have special seat belts for infants.

junior
a young or younger person
The juniors have their lunch at noon and the seniors have theirs at a quarter to one.

juvenile (formal)
a young person
Juveniles make up 20 percent of the population.

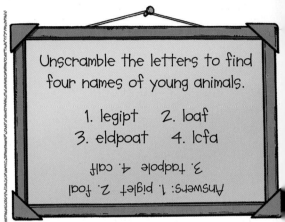

Unscramble the letters to find four names of young animals.

1. legipt　　2. loaf
3. eldpoat　　4. lcfa

Answers: 1. piglet　2. foal
3. tadpole　4. calf

kid (informal)
a child
The kids are playing together nicely.

minor
a legal term for a person who is not an adult
Minors must be accompanied by an adult.

infant

nipper (informal)
a young child
I remember when I was nipper.

teenager
someone between the ages of
thirteen and nineteen
The disco is for teenagers.

toddler
a young child just learning
to walk
*You have to have eyes in the back of
your head when there's a toddler
around.*

youngster (informal)
a young person or young
teenager
*There is nothing for the youngsters
to do in this village.*

youth
a boy or a young man,
usually when talking
about them in a
negative way
*A gangs of youths was
hanging around the chip shop.*

• young

immature
not yet fully grown or developed
*Scientists carried out the study on
both adult and immature animals.*

little
describing a sister or brother who
is younger than you
My little brother is learning to swim.

little

small
young, usually less than ten years
of age
*Dad says that when he was small
no one had computers or mobile
phones.*

**The opposite of
young is old.**

a b c d e f g h i j k l m n o p q r s t u v w x y z

Index

All the synonyms and their headwords in the thesaurus are listed alphabetically here. Simply look up the word you want to use — the headword for that entry is listed opposite in **bold** type.

Aa

a breeze	see	**Easy**
a doddle	see	**Easy**
a fortune	see	**money**
a man/woman of means	see	**Rich**
abandon	see	**Stop**
abhor	see	**Hate**
absolutely	see	**Very**
absurd	see	**Stupid**
accelerate	see	**Fast**
accept	see	**Get**
accepted	see	**Right**
accompany	see	**Take**
accurate	see	**Right**
achievement	see	**Win**
acquire	see	**Get**
activate	see	**Start**
actual	see	**Real**
admire	see	**Like**
adolescent	see	**Young**
adorable	see	**Lovely**
adore	see	**Like**
advise	see	**Tell**
affluent	see	**Rich**
afraid	see	**Frightened**
ageing	see	**Old**
ajar	see	**Open**
alike	see	**Same**
allowance	see	**Money**
ally	see	**Friend**
amazed	see	**Surprised**
amazing	see	**Good**
ambition	see	**Want**
amble	see	**Walk**
amusing	see	**Funny**
ancient	see	**Old**
anecdote	see	**Joke**
anecdote	see	**Story**
animosity	see	**Hate**
angelic	see	**Lovely**
announce	see	**Say**
announce	see	**Tell**
annoyed	see	**Angry**
another	see	**New**
antique	see	**Old**
appalling	see	**Bad**
appealing	see	**Nice**
appear	see	**Come**
apply	see	**Put**
appreciate	see	**Like**
approach	see	**Come**
appropriate	see	**Right**
approve of	see	**Like**
apt	see	**Right**
arduous	see	**Difficult**
arrange	see	**Put**
arrive	see	**Come**
artificial	see	**Pretend**
aspire to	see	**Want**
assemble	see	**Make**
assignment	see	**Job**
assorted	see	**Different**
astonished	see	**Surprised**
astounded	see	**Surprised**
at fault	see	**Wrong**
attempt	see	**Try**

Index

attractive	see	**Lovely**
attractive	see	**Nice**
authentic	see	**Real**
average	see	**Ordinary**
award	see	**Give**
awesome	see	**Good**
awfully	see	**Very**
awkward	see	**Difficult**

Bb

backbreaking	see	**Difficult**
badly off	see	**Poor**
bairn	see	**Young**
baking	see	**Hot**
balmy	see	**Hot**
banal	see	**Ordinary**
banter	see	**Joke**
bash	see	**Hit**
basic	see	**Easy**
batter	see	**Hit**
be devoted to	see	**Like**
be employed	see	**Work**
be fond of	see	**Like**
be industrious	see	**Work**
be joking	see	**Joke**
be keen on	see	**Like**
be kidding	see	**Joke**
be partial to	see	**Like**
beam	see	**Smile**
bear	see	**Carry**
beat	see	**Win**
beautiful	see	**Lovely**
beautiful	see	**Nice**
beaver away	see	**Work**
become	see	**Get**
beefy	see	**Strong**
beg	see	**Ask**
begin	see	**Start**
beginning	see	**Start**
behind someone's back	see	**Secret**

believe	see	**Think**
bellow	see	**Call**
belt	see	**Hit**
bequeath	see	**Give**
bicker	see	**Argue**
big	see	**Great**
billionaire	see	**Rich**
bin	see	**Box**
bitter	see	**Cold**
bland	see	**Ordinary**
bloomer	see	**Mistake**
bluff	see	**Pretend**
blunder	see	**Mistake**
blurt out	see	**Say**
bob	see	**Jump**
boiling	see	**Hot**
bolt	see	**Eat**
bolt	see	**Run**
bound	see	**Jump**
bowl	see	**Throw**
brainy	see	**Clever**
brand new	see	**New**
brawny	see	**Strong**
break	see	**Stop**
break down	see	**Break**
break into a smile	see	**Smile**
break off	see	**Stop**
brief	see	**Tell**
bright	see	**Clever**
brilliant	see	**Clever**
brilliant	see	**Good**
brilliant	see	**Great**
bring	see	**Carry**
bring	see	**Take**
brisk	see	**Fast**
broke	see	**Poor**
brood	see	**Think**
buddy	see	**Friend**
budge	see	**Move**
buffoon	see	**Funny**
build	see	**Make**

bulky	*see* **Big**	chore	*see* **Job**
bump	*see* **Hit**	chortle	*see* **Laugh**
burglar	*see* **Steal**	christen	*see* **Call**
burgle	*see* **Steal**	chuck	*see* **Throw**
burly	*see* **Strong**	chuckle	*see* **Laugh**
burst out laughing	*see* **Laugh**	chum	*see* **Friend**
buy	*see* **Get**	chunk	*see* **Bit**
bygone	*see* **Old**	circle	*see* **Friend**
		clandestine	*see* **Secret**

Cc

		clash	*see* **Argue**
cackle	*see* **Laugh**	classified	*see* **Secret**
cagey	*see* **Secret**	clear	*see* **Jump**
calm	*see* **Quiet**	clique	*see* **Friend**
can't bear	*see* **Hate**	cloak-and-dagger	*see* **Secret**
can't stand	*see* **Hate**	clobber	*see* **Hit**
carbon copy	*see* **Same**	clone	*see* **Same**
career	*see* **Job**	clout	*see* **Hit**
carry	*see* **Take**	clown	*see* **Funny**
cart	*see* **Carry**	clutch	*see* **Take**
carton	*see* **Box**	coins	*see* **Money**
case	*see* **Box**	collect	*see* **Get**
cash	*see* **Money**	colossal	*see* **Big**
casket	*see* **Box**	comedian	*see* **Funny**
cast	*see* **Throw**	come first	*see* **Win**
cat burglar	*see* **Steal**	come to a standstill	*see* **Stop**
catapult	*see* **Throw**	comfortable	*see* **Rich**
catch	*see* **Problem**	comical	*see* **Funny**
catch sight of	*see* **See**	command	*see* **Tell**
catnap	*see* **Sleep**	commence	*see* **Start**
cease	*see* **Stop**	comment	*see* **Say**
challenging	*see* **Difficult**	commonplace	*see* **Ordinary**
change	*see* **Money**	commute	*see* **Go**
change position	*see* **Move**	companion	*see* **Friend**
charming	*see* **Lovely**	completely	*see* **Very**
charming	*see* **Nice**	complicated	*see* **Difficult**
chat	*see* **Talk**	complication	*see* **Problem**
chatter	*see* **Talk**	component	*see* **Bit**
cheerful	*see* **Happy**	comrade	*see* **Friend**
chest	*see* **Box**	concealed	*see* **Secret**
chew	*see* **Eat**	concentrate	*see* **Think**
chilly	*see* **Cold**	conclude	*see* **Stop**

Index

concoct	*see* **Make**		cunning	*see* **Clever**
concrete	*see* **Real**		currency	*see* **Money**
confidential	*see* **Secret**		current	*see* **New**
conquest	*see* **Win**		cute	*see* **Lovely**
consider	*see* **Think**		cycle	*see* **Go**
consistent	*see* **Same**			
construct	*see* **Make**		**Dd**	
consult	*see* **Ask**		daft	*see* **Stupid**
consume	*see* **Eat**		dainty	*see* **Small**
contemplate	*see* **Think**		dart	*see* **Run**
contempt	*see* **Hate**		dash	*see* **Fast**
content	*see* **Happy**		dash	*see* **Bit**
contrasting	*see* **Different**		dash	*see* **Run**
contribute	*see* **Give**		dated	*see* **Old**
conventional	*see* **Ordinary**		dawn	*see* **Start**
conversation	*see* **Talk**		daydream	*see* **See**
converse	*see* **Talk**		dead beat	*see* **Tired**
convey	*see* **Carry**		debate	*see* **Argue**
convey	*see* **Take**		decent	*see* **Good**
cool	*see* **Cold**		decidedly	*see* **Very**
cool	*see* **Great**		defeat	*see* **Win**
correct	*see* **Right**		dejected	*see* **Sad**
counterpart	*see* **Same**		delighted	*see* **Happy**
covert	*see* **Secret**		delightful	*see* **Lovely**
crack	*see* **Break**		delightful	*see* **Nice**
crash into	*see* **Hit**		deliver	*see* **Carry**
crash out	*see* **Sleep**		deliver	*see* **Take**
crate	*see* **Box**		demanding	*see* **Difficult**
crave	*see* **Want**		deposit	*see* **Put**
crease up	*see* **Laugh**		depressed	*see* **Sad**
create	*see* **Make**		deprived	*see* **Poor**
creep	*see* **Walk**		desire	*see* **Want**
crisp	*see* **Cold**		desolate	*see* **Sad**
crony	*see* **Friend**		despise	*see* **Hate**
cross	*see* **Angry**		despondent	*see* **Sad**
cross-examine	*see* **Ask**		destitute	*see* **Poor**
crossing	*see* **Go**		detest	*see* **Hate**
crowd	*see* **Friend**		devour	*see* **Eat**
cruise	*see* **Go**		difficulty	*see* **Problem**
crumb	*see* **Bit**		dilemma	*see* **Problem**
cry	*see* **Call**		dim	*see* **Stupid**

dine	see	**Eat**
ding-dong	see	**Argue**
dinky	see	**Small**
disadvantaged	see	**Poor**
disagree	see	**Argue**
disagreeable	see	**Horrible**
disappointed	see	**Sad**
disapprove of	see	**Hate**
discuss	see	**Talk**
discussion	see	**Talk**
disdain	see	**Hate**
disgust	see	**Hate**
disgusting	see	**Horrible**
disintegrate	see	**Break**
dislike	see	**Hate**
dispute	see	**Argue**
dissimilar	see	**Different**
distressed	see	**Sad**
distressing	see	**Sad**
distinctive	see	**Different**
distinguished	see	**Great**
distribute	see	**Get**
diverse	see	**Different**
do your best	see	**Try**
dog-tired	see	**Tired**
dole out	see	**Give**
donate	see	**Give**
dopey	see	**Stupid**
dosh	see	**Money**
dote on	see	**Like**
down	see	**Drink**
down	see	**Sad**
doze	see	**Sleep**
drain	see	**Drink**
drained	see	**Tired**
draughty	see	**Cold**
draw near	see	**Come**
dread	see	**Afraid**
dreadful	see	**Bad**
dream	see	**See**
dream	see	**Want**

drift off	see	**Sleep**
drive	see	**Go**
drop	see	**Bit**
drop	see	**Stop**
drop in	see	**See**
drop off	see	**Sleep**
drowsy	see	**Tired**
drudgery	see	**Work**
drum	see	**Box**
dump	see	**Put**
duplicate	see	**Same**
durable	see	**Strong**
duties	see	**Work**
duty	see	**Job**

Ee

easy peasy	see	**Easy**
earn	see	**Get**
ecstatic	see	**Happy**
edge	see	**Move**
effortless	see	**Easy**
elderly	see	**Old**
elementary	see	**Easy**
embark on	see	**Start**
emigrate	see	**Move**
eminent	see	**Great**
enchanting	see	**Lovely**
end	see	**Stop**
endeavour	see	**Try**
enormous	see	**Big**
enormous	see	**Great**
enjoy	see	**Like**
enjoyable	see	**Good**
enjoyable	see	**Nice**
enquire	see	**Ask**
enter	see	**Come**
epic	see	**Story**
equivalent	see	**Same**
erect	see	**Make**
errand	see	**Job**
error	see	**Mistake**

Index

establish	*see*	**Start**
everyday	*see*	**Ordinary**
exact	*see*	**Right**
examine	*see*	**Look**
exceedingly	*see*	**Very**
excellent	*see*	**Good**
excellent	*see*	**Great**
exceptionally	*see*	**Very**
exclaim	*see*	**Say**
excursion	*see*	**Go**
exhausted	*see*	**Tired**
expedition	*see*	**Go**
explain	*see*	**Tell**
express	*see*	**Fast**
extremely	*see*	**Very**

F f

fable	*see*	**Story**
face lights up	*see*	**Smile**
factual	*see*	**Real**
fair	*see*	**Right**
fairy tale	*see*	**Story**
fake	*see*	**Pretend**
fall about	*see*	**Laugh**
fall apart	*see*	**Break**
false	*see*	**Wrong**
fancy	*see*	**Like**
fancy	*see*	**Want**
fantastic	*see*	**Good**
fantastic	*see*	**Great**
fashion	*see*	**Make**
fault	*see*	**Mistake**
faulty	*see*	**Wrong**
fear	*see*	**Frightened**
fearful	*see*	**Frightened**
fed up	*see*	**Sad**
fed up	*see*	**Tired**
feed	*see*	**Eat**
feel like	*see*	**Want**
fetch	*see*	**Carry**
fetch	*see*	**Get**

fetch	*see*	**Take**
feud	*see*	**Argue**
fiddly	*see*	**Difficult**
fidget	*see*	**Move**
fight	*see*	**Argue**
figure	*see*	**Money**
fine	*see*	**Good**
fine	*see*	**Nice**
finish	*see*	**Stop**
finish first	*see*	**Win**
first-class	*see*	**Great**
fitting	*see*	**Right**
flabbergasted	*see*	**Surprised**
flagging	*see*	**Tired**
flee	*see*	**Run**
fling	*see*	**Throw**
flip	*see*	**Throw**
flush	*see*	**Rich**
fly	*see*	**Go**
follow	*see*	**Get**
foolish	*see*	**Stupid**
foolish	*see*	**Wrong**
force	*see*	**Open**
form	*see*	**Make**
forty winks	*see*	**Sleep**
found	*see*	**Start**
fraction	*see*	**Bit**
fracture	*see*	**Break**
fragment	*see*	**Bit**
fragment	*see*	**Break**
freezing	*see*	**Cold**
fresh	*see*	**New**
friendly	*see*	**Nice**
frosty	*see*	**Cold**
fuming	*see*	**Angry**
furious	*see*	**Angry**
furtive	*see*	**Secret**

G g

gaffe	*see*	**Mistake**
gag	*see*	**Joke**

Index

gain	*see*	**Win**
gallop	*see*	**Run**
gambol	*see*	**Jump**
gang	*see*	**Friend**
gaping	*see*	**Open**
gargle	*see*	**Drink**
gaze	*see*	**Look**
generate	*see*	**Make**
genuine	*see*	**Real**
get cracking	*see*	**Start**
get going	*see*	**Start**
getting on	*see*	**Old**
ghastly	*see*	**Bad**
ghastly	*see*	**Horrible**
gifted	*see*	**Clever**
gigantic	*see*	**Big**
giggle	*see*	**Laugh**
glad	*see*	**Happy**
glance	*see*	**Look**
glare	*see*	**Look**
glimpse	*see*	**See**
glitch	*see*	**Problem**
globetrotting	*see*	**Go**
glum	*see*	**Sad**
go on a trip	*see*	**Go**
gobble	*see*	**Eat**
gobsmacked	*see*	**Surprised**
good-looking	*see*	**Lovely**
good-natured	*see*	**Nice**
goof	*see*	**Mistake**
gorge	*see*	**Eat**
gorgeous	*see*	**Lovely**
gossip	*see*	**Talk**
grab	*see*	**Take**
grand	*see*	**Great**
grant	*see*	**Give**
grant	*see*	**Money**
great	*see*	**Big**
great	*see*	**Good**
gremlin	*see*	**Problem**
grill	*see*	**Ask**

grin	*see*	**Smile**
grind	*see*	**Work**
groan	*see*	**Say**
grow	*see*	**Get**
gruelling	*see*	**Difficult**
guffaw	*see*	**Laugh**
guide	*see*	**Take**
gulp	*see*	**Drink**
guzzle	*see*	**Drink**

Hh

hair-raising	*see*	**Frightened**
halt	*see*	**Stop**
hand	*see*	**Give**
hanker after	*see*	**Want**
hare-brained	*see*	**Stupid**
hard	*see*	**Difficult**
hard up	*see*	**Poor**
hard-wearing	*see*	**Strong**
hare	*see*	**Run**
haul	*see*	**Carry**
have goose pimples	*see*	**Cold**
headache	*see*	**Problem**
heap	*see*	**Put**
heartfelt	*see*	**Real**
heave	*see*	**Throw**
heavy-duty	*see*	**Strong**
hibernate	*see*	**Sleep**
hiccup	*see*	**Problem**
hidden	*see*	**Secret**
hideous	*see*	**Horrible**
high-speed	*see*	**Fast**
highly	*see*	**Very**
hike	*see*	**Walk**
hilarious	*see*	**Funny**
hindrance	*see*	**Problem**
hint	*see*	**Say**
hitch	*see*	**Problem**
homesick	*see*	**Sad**
hoot with laughter	*see*	**Laugh**
hop	*see*	**Jump**

hope	*see*	**Want**
hopeless	*see*	**Bad**
horrible	*see*	**Bad**
horrid	*see*	**Horrible**
hot	*see*	**Strong**
howler	*see*	**Mistake**
huge	*see*	**Big**
humorous	*see*	**Funny**
hurdle	*see*	**Jump**
hurdle	*see*	**Problem**
hurl	*see*	**Throw**
hush-hush	*see*	**Secret**
hushed	*see*	**Quiet**

Ii

icy	*see*	**Cold**
ideal	*see*	**Right**
identical	*see*	**Same**
idiot-proof	*see*	**Easy**
idiotic	*see*	**Stupid**
idolize	*see*	**Like**
illegal	*see*	**Wrong**
imagine	*see*	**See**
imagine	*see*	**Think**
imbibe	*see*	**Drink**
immature	*see*	**Young**
immoral	*see*	**Wrong**
impersonate	*see*	**Pretend**
important	*see*	**Great**
important	*see*	**Big**
impossible	*see*	**Difficult**
impostor	*see*	**Pretend**
impoverished	*see*	**Poor**
impressive	*see*	**Good**
impulse	*see*	**Want**
in a flash	*see*	**Fast**
in high spirits	*see*	**Happy**
in jest	*see*	**Joke**
in private	*see*	**Secret**
inaccurate	*see*	**Wrong**
inappropriate	*see*	**Wrong**

inaudible	*see*	**Quiet**
incensed	*see*	**Angry**
inch	*see*	**Move**
incorrect	*see*	**Wrong**
incredible	*see*	**Surprised**
indestructible	*see*	**Strong**
indignant	*see*	**Angry**
individual	*see*	**Different**
income	*see*	**Money**
inept	*see*	**Bad**
infant	*see*	**Young**
inferior	*see*	**Bad**
inform	*see*	**Tell**
initiate	*see*	**Start**
innovative	*see*	**New**
insincere	*see*	**Pretend**
inspect	*see*	**Look**
instruct	*see*	**Tell**
intellectual	*see*	**Clever**
intelligent	*see*	**Clever**
interrogate	*see*	**Ask**
interview	*see*	**Ask**
invent	*see*	**Make**
irate	*see*	**Angry**
irresponsible	*see*	**Stupid**
irritable	*see*	**Angry**
irritated	*see*	**Angry**

Jj

jet-lagged	*see*	**Tired**
job	*see*	**Work**
jog	*see*	**Run**
jokey	*see*	**Funny**
jolly	*see*	**Happy**
journey	*see*	**Go**
junior	*see*	**Young**
just	*see*	**Right**
just out	*see*	**New**
juvenile	*see*	**Young**
joyful	*see*	**Happy**

Index

K k

keep posted	*see*	**Tell**
kid	*see*	**Young**
kind	*see*	**Nice**
kip	*see*	**Sleep**
knock	*see*	**Hit**
knock back	*see*	**Drink**
knock together	*see*	**Make**
knowledgeable	*see*	**Clever**

L l

laborious	*see*	**Difficult**
labour	*see*	**Work**
landslide	*see*	**Win**
lap up	*see*	**Drink**
large	*see*	**Big**
latest	*see*	**New**
launch	*see*	**Start**
lay	*see*	**Put**
lead	*see*	**Take**
lean	*see*	**Put**
leap	*see*	**Jump**
leg it	*see*	**Run**
legal tender	*see*	**Money**
legend	*see*	**Story**
lend	*see*	**Give**
let know	*see*	**Tell**
lifelike	*see*	**Real**
lift	*see*	**Carry**
light-hearted	*see*	**Funny**
likeable	*see*	**Nice**
limp	*see*	**Walk**
little	*see*	**Small**
little	*see*	**Young**
livid	*see*	**Angry**
loaded	*see*	**Rich**
loathe	*see*	**Hate**
lob	*see*	**Throw**
long for	*see*	**Want**
look amused	*see*	**Smile**
loot	*see*	**Steal**

lope	*see*	**Run**
love	*see*	**Like**
lovely	*see*	**Nice**
low	*see*	**Quiet**
low	*see*	**Sad**
lug	*see*	**Carry**
lukewarm	*see*	**Hot**
lunge	*see*	**Jump**

M m

mad	*see*	**Angry**
made-up	*see*	**Pretend**
magnate	*see*	**Rich**
magnificent	*see*	**Great**
magnificent	*see*	**Nice**
major	*see*	**Big**
make an effort	*see*	**Try**
make out	*see*	**See**
make-believe	*see*	**Pretend**
manufacture	*see*	**Make**
march	*see*	**Walk**
marvellous	*see*	**Good**
masquerade as	*see*	**Pretend**
massive	*see*	**Big**
match	*see*	**Same**
mate	*see*	**Friend**
mature	*see*	**Old**
meagre	*see*	**Small**
mean	*see*	**Horrible**
meditate	*see*	**Think**
mention	*see*	**Say**
mighty	*see*	**Strong**
millionaire	*see*	**Rich**
miniature	*see*	**Small**
minor	*see*	**Small**
minor	*see*	**Young**
minuscule	*see*	**Small**
minute	*see*	**Small**
mischievous	*see*	**Bad**
miserable	*see*	**Sad**
misjudge	*see*	**Mistake**

mission	*see*	**Job**
mistaken	*see*	**Wrong**
mix-up	*see*	**Mistake**
modern	*see*	**New**
morsel	*see*	**Bit**
mould	*see*	**Make**
move closer	*see*	**Come**
move nearer	*see*	**Come**
muffled	*see*	**Quiet**
mug	*see*	**Steal**
muggy	*see*	**Hot**
multimillionaire	*see*	**Rich**
mumble	*see*	**Say**
munch	*see*	**Eat**
mundane	*see*	**Ordinary**
muscular	*see*	**Strong**
muse	*see*	**Think**
muted	*see*	**Quiet**
mutter	*see*	**Say**
myth	*see*	**Story**

Nn

name	*see*	**Call**
nap	*see*	**Sleep**
narrate	*see*	**Tell**
nasty	*see*	**Bad**
nasty	*see*	**Horrible**
natter	*see*	**Talk**
naughty	*see*	**Bad**
needy	*see*	**Poor**
neutral	*see*	**Ordinary**
newcomer	*see*	**New**
newfangled	*see*	**New**
nibble	*see*	**Eat**
nick	*see*	**Steal**
nipper	*see*	**Young**
nippy	*see*	**Cold**
nippy	*see*	**Fast**
nod off	*see*	**Sleep**
noiseless	*see*	**Quiet**
nothing special	*see*	**Ordinary**

notice	*see*	**See**
noticeably	*see*	**Very**
normal	*see*	**Ordinary**
notify	*see*	**Tell**
novel	*see*	**New**
novel	*see*	**Story**

Oo

obnoxious	*see*	**Horrible**
observe	*see*	**Look**
obtain	*see*	**Get**
occupation	*see*	**Job**
off the latch	*see*	**Open**
one-liner	*see*	**Joke**
open	*see*	**Start**
open-mouthed	*see*	**Surprised**
opposite	*see*	**Different**
operate	*see*	**Work**
order	*see*	**Tell**
original	*see*	**New**
out of order	*see*	**Wrong**
outing	*see*	**Go**
outset	*see*	**Start**
outstanding	*see*	**Good**
overeat	*see*	**Eat**
overjoyed	*see*	**Happy**
oversight	*see*	**Mistake**

Pp

pack	*see*	**Box**
packet	*see*	**Box**
packing case	*see*	**Box**
page	*see*	**Call**
painless	*see*	**Easy**
pal	*see*	**Friend**
panic	*see*	**Frightened**
parable	*see*	**Story**
part	*see*	**Bit**
particularly	*see*	**Very**
pass	*see*	**Throw**
pass on	*see*	**Give**

Index

pause	see	**Stop**
peaceful	see	**Quiet**
peek	see	**Look**
peep	see	**Look**
peer	see	**Look**
pelt	see	**Throw**
penniless	see	**Poor**
perfect	see	**Right**
persevere	see	**Try**
persist	see	**Try**
personal	see	**Secret**
petite	see	**Small**
petrified	see	**Frightened**
petty	see	**Small**
phone	see	**Call**
pick a lock	see	**Open**
pickpocket	see	**Steal**
picture	see	**See**
picturesque	see	**Lovely**
piece	see	**Bit**
pile	see	**Put**
pilfer	see	**Steal**
pinch	see	**Bit**
pinch	see	**Steal**
pioneering	see	**New**
piping hot	see	**Hot**
play-act	see	**Pretend**
playmate	see	**Friend**
place	see	**Put**
plead	see	**Ask**
pleasant	see	**Lovely**
pleasant	see	**Nice**
pleased	see	**Happy**
pleasing	see	**Nice**
plod	see	**Walk**
plonk	see	**Put**
poach	see	**Steal**
pocket money	see	**Money**
pointless	see	**Stupid**
polish off	see	**Drink**
ponder	see	**Think**

poor	see	**Bad**
pop	see	**Put**
portion	see	**Bit**
pose as	see	**Pretend**
position	see	**Put**
post	see	**Job**
pounce	see	**Jump**
pound	see	**Hit**
poverty-stricken	see	**Poor**
powerful	see	**Strong**
practical joke	see	**Joke**
prank	see	**Joke**
precise	see	**Right**
present	see	**Give**
pretty	see	**Lovely**
prise	see	**Open**
proceed	see	**Come**
produce	see	**Make**
profession	see	**Job**
project	see	**Job**
pronounce	see	**Say**
prop	see	**Put**
proper	see	**Real**
proper	see	**Right**
prosperous	see	**Rich**
pummel	see	**Hit**
pump	see	**Ask**
pun	see	**Joke**
punch	see	**Hit**
punchline	see	**Joke**
pungent	see	**Strong**
puny	see	**Small**
purchase	see	**Get**
push yourself	see	**Work**
put it on	see	**Pretend**
put together	see	**Make**
put up	see	**Make**

Qq

quack	see	**Pretend**
quarrel	see	**Argue**

Index

quench	see	**Drink**
query	see	**Ask**
question	see	**Ask**
quick	see	**Clever**
quick	see	**Fast**
quickly	see	**Fast**
quip	see	**Joke**
quit	see	**Stop**
quite	see	**Very**
quiz	see	**Ask**

Rr

rabbit on	see	**Talk**
race	see	**Run**
rapid	see	**Fast**
reach	see	**Come**
real-life	see	**Real**
really	see	**Very**
receive	see	**Get**
recent	see	**New**
reckon	see	**Think**
recoil	see	**Jump**
reflect	see	**Think**
regard	see	**Think**
relate	see	**Tell**
relocate	see	**Move**
remark	see	**Say**
remarkably	see	**Very**
report	see	**Tell**
repulsive	see	**Horrible**
request	see	**Ask**
resemble	see	**Same**
resentful	see	**Angry**
responsibility	see	**Job**
rest	see	**Put**
retire	see	**Sleep**
retire	see	**Stop**
revolting	see	**Horrible**
reward	see	**Give**
rib-tickling	see	**Funny**
riddle	see	**Joke**

ridiculous	see	**Stupid**
ring	see	**Call**
roam	see	**Walk**
roar with laughter	see	**Laugh**
roasting	see	**Hot**
rob	see	**Steal**
robber	see	**Steal**
robust	see	**Strong**
role	see	**Job**
routine	see	**Ordinary**
row	see	**Argue**
run	see	**Work**
run-of-the-mill	see	**Ordinary**
rush	see	**Fast**
rush	see	**Run**

Ss

safe	see	**Box**
saga	see	**Story**
sail	see	**Go**
sample	see	**Try**
satirical	see	**Funny**
satisfied	see	**Happy**
saunter	see	**Walk**
scalding	see	**Hot**
scamper	see	**Run**
scared	see	**Frightened**
scary	see	**Frightened**
scatter	see	**Throw**
scoff	see	**Eat**
scorching	see	**Hot**
scream	see	**Call**
scrutinize	see	**Look**
scurry	see	**Run**
scuttle	see	**Run**
second-hand	see	**Old**
section	see	**Bit**
seek	see	**Try**
seething	see	**Angry**
segment	see	**Bit**
seize	see	**Take**

Index

send for	*see*	**Call**
senior	*see*	**Old**
serious	*see*	**Bad**
set	*see*	**Friend**
set in motion	*see*	**Start**
set up	*see*	**Start**
sham	*see*	**Pretend**
share out	*see*	**Give**
shatter	*see*	**Break**
shattered	*see*	**Tired**
shepherd	*see*	**Take**
shriek	*see*	**Call**
shift	*see*	**Move**
shivering	*see*	**Cold**
shrink	*see*	**Small**
shrivel	*see*	**Small**
shocked	*see*	**Surprised**
shocking	*see*	**Horrible**
shoplifter	*see*	**Steal**
shout	*see*	**Call**
shout	*see*	**Say**
show up	*see*	**Come**
siesta	*see*	**Sleep**
silent	*see*	**Quiet**
silly	*see*	**Stupid**
similar	*see*	**Same**
simper	*see*	**Smile**
simple	*see*	**Easy**
sincere	*see*	**Real**
sinful	*see*	**Wrong**
sip	*see*	**Drink**
sizeable	*see*	**Big**
skint	*see*	**Poor**
skip	*see*	**Jump**
slap	*see*	**Hit**
slapstick	*see*	**Funny**
slave away	*see*	**Work**
sleepy	*see*	**Tired**
slice	*see*	**Bit**
sling	*see*	**Throw**
slip	*see*	**Give**

slip	*see*	**Mistake**
sliver	*see*	**Bit**
slog	*see*	**Work**
sluggish	*see*	**Tired**
slumber	*see*	**Sleep**
slurp	*see*	**Drink**
smack	*see*	**Hit**
small	*see*	**Young**
small talk	*see*	**Talk**
smart	*see*	**Clever**
smash	*see*	**Break**
smile from ear to ear	*see*	**Smile**
smirk	*see*	**Smile**
snack	*see*	**Eat**
snag	*see*	**Problem**
snap	*see*	**Break**
snarl	*see*	**Say**
snatch	*see*	**Take**
sneer	*see*	**Smile**
snigger	*see*	**Laugh**
snooze	*see*	**Sleep**
snort with laughter	*see*	**Laugh**
soft	*see*	**Quiet**
solid	*see*	**Real**
sound out	*see*	**Ask**
spat	*see*	**Argue**
speak	*see*	**Say**
speech	*see*	**Talk**
speechless	*see*	**Quiet**
speechless	*see*	**Surprised**
speedy	*see*	**Fast**
spicy	*see*	**Hot**
spicy	*see*	**Strong**
splendid	*see*	**Good**
splinter	*see*	**Break**
split	*see*	**Break**
spooky	*see*	**Frightened**
spot	*see*	**See**
spot on	*see*	**Right**
sprint	*see*	**Run**
spring	*see*	**Jump**

Index

spy	see	**See**		super	see	**Very**
spy on	see	**Look**		superb	see	**Good**
squabble	see	**Argue**		supersonic	see	**Fast**
squint	see	**Look**		support	see	**Carry**
squirm	see	**Move**		suppose	see	**Think**
stack	see	**Put**		survey	see	**Ask**
staggering	see	**Surprised**		suspect	see	**Think**
stall	see	**Stop**		swagger	see	**Walk**
stand	see	**Put**		swallow	see	**Drink**
stand-up	see	**Funny**		sweet	see	**Lovely**
standard	see	**Ordinary**		sweltering	see	**Hot**
stare	see	**Look**		swift	see	**Fast**
start	see	**Jump**		swig	see	**Drink**
startled	see	**Frightened**		swing	see	**Move**
startled	see	**Surprised**		synonym	see	**Same**
state-of-the-art	see	**New**				
still	see	**Quiet**		**T t**		
stir	see	**Move**		taciturn	see	**Quiet**
straightforward	see	**Easy**		take	see	**Carry**
streetwise	see	**Clever**		taken aback	see	**Surprised**
strenuous	see	**Difficult**		tale	see	**Story**
strew	see	**Throw**		talented	see	**Clever**
stride	see	**Walk**		talented	see	**Good**
strike	see	**Hit**		tally	see	**Same**
strive	see	**Try**		tangible	see	**Real**
stroll	see	**Walk**		target	see	**Want**
struggle	see	**Try**		task	see	**Job**
study	see	**Look**		taste	see	**Try**
stunning	see	**Lovely**		tea chest	see	**Box**
stunned	see	**Surprised**		tear	see	**Run**
sturdy	see	**Strong**		tease	see	**Joke**
subdued	see	**Quiet**		teenager	see	**Young**
success	see	**Win**		tell	see	**Say**
suitable	see	**Right**		terrible	see	**Bad**
sultry	see	**Hot**		terribly	see	**Very**
sum	see	**Money**		terrific	see	**Great**
summon	see	**Call**		terrified	see	**Frightened**
sundry	see	**Different**		test	see	**Try**
sunny	see	**Happy**		the haves	see	**Rich**
sunny	see	**Nice**		thick	see	**Stupid**
super	see	**Great**		thief	see	**Steal**

Index

thrash	*see*	**Hit**
thrilled	*see*	**Happy**
thriller	*see*	**Story**
thump	*see*	**Hit**
tiff	*see*	**Argue**
tight-lipped	*see*	**Quiet**
tiny	*see*	**Small**
tiptoe	*see*	**Walk**
tired out	*see*	**Tired**
titchy	*see*	**Small**
titter	*see*	**Laugh**
toasty	*see*	**Hot**
toddler	*see*	**Young**
toil	*see*	**Work**
top secret	*see*	**Secret**
toss	*see*	**Throw**
tote	*see*	**Carry**
tough	*see*	**Difficult**
tough	*see*	**Strong**
tour	*see*	**Go**
trade	*see*	**Job**
tragic	*see*	**Sad**
transfer	*see*	**Move**
transport	*see*	**Carry**
transport	*see*	**Move**
transport	*see*	**Take**
travel	*see*	**Go**
trek	*see*	**Walk**
tricky	*see*	**Difficult**
triumph	*see*	**Win**
trivial	*see*	**Small**
true	*see*	**Real**
true	*see*	**Right**
truly	*see*	**Very**
trunk	*see*	**Box**
tuck in	*see*	**Eat**
turn	*see*	**Get**
turn up	*see*	**Come**
tycoon	*see*	**Rich**
typical	*see*	**Ordinary**
typo	*see*	**Mistake**

Uu

ultra	*see*	**Very**
unacceptable	*see*	**Wrong**
unalike	*see*	**Different**
unbolt	*see*	**Open**
unbutton	*see*	**Open**
uncomplicated	*see*	**Easy**
undercover	*see*	**Secret**
underprivileged	*see*	**Poor**
understand	*see*	**Get**
undertaking	*see*	**Job**
unexpected	*see*	**Surprised**
unfasten	*see*	**Open**
unfold	*see*	**Open**
unhappy	*see*	**Sad**
uniform	*see*	**Same**
unique	*see*	**Different**
unlike	*see*	**Different**
unlock	*see*	**Open**
unpleasant	*see*	**Horrible**
unremarkable	*see*	**Ordinary**
unscrew	*see*	**Open**
untrue	*see*	**Wrong**
unwise	*see*	**Stupid**
unwrap	*see*	**Open**
unzip	*see*	**Open**
up to date	*see*	**New**
up to the minute	*see*	**New**
upset	*see*	**Sad**
used	*see*	**Old**
useless	*see*	**Bad**
user-friendly	*see*	**Easy**
usual	*see*	**Ordinary**

Vv

varied	*see*	**Different**
various	*see*	**Different**
vast	*see*	**Big**
vault	*see*	**Jump**
verbatim	*see*	**Same**
veteran	*see*	**Old**

Index

victory	*see*	**Win**
view	*see*	**Look**
vile	*see*	**Horrible**
vintage	*see*	**Old**
visit	*see*	**Come**
visit	*see*	**See**
visualize	*see*	**See**
vocation	*see*	**Job**
voyage	*see*	**Go**

Ww

wacky	*see*	**Stupid**
wade	*see*	**Walk**
waffle	*see*	**Talk**
walkover	*see*	**Win**
wander	*see*	**Walk**
warm	*see*	**Hot**
warn	*see*	**Tell**
watch	*see*	**Look**
wealth	*see*	**Money**
wealthy	*see*	**Rich**
weary	*see*	**Tired**
wedge	*see*	**Bit**
weigh up	*see*	**Think**
well-heeled	*see*	**Rich**
well-off	*see*	**Rich**
well-to-do	*see*	**Rich**
whack	*see*	**Hit**
whim	*see*	**Want**
whisper	*see*	**Say**
whodunnit	*see*	**Story**
whopping	*see*	**Big**
wicked	*see*	**Wrong**
wide open	*see*	**Open**
wiggle	*see*	**Move**
win easily	*see*	**Win**
win hands down	*see*	**Win**
wintry	*see*	**Cold**
wise	*see*	**Clever**
wisecrack	*see*	**Joke**
wish	*see*	**Want**

withdraw	*see*	**Take**
witness	*see*	**See**
witter	*see*	**Talk**
witty	*see*	**Funny**
wolf	*see*	**Eat**
wonderful	*see*	**Good**
wonderful	*see*	**Great**
word for word	*see*	**Same**
worn out	*see*	**Tired**
worship	*see*	**Like**
would like	*see*	**Want**
wriggle	*see*	**Move**
writhe	*see*	**Move**

Yy

yell	*see*	**Call**
yawning	*see*	**Open**
youngster	*see*	**Young**
youth	*see*	**Young**
yearn for	*see*	**Want**
yarn	*see*	**Story**
zip	*see*	**Run**

Acknowledgements

Dreamstime.com
Front cover (kitten) Isselee, (rabbit) Jonnysek;
23 Museman; 26 Egal; 62(b) Mirkamoksha;
145(l) Jonnysek; 188 Mrmarshall

Fotolia.com
Back cover (frog) alle, (guitar) Stefan Balk, (ice cream) JLV Image Works; 17 Andrew Bruce;
19 Tomasz Trojanowski; 31(t) NiDerLander;
43 JLV Image Works; 44 Joe Gough; 50(b)
Maksim Shebeko; 70 Stefan Balk; 86(t) Alx; 94
Fatman73; 105 Oleg Belyakov; 120(t); 126(l)
Joellen Armstrong; 136 FBC24; 138 Joe Gough;
140 klikk; 157 ivan kmit; 182(l) Malena und
Philipp K, (r) Eric Isselée

iStockphoto.com
25 DNY59; 32(t) Gary Wales; 41 coloroftime;
50(t) Jan Rysavy; 54 Seb Chandler; 73 P_Wei;
91(t) Tony Campbell; 116 Skeezer

Shutterstock.com
8 Kacso Sandor; 13 Richard Peterson;
22 violetkaipa; 24 Eric Isselée; 31(b) Eric Isselée;
35 I lomeStudio; 38 Jose AS Reyes; 49 alarifoto;
64 Dudarev Mikhail; 67 haveseen; 72 Subbotina
Anna; 75 Andrew Buckin; 77(t) Vladimir Wrangel,
(bl) Siberian Lena, (br) Golden Pixels LLC;
78 Stephen Mahar; 80 Madlen; 81(t) Vishnevskiy
Vasily, (b) Christopher Halloran; 82(t) Oleg
Zhevelev, (b) Loskutnikov; 84 terekhov igor;
85(l–r) jojof, RoJo Images, Geanina Bechea;
86(b) vilainecrevette; 88(t) Valentyn Volkov,
(b) michaeljung; 89(l) Kbiros, (r) Smileus;
91(b) Iwona Grodzka; 92 Eric Isselée; 95 Nata
Sdobnikova; 96(t) maxstockphoto, (b) Krasowit;
98 Atlaspix; 99 Vishnevskiy Vasily; 100 Sergieiev;
103(t) Borislav Borisov, (b) Mark William Penny;
107 viewgene; 108 Yurchyks; 110 Euro Color
Creative; 111 andere; 113 Vakhrushev Pavel;
117(l) marilyn barbone, (r) ULKASTUDIO;
119 infografick; 120(b) Nattika; 122 DM7;
123 Vitaly Titov & Maria Sidelnikova;
124(l) John Carnemolla, (r) alarifoto; 125
MaszaS; 126(r) tale; 128(t) Morgan Lane
Photography, (b) Elena Schweitzer; 129 Yasonya;
130(l) Eric Isselée, (r) Kotkin Vasily;
131 L_amica; 132 Granite; 133 Sandra van der
Steen; 134(t) Mayovskyy Andrew, (b) Smit;
135(t) sevenke, (c) Morgan Lane Photography,
(b) Nattika; 136 FBC24; 137 Mirek Srb; 139 Elena
Schweitzer; 141(t) Stanislav Fridkin,
(c) Algecireño, (b) Warren Goldswain;
142 fivespots; 144 Jim Barber; 145(r) ssuaphotos;
146 Snezana Skundric; 147 Fotokostic; 148 Eric
Isselée; 150 charles taylor; 151 design36;
154(l) Mandy Godbehear, (r) Robyn Mackenzie;
155 Miramiska; 159 Nadezda; 160(t) SergiyN,
(b) Brandelet; 161 Tomasz Trojanowski;
163(t) Kletr, (b) Galushko Sergey; 165 Aleksandra
Duda; 166(t) Fotokostic, (b) Palto; 167 akva;
170(t) Franck Boston, (b) Sergii Figurnyi;
178 ZouZou; 179 Orla; 181 Gelpi; 184 Beata
Becla; 187 irin-k